MW00466685

STORIES OF PEOPLE & CIVILIZATION

EGYPTIAN

ANCIENT ORIGINS

FLAME TREE PUBLISHING
6 Melbray Mews, Fulham,
London SW6 3NS, United Kingdom
www.flametreepublishing.com

First published and copyright © 2023
Flame Tree Publishing Ltd

23 25 27 26 24
1 3 5 7 9 10 8 6 4 2

ISBN: 978-1-80417-576-7

Cover and pattern art was created by Flame Tree Studio, with elements courtesy of Shutterstock.com/svekloid/OlgaChernyak. Additional interior decoration courtesy of Shutterstock.com/Gorbash Varvara.

Judith John (Glossary) is a writer and editor specializing in literature and history. A former secondary school English Language and Literature teacher, she has subsequently worked as an editor on major educational projects, including *English A: Literature* for the Pearson International Baccalaureate series. Judith's major research interests include Romantic and Gothic literature, and Renaissance drama.

Special thanks to Jason Emerson.

The text in this book is compiled and edited, with a new introduction, from elements of the following: *History of Egypt from the Earliest Times to the End of the XVIIIth Dynasty*, Vol. II by James Baikie (The Macmillan Company, 1929); *Tutankhamen: Amenism, Atenism and Egyptian Monotheism* by E.A.W. Budge (Dodd, Mead & Co., 1923); *The History of Antiquity*, Vol. 1, Max Duncker (Richard Bentley & Son, 1877); *A Thousand Miles up the Nile*, Amelia Ann Blanford Edwards (New York, E.P. Dutton, 1888); *Ancient Egypt from the Records*, M.E. Monckton Jones (E.P. Dutton, 1923); *An Account of Egypt* by Herodotus, translated By G.C. Macaulay (Macmillan, 1890); *Predecessors of Cleopatra*, Leigh North (Broadway Publishing Co., 1906); *A History of Egypt During the XVIIth and XVIIIth Dynasties*, Vol 2 by W.M. Flinders Petrie (Methuen & Co., 1896); *Ancient Egypt* by George Rawlinson (T. Fisher Unwin, 1886); *A Manual of Ancient History* by M.E. Thalheimer (Van Antwerp, Bragg & Co., 1872); *The Historians' History of the World in Twenty-Five Volumes*, Volume 1: *Prolegomena; Egypt, Mesopotamia*, ed. Henry Smith Williams (The Outlook Company/The History Association, 1905).

A copy of the CIP data for this book is available
from the British Library.

Designed and created in the UK | Printed and bound in China

STORIES OF PEOPLE & CIVILIZATION

EGYPTIAN

ANCIENT ORIGINS

With a New Introduction by

CHARLOTTE BOOTH

Further Reading and

Lists of Ancient Kings & Leaders

CONTENTS

STORIES OF PEOPLE & CIVILIZATION

7

STORIES OF PEOPLE & CIVILIZATION
EGYPTIAN
ANCIENT ORIGINS

SERIES FOREWORD

Stretching back to the oral traditions of thousands of years ago, tales of heroes and disaster, creation and conquest have been told by many different civilizations, in ways unique to their landscape and language. Their impact sits deep within our own culture even though the detail in the stories themselves are a loose mix of historical record, the latest archaeological evidence, transformed narrative and the unwitting distortions of generations of storytellers.

Today the language of mythology lives around us: our mood is jovial, our countenance is saturnine, we are narcissistic and our modern life is hermetically sealed from others. The nuances of the ancient world form part of our daily routines and help us navigate the information overload of our interconnected lives.

The nature of a myth is that its stories are already known by most of those who hear or read them. Every era brings a new emphasis, but the fundamentals remain the same: a desire to understand and describe the events and relationships of the world. Many of the great stories are archetypes that help us find our own place, equipping us with tools for self-understanding, both individually and as part of a broader culture.

For Western societies it is Greek mythology that speaks to us most clearly. It greatly influenced the mythological heritage of the ancient Roman civilization and is the lens through which we still see the Celts, the Norse and many of the other great peoples and religions. The Greeks themselves inherited much from their neighbours, the Egyptians, an older culture that became weary with the mantle of civilization.

Of course, what we perceive now as mythology had its own origins in perceptions of the divine and the rituals of the sacred. The earliest civilizations, in the crucible of the Middle East, in the Sumer of the third millennium BCE, are the source to which many of the mythic archetypes can be traced. Over five thousand years ago, as humankind collected together in cities for the first time, developed writing and industrial scale agriculture, started to irrigate the rivers and attempted to control rather than be at the mercy of its environment, humanity began to write down its tentative explanations of natural events, of floods and plagues, of disease.

Early stories tell of gods or god-like animals who are crafty and use their wits to survive, and it is not unreasonable to suggest that these were the first rulers of the gathering peoples of the earth, later elevated to god-like status with the distance of time. Such tales became more political as cities vied with each other for supremacy, creating new gods, new hierarchies for their pantheons. The older gods took on primordial roles and became the preserve of creation and destruction, leaving the new gods to deal with more current, everyday affairs. Empires rose and fell, with Babylon assuming the mantle from Sumeria in the 1800s BCE, in turn to be swept away by the Assyrians of the 1200s BCE; then the Assyrians and the Egyptians were subjugated by the Greeks, the Greeks by the Romans and so on, leading to the spread and assimilation of common themes, ideas and stories throughout the world.

The survival of history is dependent on the telling of good tales, but each one must have the 'feeling' of truth, otherwise it will be ignored. Around the firesides, or embedded in a book or a computer, the myths and legends of the past are still the living materials of retold myth, not restricted to an exploration of historical origins. Now we have devices and global communications that give us unparalleled access to a diversity of traditions. We can find out about Indigenous American, Indian, Chinese and tribal African mythology in a way that was denied to our ancestors, we can find connections, plot the archaeology, religion and the mythologies of the world to build a comprehensive image of the human experience that is both humbling and fascinating.

The books in this series introduce the many cultures of ancient humankind to the modern reader. From the earliest migrations across the globe to settlements along rivers, from the landscapes of mountains to the vast Steppes, from woodlands to deserts, humanity has adapted to its environments, nurturing languages and observations and expressing itself through records, mythmaking stories and living traditions. There is still so much to explore, but this is a great place to start.

Jake Jackson
General Editor

STORIES OF PEOPLE & CIVILIZATION EGYPTIAN ANCIENT ORIGINS

INTRODUCTION
& FURTHER READING

INTRODUCTION TO EGYPTIAN ANCIENT ORIGINS

THE EVOLVING NATURE OF EGYPTIAN CULTURE

A **common misconception** about ancient Egypt is that it can be captured in a moment. It is often perceived as having a homogenous language, culture and religion, with people stating confidently, 'the ancient Egyptians did/believed this'.

However, this simply is not the case.

The shear longevity of ancient Egyptian history and culture is difficult to comprehend. Many aspects of the culture which appear ancient to us also appeared ancient to the Romans. The pyramids at Giza, for example, built 4,500 years ago, were already more than 2,500 years old when Cleopatra and Julius Caesar gazed upon them. This means that Cleopatra and Caesar are closer in history to us than the Pyramids were to them.

Did these structures inspire similar thoughts in Caesar and Cleopatra as they did in the American traveller John Lloyd Stephens in 1836? He describes how

thousands of years roll through his mind, and thought recalls the men who built them, their mysterious uses, the poets, historians, philosophers, and warriors who have gazed upon them with wonder like his own.

Even temple building in Egypt spanned millennia, with the Karnak temple complex in Luxor taking more than 2,000 years to build. The earliest structures date to the twelfth dynasty in the Middle Kingdom (2040–1782 BCE), although these were built on the remnants of earlier buildings. The complex was then continually added to and updated until the Roman period, when a set of baths were constructed on the site. The majority of the temple standing dates from the New Kingdom, but the temple, like the Egyptian culture, religion and language, was constantly evolving.

Anyone looking for the 'origin' of ancient Egypt is therefore doomed to failure. With more than 3,000 years of history before the Roman invasion, every aspect of culture and language evolved to create a dynamic and fascinating culture which has intrigued the world for the past 2,000 years.

WHAT IS EGYPTOLOGY?

Due to this complex and dynamic culture, the discipline of Egyptology is divided into specialisms, invariably based on dates or topics; there are consequently specialists in language, religion or specific periods in history, such as the New Kingdom or the Graeco-Roman period.

However, in general, Egyptology and the 'ancient Egyptian' culture refers to the pharaonic period spanning from the first dynasty (3150–3050 BCE) through to the death of Cleopatra VII (30 BCE).

These dates, however, do not represent a hard beginning and end of Egyptian culture. The pre-dynastic period, for example, demonstrates the beginnings of religious and funerary beliefs as well as the foundations of culture and language as we recognize it. Nor did the arrival of the Romans spell the end of Egyptian beliefs and practices. It just changed them, with deities such as Isis still being worshipped well into the fifth century in Egypt and abroad.

Throughout the 3,000 years that spanned the time of the first dynasty to the Roman annexation nothing remained static, from language to beliefs, from food to technology. Despite this, the whole period is defined as 'ancient Egypt' and forms part of the rich tapestry of Egyptian history.

CHANGES IN EGYPTOLOGY

Egyptology as a discipline is only about 200 years old. It has seen the systematic study of the ancient Egyptian civilization develop into a well-respected science.

Being an active Egyptologist in the nineteenth century was relatively straightforward, in the sense that anyone with sufficient money and time could get a concession to excavate. As a discipline, it can be said to have originated with the Rosetta Stone and decipherment of hieroglyphs in 1822 by Jean-Francois Champollion, but it was not until the end of the nineteenth century that Egyptology was available as a separate discipline taught in universities in the UK and the wider world. Egyptology is now generally part of the archaeology departments of many universities.

Although all scholars, archaeologists, historians and Egyptologists for the past two centuries claimed to want to discover the truth about this ancient civilization, those in the eighteenth and nineteenth centuries were generally looking at the ancient society through very specific and biased lenses.

Even though there was no official route into Egyptology until the end of the nineteenth century, a certain element of snobbery did exist; anyone entering the discipline without a university education for instance (no matter how unrelated the subject), was not considered an Egyptologist. This was even extended to Howard Carter, who was neither a historian nor an archaeologist but had entered the field as an artist. He worked with Flinders Petrie at Amarna recording the images and there was taught excavation techniques. Carter's grounding in the discipline eventually led to the greatest discovery of all time. Throughout his life and career Carter's lack of a university education was held against him.

EARLY EGYPTOLOGY

Most 'professional' Egyptologists in the nineteenth century came from a Classics background and were trying to reconcile the ancient Egyptian culture with the Greek and Roman cultures even though it was thousands of years older. Erman (1894), for example, states 'the Greeks may have enjoyed a richer and more happy civilization than the Egyptians' – a rather bizarre statement based on his comparison between the land and lifestyles of these two countries.

Other scholars had strong Christian beliefs and sought to match the archaeology of Egypt with certain biblical stories. In the 1830s and 1840s, for example, Egypt was more associated with Jewish slavery, Moses and the parting of the Red Sea than anything else. Egypt is mentioned in the Bible more than 600 times, and early scholars wanted to find the truth behind these references.

As with any discipline, Egyptology is constantly evolving, growing and improving. The scholars of the nineteenth century were using the knowledge they had gleaned from classical texts, as well as the new archaeological techniques which were introduced to construct a history that made sense. Over the past 200 years, as technology has evolved and skills have been built upon, our knowledge of ancient Egyptian culture continues to evolve.

THE CONSTANT NILE

Even in a fast-changing civilization there were some constants which formed the foundations of its culture and lifestyle. The most important one was the Nile, an element which formulated the country, the religion, transportation and irrigation, and is discussed in some detail in the first section of this book. It has been studied and measured for centuries, long before the advent of Egyptology, as the heart blood of this great nation.

The Nile runs through or along the borders of 10 African countries including Egypt. It is the longest river in the world at 6,650 kilometres, and has three main tributaries: the White Nile, Blue Nile and Atbara. It flows from south to north, which is why southern Egypt is known as Upper Egypt and northern Egypt is known as Lower Egypt.

Once the river reaches Cairo, it fans out into a series of canals which forms the Delta region. The rich silt in this part of Egypt makes it the most fertile and has been used for agriculture for millennia. It was this rich silt from the Nile that ensured Egypt was able to thrive as a country; as Herodotus observed, Egypt was 'a land won by the Egyptians and given them by the Nile'.

INUNDATION

Throughout its long history the inhabited part of Egypt has been close to the banks of the Nile, in 2020 covering a total area of only 39,700 square kilometres. However, this is considerably more than in ancient times. One constant is that the arable land forms a clear strip on either side of the Nile, even if today much of this is artificially irrigated.

Rainfall in Egypt is rare; even the wettest part of the Delta receives only 100–200 millimetres a year. This means the survival of its inhabitants was completely dependent on the annual inundation of the Nile.

The Nile started to swell in June at Aswan, slowly rising in height and volume until September. It would then take a few weeks to subside, distributing rich fertile silt across the land. Although an important time of the year, it could also be stressful. If the inundation was too high, it would ruin the soil and there would be famine. Yet if the Nile was too low the land would not be fertilized and there would also be famine. It was thus a fine balance which led to both practical and religious practices to predict and control it. The inundation was an integral part of the calendar, with New Year falling on the day the flood started, and the river featured in many religious beliefs and practices.

IDLE HANDS

With agricultural land a few feet under water for four months of the year, those who worked the land were often conscripted to work on state monuments.

Excavations and research have shown that many of the workers who built the pyramids at Giza were corvée labourers. They were paid and fed well, and they had work ensured for four months at a time when they were unable to work their fields.

This contradicts the often-stated belief, introduced by Herodotus (*c.* 425 BCE), that slaves built the pyramids. This idea was then reiterated in the Bible and took root. However, excavations of the workers' village at Giza show that the workers were better fed than most Egyptians; they consumed meat daily, including beef, goat and sheep, and also had access to medical care. Many of the workers were also given permission to build their own tombs at the site – to be buried in the shadow of the king's tomb was considered a great honour. The corvée labourers then returned to their fields in October to start the important work of food production, leaving the permanent workers at the site.

ASWAN HIGH DAM

Egypt today, although still situated within close proximity to the Nile, is no longer reliant on the inundation for agriculture.

The Aswan Low Dam was built in 1902. It went some way towards controlling the flood waters and creating a more stable environment, even though there was still an annual increase in water along the Nile. However, by the 1960s the dam was working to capacity and had become no longer as effective at controlling the water levels.

This resulted in the development of the Aswan High Dam. It was much bigger and would be more effective at controlling flooding, providing water for irrigation all year round as well as providing a source of power through hydroelectricity. Since it was opened in 1971, the Nile no longer floods, but instead remains at a consistent level throughout the year.

THE NATURE OF DUALITY

The Nile, as such a vital element of life, running straight through the centre of the entire country, was integral to the political and religious divisions of Egypt, as well as to the names associated with certain aspects of the landscape.

As mentioned above, the direction of flow of the Nile led to southern Egypt being known as Upper Egypt and the north as Lower Egypt.

Upper Egypt started at the cataracts in Aswan. For some, Lower Egypt started at Asyut, although politically the king needed to rule Memphis, near Cairo, to be said to be the King of Lower Egypt, which suggests that this was the real dividing line.

The black, fertile soil deposited by the Nile every year after the inundation gave Egypt the name Kemet, or Black Land. The desert, which formed a stark line at the edge of the fertile strip of land, was considered a desolate, chaotic place known as Deshret, the Red Land.

The perfect north/south direction of the river made the division of east and west bank conclusive: the east bank was associated with the rising sun and the living, and the west bank associated with the setting sun and the dead. A temple on the west bank, for example, is more likely to be a funerary temple, one on the east bank to be a 'living' god and a cult for the living. There are, of course, always exceptions.

These divisions, while logical, were also the foundations of the dual nature of Egyptian religion. Here duality and opposites were a means of maintaining the cosmic equilibrium, known as Maat, meaning you could not have order (Horus) without chaos (Seth), and a king (male) always needed a queen (female). Pages 185–209 explore the reign of Hatshepsut, who decided that the role of queen was not powerful enough for her and took the role of king instead. This proved disastrous for the balance provided by duality.

NOMES

A more political division, which had its roots in the pre-dynastic tribal culture, were the 'nomes'. These were like counties or states, dividing the country into manageable regions. There were 22 of them in Upper Egypt and 20 in Lower Egypt. Although they were more or less static, the boundaries and capital cities changed over the centuries.

Each nome was governed by their own mayor and a council, and they had their own capital city. Each nome also had their own cult god and the associated practices and festivals. The local mayor was responsible for taxation, law and order and religious laws. Everything was dealt with internally, although ultimately all were under the jurisdiction of the king and central government. These are discussed further by Erman from page 55 onwards.

Before the unification of Egypt by Narmer (identified as Menes in many older texts and throughout this book) in Dynasty 0 (approx. 3100 BCE), Egypt was ruled by a number of local chieftains who were in control of a small area. Narmer decided to start uniting these areas through a series of battles. By winning these he deposed the individual chieftain and took control of his tribal region, eventually gaining control over all of Egypt. This early period of Egyptian history is discussed by Rawlinson on page 96 .

KING OF UPPER AND LOWER EGYPT

The unification of Egypt was a key feature of kingship throughout the pharaonic period, from the time of Narmer to Cleopatra VII. For a king to be recognized he must be a dual king – the king of Upper and Lower Egypt. Not every king achieved this, and many of them were erased from history by their descendants.

Every king had five titles, two of which refer to the importance of the duality of the role.

The classical order of the names and titles was as follows:

1. **The Horus name:** this title was represented in a *serekh* frame, with the god Horus seated on top.

2. **He of the Two Ladies:** this referred to the vulture goddess Nekhbet, from el Kab in Upper Egypt and the cobra goddess Wadjet from Buto in Lower Egypt. It emphasized the importance of being a dual king.

3. **The Golden Horus name:** this name was represented by Horus sitting on the sign for gold. There are still some questions about its true meaning.

4. **The Throne name (in a cartouche) and He of the sedge and the bee:** this is the first name to be written in a cartouche and was announced at the king's coronation. The sedge and the bee represent Upper and Lower Egypt.

5. **The Birth name (in a cartouche) with Son of Ra:** this was the king's birth name, but it was the title 'Son of Ra' that emphasized his divinity and his right to rule.

If a king only ruled the north or the south of the country, he was unable to use the two titles associated with duality. This meant that he was not a true king of Egypt.

CHRONOLOGY

Any kings who did not rule a unified Egypt could therefore be erased from history by those who followed them. This was also applied to any rulers considered to be controversial or who went against the rule of Maat (cosmic balance).

This was only really possible due to the dating system which was in place throughout the pharaonic period. There was no centralized dating system; Year 1 coincided with the ascension to the throne of a particular king and continued until his death (e.g. year 12 of Ramses II or year 4 of Tutankhamun) and the ascension of the next king. Unfortunately the date of death was often not recorded, so creating a chronology is reliant upon archaeology and the latest known date of a particular king.

This has led to different and changing chronologies throughout Egyptian history. It also goes some way towards explaining why every book (including this one) has different dates for specific reigns. The dates they use are dependent on their source chronology and how up to date this is, as well as which version of Egyptian chronologies are accepted by the author.

One would think that chronology would be more concrete than what a particular scholar believes, but there are so many uncertainties in Egyptology – especially when it comes to co-rulers and reign lengths – that there will always be discussions. For example, there has been an ongoing debate for decades about whether Akhenaten was followed on the throne by Smenkhkare or whether the two kings co-ruled for a period. If they co-ruled, this knocks a few years off the timeline. That may not seem too much of a problem, but multiplying this issue over the dozens of potential co-rulers can shift a chronology by a century or more.

Further challenges occur where kings were erased from history altogether. A perfect example is that, according to Egyptian records, Amenhotep III was followed on the throne by Horemheb. However, archaeology has shown that between these two kings came Akhenaten, Smenkhkare, Ay and Tutankhamun, ruling for a combined period of approximately 29 years. Horemheb's official reign length is thought to include all of these kings' years on the throne as well as his own.

As you can imagine, this can be very confusing – not only for scholars who are trying to unravel these dates, but also for interested readers who may not understand why there are large discrepancies.

DYNASTIES

Thankfully, however, a dynastic system was created by Manetho, writing in the third century BCE. This at least provides a framework for the chronology and enables us to place kings and activities into a dynasty, even without a concrete date.

Manetho's system divides the pharaonic period into 31 dynasties, with the idea that each one represented one royal family. These 31 dynasties are then further divided into three main periods, known as the Old Kingdom, Middle Kingdom and New Kingdom.

The transition between these Kingdoms was rarely smooth, so each is separated by an Intermediate Period (First, Second and Third) which represents a period of political instability and unrest. Following the Third Intermediate Period was the unstable Late Period, a time characterized by Persian and Libyan invasions and outlined in the final chapter.

The instability of the Late Period made it easy for Alexander the Great to invade Egypt (332 BCE). This event saw the start of the Ptolemaic Period, which had 15 kings called Ptolemy and two queens, Berenice IV and Cleopatra VII. This period ended with the Roman annexation of Egypt in 30 BCE.

DYNASTIC CHALLENGES

There is no denying that Manetho's system makes studying Egypt a lot easier, but the challenges associated with it remain. These are due to the evolving nature of archaeology and the information we have about the culture.

A major challenge is the starting point, as the pre-dynastic period was only discovered in 1890. This means that the first dynasty no longer represented the start of Egyptian history. Dynasty 0 was therefore added to accommodate Narmer's unification and this early period of Egyptian history. The rest of the pre-dynastic is defined by region (e.g. Naqada I, II, III). At least four of the scholars in this book were writing before this discovery was made, and so had no concept of history prior to the first dynasty.

Further challenges include where to put the kings within the dynastic framework. For example, Horemheb is always placed at the end of the eighteenth dynasty as the last king of the Amarna period. However, Ramses I, the first king of the nineteenth dynasty, and his son Sety I revered Horemheb as the start of their line, which would make him the first king of the nineteenth dynasty (according to their own wishes). You could argue that he isn't related to Ramses I, but he wasn't related to Tutankhamun or Ay either. So where should he be placed?

Further challenges arise as archaeology makes new discoveries. In 2014, for example, the first instance of a royal name, Woseribre Senebkay, was discovered. The name was in a tomb dated to the Second Intermediate Period in Abydos. The Second Intermediate Period had five overlapping dynasties ruling from different parts of the country, so ensuring that he is placed in the correct dynasty, and shifting the chronology accordingly, is a complex process.

HISTORY IN CONTEXT

These dynasties enable us to put key aspects of Egyptian history into a rough chronology without having any idea of dates. The wonderful thing about ancient Egypt is that there are a number of key events which the majority of people will be able to name, even with only a rudimentary knowledge of Egyptian history. These include:

Pyramids at Giza

Everyone who goes to Egypt wants to stand in front of the Great Pyramid of Giza, built by Khufu (2589–2566 BCE) of the fourth dynasty, and for the past two millennia hundreds of theories have arisen as to why and how they were built. However, the Great Pyramid is one of more than 130 known pyramids in Egypt and one of nine at Giza. It is the biggest and represents the pinnacle of pyramid building, a practice that started a century earlier with the third-dynasty king Djoser's step pyramid at Saqqara, with subsequent pharaohs working towards building a straight-sided pyramid which varying degrees of success. These are discussed on pages 107–108, and from page 114.

Notable Kings

There are a handful of kings, primarily from the New Kingdom, who have stood the test of time. They include:

Hatshepsut (1498–1483 BCE), the first female pharaoh.

Amenhotep III (1386–1349 BCE), the king who ruled during a golden era of Egyptian history. He was referred to by the Greeks as Memnon, in reference to Homer's *Odyssey*, where the mother of King Memnon, Eos, cried at dawn mourning his death. The Colossi of Memnon, which once stood at the entrance to the temple of Amenhotep III, made a sound every day at dawn following damage caused by an earthquake.

Akhenaten (1350–1334 BCE), the king who abandoned the traditional gods in favour of Aten, the sun disc, and is often called a monotheist.

Tutankhamun (1134–1325 BCE), who reinstated the traditional religion after the reign of his father, Akhenaten. He was thrown into the limelight when his almost intact tomb was discovered in 1922.

Ramses II (1279 BCE), who is often thought to be the pharaoh of the Bible. He was a prolific builder and one of the longest reigning Egyptian kings.

Cleopatra VII (51–30 BCE), who was the last queen of the so-called pharaonic period. She famously had romantic relationships with Julius Caesar and Marc Antony; after her death Egypt experienced annexation by the Romans.

ADVANCING KNOWLEDGE

While the ancient Egyptian culture and society apparently 'ended' with the Roman annexation in 30 BCE, the culture in fact just changed and continued to evolve. There are elements of the modern culture and the language (Coptic) which have their roots firmly in the ancient past.

Nothing is static – a fact that also applies to the study of ancient Egypt.

In November 2022 we celebrated the centenary of the discovery of the tomb of Tutankhamun by Howard Carter and Lord Carnarvon – one of the most important archaeological discoveries of all time. It taught us a great deal about the funerary culture of the Egyptians, being one of the only almost intact tombs discovered. Howard Carter's account of the excavation is also the latest work covered in this book.

However, in the subsequent century since Tutankhamun's tomb, discoveries have kept coming. While they may not be as shiny as Tutankhamun, they have advanced the discipline greatly and given us an insight into the Egyptians that they themselves did not have. Take the medical advancements we have seen in the twentieth century, which can also be applied to the study of mummies. This has led to DNA testing of the mummies of the two brothers in Manchester determining their relationship, which had been debated for centuries, as well as extracting the DNA of parasites within mummies.

From a historical point of view, the excavations at Tell el-Dab'a/Avaris in the Delta have advanced our knowledge. This site was the northern capital of Ramses II (Pi-Ramesse), the site of a palace with Minoan bull leaping figures and, more importantly, the capital city of the Hyksos. When Duncker was writing about the Hyksos in 1877 (*see* pages 155–167), excavations at the site had not yet started. He was therefore basing his text on Manetho, who was writing 1,300 years after the Hyksos period had ended. The discoveries of Manfred Bietak in the 1960s and 1970s at Avaris and Tell el-Dab'a have completely rewritten the Hyksos period of Egyptian history, offering insights into their origins, beliefs and gradual take-over of Upper and Lower Egypt. They were not the invading hordes of Manetho, but had instead arisen from a community that had lived in the Delta for more than a century.

As mentioned above, Herodotus's claim that the pyramids at Giza were built by slaves has been debunked through continued and extensive excavation at the site uncovering the workmen's village and their tombs. The work was started in the 1980s by the Oriental Institute and continues today, uncovering detailed information about how the structures were built and by whom, as well as where the workers slept and what they ate. Much of the work written about the pyramids prior to these excavations was based on Herodotus, who was writing about them 2,000 years after they were built, as well as other observations by travellers over the centuries regarding dimensions and building methods.

Throughout the last century there have been many new archaeological discoveries. These include the unique Tanis silver coffins found in the late 1930s just as the Second World War broke out, the Valley of the Golden Mummies in 1996, comprising 250 Graeco-Roman mummies, and the discovery of a tomb of an unknown queen, Neith, at Saqqara in November 2022.

PART OF EVOLVING HISTORY

In the following pages we will be given a snapshot of Egyptological and historical thought on the history of Egypt as it stood between the middle of the nineteenth century through to the discovery of Tutankhamun in 1922. We will hear from W.M. Flinders Petrie, the Father of Egyptian Archaeology, writer turned Egyptologist Amelia Edwards and Howard Carter, the discoverer of Tutankhamun. Additionally, we will read the work of historian and politician Max Duncker, historian and theologian George Rawlinson and writer Leigh North. Each of these writers present the best scholarship of their time, with much of it based on classical texts such as Herodotus (fifth century BCE), Manetho (third century BCE) and Diodorus (first century BCE), and explore how that corresponded with the archaeological findings of the time and the understanding gleaned from the newly deciphered hieroglyphic language.

While much of the information they offered is perhaps outdated, with archaeology, technology and research advancements telling us more about the ancient Egyptian culture than we once thought was possible, these scholars are part of the evolving journey that is ancient Egypt and Egyptology. The work that archaeologists and researchers are doing today may seem naïve and outdated in another century, so great are the advances in scientific techniques. Yet it is through such research, publication and updating that we will one day fully understand this fascinating, diverse and rich culture that has fired imaginations since Caesar (47 BCE), Napoleon (1798 CE) and Morgan Freeman (2015 CE) gazed at the pyramids and marvelled at their antiquity.

FURTHER READING

Baines, John and Jaromir Malek, *Atlas of Ancient Egypt* (Time Life UK, 1994)

Booth, Charlotte, *Ancient Egyptians for Dummies* (John Wiley, 2007)

Clayton, Peter, *Chronicle of the Pharaohs* (Thames and Hudson, 1994)

David, Rosalie, *Religion and Magic in Ancient Egypt* (Penguin, 2002)

Gardiner, Alan, *Ancient Egyptian Grammar* (Oxford University Press, 1957)

Gardner Wilkinson, John, *The Ancient Egyptians: Their Life and Customs* (Senate Books, 1994 (1837))

Hawass, Zahi, *The Great Book of Ancient Egypt: In the Realm of the Pharaohs* (White Star, 2019)

Ikram, Salima and Aiden Dodson, *The Mummy in Ancient Egypt: Equipping the Dead for Eternity* (Thames and Hudson, 1998)

Janssen, Rosalind and Jac Janssen, *Growing Up in Ancient Egypt* (The Rubicon Press, 1990)

Janssen, Rosalind and Jac Janssen, *Getting Old in Ancient Egypt* (The Rubicon Press, 1996)

Kemp, Barry, *Ancient Egypt; Anatomy of a Civilisation* (Routledge, 2018)

Lehner, Mark and Zahi Hawass, *Giza and the Pyramids* (Thames and Hudson, 2017)

Oakes, Lorna and Lucia Gahlin, *Ancient Egypt: An Illustrated History* (Lorenz Books, 2018)
Romer, John, *A History of Ancient Egypt: From the First Farmers to the Great Pyramid* (Penguin, 2013)
Shaw, Ian, *The Oxford History of Ancient Egypt* (Oxford University Press, 2004)
Tyldesley, Joyce, *The Penguin Book of Myths and Legends of Ancient Egypt* (Penguin, 2011)

Charlotte Booth (Introduction) has a PhD in Egyptology from University of Birmingham, where she studied paper squeezes and their value as an archaeological tool. She obtained her BA (Hons) and MA from UCL in Egyptian Archaeology. She worked in Cairo for the EAIS project and in Luxor for ARCE. She has published extensively in Egyptology including 17 books, and numerous articles and papers.

DESCRIBING ANCIENT EGYPT

One of the constants in Egypt for the past 5,000 years has been the landscape. Learning about this landscape provides a strong foundation for understanding religious beliefs, cultural practices and the development of the country. The central aspect of the Egyptian landscape is the Nile and the success and longevity of Egypt is due to its abundance.

This environment helped to form the complex and diverse religious practices of the Egyptians as they tried to make sense of their world. Petrie introduces us to the creation of the world according to Egyptian mythology, and Herodotus introduces us to the sacred animals incorporated into their religion.

The success of the Egyptian culture is also due to the people who lived, worked, worshipped and died there. In this chapter we are introduced to the people as a population, as well as to how they were depicted in art and differentiated from those who lived in surrounding areas. Petrie and Herodotus introduce the concepts of cultural practices such as marriage and gender divisions which were essential aspects of everyday life.

THE LAND OF EGYPT

Geology of the Country

The Nile receives its last great tributary, the Blue Nile, near Khartum, in about the 17th degree of north latitude. Above the town the river flows quietly through grassy plains; below, the stream changes its peaceful character, as it makes its way through the great tableland of the north of Africa, and in an immense bend of over 1,528 kilometres (950 miles) forces a passage through the Nubian sandstone. In some places where the harder stone emerges through the sandstone, the river, even after thousands of years, has not succeeded in completely breaking through the barrier, and the water finds its way in rapids between the hard rocks.

There are 10 of these so-called cataracts, and they play an important and sometimes an unhappy part in the development of Egypt and the Sudan. It is owing to them that intercourse by boats is rendered almost impossible between the Upper and Lower Nile except during high Nile, and even then there is risk of accidents happening to larger boats passing through these rapids. The last of these cataracts is 11 kilometres (seven miles) long, and forms the natural boundary of Egypt proper; close to it is situated the town of Assuan, the old Syene.

Below Assuan the character of the country again changes, and the valley, which in Nubia never exceeded 8 to 14 kilometres (five to nine miles) in width, broadens out, its greatest extent being, in one place, as much as 53 kilometres (33 miles) from side to side. The reason for this change is that at Gebel Silsileh, some way below Assuan, the sandstone (found throughout Nubia) gives way to limestone, which forms cliffs bounding the river for nearly 765 kilometres (475 miles). When the Nile reaches the Delta, the limestone again gives place to later geological formations.

Thus, Egypt in its entire length is framed in rocky walls, which sometimes reach a height of 965 to 1,287 kilometres (600 to 800 feet); they form the stereotyped horizon of all landscape views in this country. These limestone hills are not mountains in our sense of the word. Instead of rising to peaks, they form the edge of a large tableland with higher plateaus here and there. This tableland is entirely without water, and is covered with the sand of the desert, which is continually trying to trickle down into the Nile, by channels grooved in the steep monotonous wall. On the west this barren plateau joins the shifting sand dunes of the Sahara, which have never been thoroughly explored. About 150 kilometres (95 miles) from the river, and running parallel with it, are some remarkable dips in this tableland. These 'oases' are well watered and very fruitful, but with these exceptions there is no vegetation in this desolate waste, which from old times has been called the Libyan desert. To the east of the Nile is a similar limestone plateau called the Arabian desert. Further inland it changes into a high mountainous country with bold peaks of granite, porphyry, gneiss and other crystalline rocks rising sometimes to the height of 1,800 metres (6,000 feet). This magnificent range of mountains stretches along the Red Sea, and though very barren owing to the lack of rain, yet the country presents a more cheerful aspect than the Libyan desert. Springs of water are rare, but a dampness arises from the proximity of the sea, so that hardy desert plants grow everywhere, and in many places small oases are found which provide food for the wild animals and for the cattle of the nomadic tribes. The heat, however, and the want of water, make it most difficult to live in these mountains on the east of the Nile, and we cannot help admiring the courage and perseverance of the ancient Egyptians, who maintained hundreds of labourers working the large stonepits and quarries in this vast rocky waste.

To return to the Nile valley – had the river merely forced its way through the Nubian sandstone and the Egyptian limestone, the valley could never have attained its wonderful fertility under the rainless glowing sky of Egypt, where decomposition of all vegetation is so rapid. But the Nile is not solely the outflow of the great lakes of tropical Africa; it also receives from the west all the waterflow from the high mountains of Abyssinia; and the mountain torrents, laden with rocky debris, dash down the sides of the hills in the rainy season, and form the two great streams of the Blue Nile and the Atbara which flow into the Nile near Khartum and Berber. Thus, in the middle of the summer the river gradually rises so high that the banks can no longer contain the vast quantity of water and mud. The river overflows slowly, and after some months slowly retreats again into its bed. While the water of the inundation covers the valley the mud in the water is of course deposited, and when the stream has retreated, the country is left covered with a thin coating of this mud composed of the finest stone dust from the Abyssinian mountains; it is this black Nile mud which has caused, and which renews each year, the fertility of Egypt. It now forms the soil of Egypt; and from Khartum to the sea the deposit of mud in the valley has reached the height of nine metres (30 feet), and in this mud the Nile has hollowed its present bed.

In another respect also the Nile is the lifeblood of Egypt; it provides water for the country, for, as in the neighbouring deserts, there is no rainfall. On the coast of the Delta and for some miles southwards rain falls in the same way as in the other coast lands of the Mediterranean; but, with the exception of rare storms, this is never the case in Upper Egypt. There are also no springs nor brooks, so that for water the country depends entirely on the great river from the far south.

Climate and Inundation

The climate of Egypt is more uniform than that of other Mediterranean countries, owing to the absence of the rainy season, which corresponds to our winter. From December to March the air is cool, and at night sometimes the temperature may almost go down to freezing point, but during eight months of the year it is very hot, and in July the thermometer rises to 43 degrees Celsius (110 degrees Fahrenheit) in the shade. Several causes combine to produce this difference of temperature. The hot south-east wind blows only from the middle of February to the middle of June, but this wind often rises to a hurricane, filling the air and covering the plants with dust; during the rest of the year even in the hottest season the northwest wind mitigates the intense heat of the day; the ancient Egyptians thought it one of the best things in life to 'breathe its sweet breath'. The inundation has still more effect on the climate than the wind, and many other instances. The stream begins to rise in the beginning of June; it becomes a mighty torrent by the end of July; from the end of September to the end of October the water reaches its highest level, after which time it retreats more and more rapidly. In January the stream is back once more in its old bed, but it goes on subsiding till the summer. This inundation, which we must not imagine to overflow the whole country, spreads abroad coolness, dampness and fertility; the country revives from the oppression of the summer heat, and we easily understand why the old Egyptians should fix their New Year's Day on the 15th of September, the time of highest Nile.

The days of inundation were, however, days of anxiety and care. The fate of the whole country hung in the balance, for if the water rose insufficiently but one-tenth part, the canals carrying the water to the higher level did not fill, and the result was the failure of the crops and famine. Again, if the inundation rose even slightly too high, sad devastation ensued; embankments and dikes were thrown down, and freshly cultivated fields, supposed to be beyond the reach of the water, were covered by the inundation. From the earliest times therefore, the rise of the Nile was closely watched and controlled by government officials, who regulated the yearly taxes by the result of the inundation. Nilometers were also constructed – these were wells in which the height of the water was marked as in a measure or water-gauge; they were under the special protection of the State. In old times as now, the height of the inundation was officially notified; and then also, as at the present day, suspicions were often aroused that the official statement was exaggerated. [...] At the present day, on account of the ground level of Egypt having been raised by the mud deposit, a yet higher inundation is needed to ensure a good harvest to the country.

Flora and Fauna

From the fertility of the Egyptian soil we might expect a specially rich flora, but notwithstanding the luxuriant vegetation, no country in the same latitude has so poor a variety of plants. There are very few trees. The sycamore or wild fig and the acacia are the only common forest trees, and these grow in an isolated fashion somewhat as the lime or chestnut tree grows with us. Besides these there are fruit trees, such as the date and doum palms, the fig tree and others. The scarcity of wood is quite a calamity for Egypt. It is the same with plants; herbs and vegetables reign in this land of cultivation, and wildflowers are scarcely to be found. [...] Even the streams, the numerous watercourses and canals, are poorer in vegetation than one would expect under this southern sky.

The present aspect of Egypt is pleasant though monotonous; the gleaming water of the broad river flows peacefully through the green fields, and the Delta also, intersected by numerous canals, looks very much like a rich well-cultivated European plain. We scarcely realize that we are on African soil, and on the banks of a river flowing from the heart of the tropics. In prehistoric times, however, the aspect of Egypt was doubtless very different, and probably resembled that of the present valley of the Nile in the interior of Africa. The banks were covered by primaeval forests, the river changed its bed from time to time, leaving behind stagnant branches; the surface of the water was covered with luxuriant weeds, the gigantic papyrus rushes made an impenetrable undergrowth, until the stream broke through them and carried them as a floating island to another spot. These swamps and forests, inhabited by the crocodile, buffalo and hippopotamus, have been changed into peaceful fields, not so much by an alteration in the climate, as by the hand of man working for thousands of years. The land has been cleared by the inhabitants, each metre has been won with difficulty from the swamp, until at last the wild plants and the mighty animals which possessed the country have been completely exterminated. The hippopotamus is not to be seen south of Nubia, and the papyrus reeds are first met with in the ninth degree of latitude.

In the first historical period, 3000–2500 BCE, this clearing of the land had been in part accomplished. The forests had long ago disappeared, and the acacias of Nubia had to furnish the wood for boatbuilding; the papyrus, however, was still abundant. The 'backwaters', in which these rushes grew, were the favourite resorts for sport, and the reed itself was used in all kinds of useful ways. The same state of things existed in the time of Herodotus. In the time of which we shall treat, Egypt was not so over-cultivated as now, though the buildings were no less extensive.

Character of the Country; Its Influence on the Nation

The climate of Egypt would seem to make life easy to mankind, the weather provides him with no grievance, the fields bear rich crops throughout the year, the cattle are never in want of pasture, the river is stocked with fish in abundance. We should therefore expect to find a people spending their lives cheerfully and brightly, somewhat after the fashion of the Homeric heroes. Yet the Egyptian labourer, both of the present and of the past, has always been a creature with little pleasure in his life, who does his work in a serious and indeed listless way, rather like his ox or his ass. The Egyptian nation has not the light-heartedness of the Greek, though the sky of Egypt smiles more brightly than that of Hellas. There is good reason for this difference of character. However easy the life of the Egyptian labourer may appear, it is really a hard one, and each day has its toil. He must never neglect his field, he must ever work hard – above all, before and during the time of inundation. The general opinion that the Nile overflows to right and left, making the country like a lake, in which the mounds of villages appear like islands, is not the truth, at least not in the case of the inundation of average height. Earnest work is needed to regulate the irrigation of the fields. The water is drawn off first into large canals, and thence into small trenches, in order to obtain the full benefit of the inundation. Dams are constructed to divide the land to be flooded into large or small parts, these are opened to the water at the right time, and the water is retained at will, or allowed to flow back into the canals by means of sluices. Some fields, completely out of the reach of the inundation, have to be irrigated entirely by means of hydraulic works.

All this labour, which falls now to the lot of the modern fellah, had also to be done in the old time, and doubtless must have been a heavy burden to the Egyptian people. The making of the canals, dikes and sluices taxed the ingenuity of the nation, and accustomed the people to systematic work. As this system could only be carried out by large bodies of men, it was impossible that the old inhabitants of the Nile valley should consist of free peasants like those of Germany in the old time. The hard logic of facts teaches us that an autocratic government is always necessary in order to control and regulate irrigation. In fact, the earliest knowledge we have of the conditions of life in Egypt shows us a strict administration of political and agrarian relations; a state in which the individual was of little account, but in which much help was given by the government in the establishment of works for the public good, and in the superintendence of practical details.

The Greeks may have enjoyed a richer and happier civilization than the Egyptians, but the practical work of the latter people stands higher than that of the former. In making comparisons between the youthful joyous art of Greece and the severe sober art of Egypt we must remember that the latter sprang to life on the sad soil of the Nile valley, where hard work is required of everyone. We must also, if we would avoid being unjust to the Egyptian people, make allowance for one other feature of their life, the landscape which surrounded them. The Greek, with his mountains, round which the sea foamed and the winds blew, with his green forests and his flower-decked meadows, created for himself the joyous forms of the youthful gods of Olympus, with their human feelings and sufferings. The horrors and the grandeur of the desert influenced the Semitic nomads, and deepened in them the religious feeling which permeates the purest form of religion. The landscape of Egypt on the contrary was monotonous; everywhere the fertile green fields were intersected by numerous watercourses, here and there grew clumps of palms; and ever the same horizon, the wall of the limestone mountains, bounded the view.

This is not a landscape calculated to awaken the inspiration of the soul; unconsciously the dweller in this country will become sober and prosaic, and his gods will be pale forms with whom he has no sympathy. In fact, the Egyptian peasant could scarcely understand a living personal relationship between the individual and the deity. If fancy were here allowed free course, the spirits and ghosts she would create would not resemble such forms as the friendly angel leading the people through the wilderness, nor the avenging angel stretching his hand over the sinful town to strike it with the plague, nor the ghost of the night, luring the wanderer to his destruction; but they would be frog-headed fiends, fiends with heads twisted awry, human-faced birds, snakes with four legs, repulsive childish forms, which can awaken neither pleasure nor fear.

Thus, the Egyptian grew up under conditions unfavourable to the development of his spiritual life, but such as would fortify his understanding and practical industry. Foreign influence affected him little, for he lived secluded from the rest of mankind. On the cast and on the west was the desert, on the north were the swamps of the Delta, on the south the rapids of the Nile and the narrow passes of Nubia. The Bedouins of the Syrian desert and the Libyans of the eastern Sahara visited Egypt, and drove their flocks into the Delta, but it was only in later times that they gained any political power there, and the predatory incursions of early ages were much like those of the present day. There was little opportunity for friendly intercourse with foreign nations, for the neighbouring countries were far less fertile than Egypt, and their civilization developed much later. It was only in the time of the New Kingdom that the people of Syria, Asia Minor and Nubia attained a civilization at all resembling that of Egypt; before that time they were barbarians despised by the Egyptians; the Chaldeans, whose civilization was as old and at the same time equalled that of the Nile valley, were too far off.

The undisturbed repose in which life in Egypt developed was in many respects happy for the nation; yet there is the reverse side to the picture. The Egyptians were the least warlike of all the nations of the ancient East. Their contests with the Bedouins can scarcely be called warfare, and the internal struggles were always of a subordinate character, owing to the curious long form of the country. The Egyptians therefore had no heroes of war whom they could celebrate in song; their heroes, like those of the Chinese, were wise kings and princes of old time; they never experienced the invigorating influence of a great national war.

Equally unfortunate was the fact that they never learnt to carry on commerce with foreign nations. There were no harbours on the north of the Delta, and the currents off the coast made it very dangerous for ships, while the harbours of the Red Sea could only be reached by four days of desert travelling. The cataracts made it difficult to visit the countries of the Upper Nile. Thus, commerce was always somewhat strange to the Egyptians, who gladly left it to the Phoenicians; and the 'Great Green One', i.e., the ocean, was at all times a horror to them. Compared with the Phoenicians, their naval expeditions were insignificant, while in their agriculture, their arts and manufactures, they rose to true greatness.

The Twofold Division of the Country

Egypt played such an important part in the history of the world that involuntarily we are apt to consider the country as one of considerable size. Yet it is a small state, for notwithstanding its length of 900 kilometres (570 miles), it only contains about 32,300 square kilometres (12,500 square miles), and is therefore somewhat smaller than Belgium. Even including the 1,600 kilometres (1,000 miles) between the first cataract and Khartum, this would only increase the kingdom of Egypt by about 2,900 square kilometres (1,125 square miles), the upper valley being very narrow. It was the exceeding fertility of the country which made Egypt so important. This small country is naturally divided into two very different parts. The larger division, the Delta, is a broad swamp intersected with canals, the climate is influenced by the sea, and there is a regular rainy season in the winter. The smaller part, the Nile valley, is as a rule without rain, and it has one great waterway, the stagnant branches and canals being scarcely worth consideration.

This is the present aspect of the country, and in past times it differed little, except that both divisions were swampier than now. It follows naturally that the dry climate of the south was more favourable to cultivation than the swamps of the north. When the primaeval forest was once cleared, there was little left in Upper Egypt to interfere with the tillage of the soil. In the Delta, on the contrary, thousands of years passed before the swamps were converted into arable land. This work is not yet completed, and indeed many parts of the Delta which were formerly under cultivation are now lost. The brackish waters of Lake Menzaleh (called Lake Manzala today) now cover a surface of over 2,500 square kilometres (1,000 square miles), but in old times part of this district was one of the most productive in the country.

Scholars have surmised from the foregoing facts that Upper Egypt was the home of Egyptian civilization, and that agriculture, the industrial crafts and art flourished there while the Delta was still a forest swamp, the dwelling-place only of the hunter and the shepherd. Traces are not wanting to confirm this view. Herodotus tells us a legend which he heard when travelling in Egypt, according to which 'the Theban nome' in Upper Egypt was alone inhabited in the time of Menes the first king. All the rest of the country was a swamp, and the Delta was not even in existence. Though this can scarcely have been true of the time of Menes (about 3,200 BCE), yet this legend contains the truth that Lower Egypt remained a land of swamps far later than was the case with Upper Egypt. We learn the same from the fact that it was in comparatively late times that Lower Egypt played an important part in the history of the country.

In the time of the Old Kingdom (*c.* 3,000–2,500 BCE) we read that the flocks of the rich were driven at times into the Delta, which was therefore considered to be pastureland as compared with the corn lands of Upper Egypt. The name also by which the Delta is known, 'the northern country', stamps it as an annexation to Egypt proper, which at Memphis was called 'the south' without the addition of the word country. Upper Egypt was also always put first before the larger Delta; the south was said to be in front, the north lay behind. From these facts we conclude, that in the time of the Old Kingdom the Delta was far behind the southern part of the country in civilization. The civilization of Lower Egypt progressed but slowly. We find traces of this process in the names of the towns, many of which were named after some of the old famous places in Upper Egypt, e.g., Thebes and Edfu. Colonists from the south carried the names of their old homes to their new settlements, in the same way as our colonists have done in America.

Under the New Kingdom (about 1,300 BCE) much progress

seems to have been made in the east of the Delta, which rose to importance, through being the highway to Syria; the old town of Tanis became the capital, and other towns were founded at different places. The west of the Delta was in a great measure in the hands of the Libyan nomads till the seventh century BCE, when the chief town Sais became the seat of government under the family of Psammetichus, and after the foundation of Alexandria this new city assumed the lead for 1,000 years. Even as late as the Middle Ages the 'Bushmur', a swampy district, was scarcely accessible; it was inhabited by an early non-Egyptian race, with whom neither the Greek nor the Arab rulers had much to do.

Throughout the ages of antiquity there existed, between Upper and Lower Egypt, a certain rivalry which probably arose in the time when the one was so far behind the other in civilization. In old times also they were separated politically; they spoke two different dialects; and though they honoured several identical gods under different names, others were peculiar to one half of the kingdom. This contrast between Upper and Lower Egypt was emphasized in many ways by the people. The 'two countries' were under the protection of different goddesses; the Delta under that of the snake goddess Uad't, while Upper Egypt was ruled by the snake goddess Nechebt. In mythical ages the land was given to different gods as a possession; the Delta to Set, Upper Egypt to Horus.

Different plants were characteristic of each part of the country: the papyrus grew thickly in the Delta, the flowering rush in Upper Egypt and these two plants were used for armorial bearings, a flowering rush for Upper Egypt, and a papyrus plant for the Lower Country. The flowers of these two plants became emblematic of the north and south, and in decorative representations the captives of the north were bound with a rope ending in the blossom of a papyrus, those of the south with one whose end was formed of the flowering rush.

Density of the Population

I have already said that the historical importance of Egypt was owing to its fertility; the dense population of the country was also due to the same cause. The population is now somewhat over five million (exact statistics are not to be obtained), and in the old time it is supposed to have been higher. Only countries as highly developed as Belgium or Saxony [north-western Germany] are so thickly populated.

We should expect the inhabitants, when so closely crowded together, to be essentially welded into one nation, but the length of Egypt prevented this result; the inhabitants of one district had neighbours on two sides only, and the people of the Delta had a wearisome journey before reaching Upper Egypt. Therefore we find in Egypt the development of individual townships.

Each district or province had its chief god and its own traditions; the inhabitants were often at war with their neighbours, and when the central government was weak, the kingdom became subdivided into small principalities.

The districts were of very small extent, the average size of those of Upper Egypt about 700 square kilometres (270 square miles); those of the Delta were rather larger, yet these provinces were of more importance than their size would indicate, as the population of each would probably average 300,000 souls.

The Nomes or Provinces

Upper Egypt was divided in old times into about 20 provinces or *nomes* as they were called by the Greeks; the division of the Delta into the same number is an artificial one of later date, as is proved by there being the same number for a country a quarter as large again. The official list of these provinces varied at different times, sometimes the same tract of land is represented as an independent province, and sometimes as a subdivision of that next to it. The provinces were government districts, and these might change either with a change of government or for political reasons, but the basis of this division of the country was always the same, and was part of the flesh and blood of the nation. The names of the nomes are very various – some are such as would naturally occur to the mind of a primitive people; thus in Upper Egypt we find the province of the 'hare', of the 'gazelle', two of the 'sycamore', two of the 'palm', one of the 'knife', whilst the most southern portion was called simply the 'land in front'. In the Delta (the home of cattle breeding) we find the province of the 'black ox', of the 'calf', etc. Other names were derived from the religion; thus the second nome of Upper Egypt was called 'the seat of Horus', the sixth 'his mountain', and the 12th in the Delta was named after the god Thoth. […]

Upper Egypt

The natural boundary of Egypt on the south was always the so-called first cataract, those rapids seven miles long, in the 24th degree of latitude, where the Nile breaks through the mighty granite barrier. The district of the cataract was inhabited in old times as at present by Nubians, a non-Egyptian race, and the sacred island of Philae at the southern end of the cataract, where the later Egyptians revered one of the graves of Osiris, is in fact Nubian soil. These rapids were of the highest importance for strategic purposes, and the early Egyptians strongly fortified the town of Syene on the east bank so as to be able to blockade the way into Egypt by land, as well as to protect the quarries where from the earliest ages they obtained all their splendid red granite for obelisks and other monuments. The buildings in Egypt occupied so much of the attention of the state that immense importance was attached to the unobstructed working of these quarries.

The capital of this first province of Egypt was not Syene, but the neighbouring town of *Abu*, which name signifies 'ivory town' (Greek Elephantine). To the island on which this town was situated the Nubians of old brought the ivory obtained in their elephant hunts, in order to exchange it for the products of Egypt. Even in Roman times this town was important for commerce, as the place where the custom duties were paid.

Forty-five kilometres (28 miles) farther to the north on the east bank was the town of *Nubit* (Ombos), where stood the sanctuary of the crocodile god Subk, and 22 kilometres (14 miles) beyond lay Chenu, the old Silsilis, the modern Silsilch, at the point where the sandstone hills narrow the bed of the river before giving place to the limestone. Like Syene, Silsilis was important because of the great quarries close to the town. Silsilis was the easiest point from Memphis or Thebes, where hard stone was to be obtained; and here were quarried those gigantic blocks of sandstone which we still admire in the ruins of the Egyptian temples.

Whilst the 'land in front', or the first province, owed its importance to the quarries and to trade, that of the second province, called 'the exaltation of Horus', was, as the name signifies, purely religious. Horus, in the form of the winged disk, here obtained his first victory over Set, and here therefore was built the chief sanctuary of this god. The present temple of Edfu is still dedicated to him; it is in good preservation and stands on the site of the ancient Debḥot, but a building of Ptolemaic time has taken the place of the sanctuary erected by the old kings.

In the third nome, the shield of which bore the head-dress of the ram-headed god Chnum, three towns are worthy of mention: first, the old *Enit* (Esneh), the religious centre, where, as at Edfu, a late temple occupies the site of the old building; secondly, the town of Nechebt (El Kab); few towns have played such a leading part in Egypt as this great fortress, the governors of which during their time of office were equal in rank with the princes of the blood. El Kab was also important for the worship of the patron goddess of the south, Nechebt, sometimes represented as a vulture, sometimes as a snake. Numerous inscriptions by pilgrims testify to the honour in which this goddess was held in old times, and even the Greeks resorted to El Kab in order to pray to 'Eileithyia'. Thirdly, on the northern border of the nome, on the west bank, lay the very ancient town of On, distinguished from other places of the same name, as 'On of the god Mont'. On suffered the same fate as many other towns in all countries. Owing to political circumstances, the neighbouring town of Thebes rose from a country town to be the 'town of the Hundred Gates', the capital of the whole kingdom. On then lost all her power, and it was only when, after 1,000 years of splendour, Thebes fell into decay, that On of Mont rose again to importance as the Hermonthis of the Greeks. Erment is now a flourishing town, while the site of her great rival is occupied only by villages.

We now come to that town whose ruins form the greatest of all the wonders of Egypt, and whose buildings seem to have been erected by a race of giants. Thebes cannot boast of the age of Memphis, nor of the sacred character of Abydos or Heliopolis, but she had the good fortune to be the capital of the country during those centuries when Egypt was a mighty power in the world. Therefore she herself became the ruler of the world, the Rome of the ancient cast, of which the Hebrew prophet cried in astonishment: 'Ethiopia and Egypt were her strength, and it was infinite; Put and Lubim (Arabia and Libya) were thy helpers.' The political power of Thebes was also shown by the buildings of the town, which surpassed in magnificence all those of ancient or modern capitals. Thebes attained this splendour at a comparatively late date, being at first only an obscure provincial town devoted to the worship of Amon; neither the town nor the god is mentioned in the older sacred books. About 2000 BCE we first find a royal residence established here from time to time; but it was not till 1500 BCE that the town began to flourish, and nearly all the antiquities found at Thebes belong to this later period.

The old town of Thebes, called *Ueset*, was on the eastern bank, and stretched inland from the present ruins of Karnak. The harbour quarter of the town was close to the modern Luxor. When the town became the seat of government, the kings turned their energies to the building of the temple of the Theban god Amon, in order to make the simple dwelling place of this comparatively obscure god worthy of the principal deity of the kingdom. One generation after another added to the buildings of *Epet* (the name of the temple), and in the course of centuries a gigantic sanctuary arose, the ruins of which, near the village of Karnak, stretch for more than half a mile in length. The central of the three great temple enclosures measures about 450 metres (1,500 feet) in width, and about the same in length; the building itself being about 300 metres (1,000 feet) by 90 metres (300 feet) wide. A second great temple was erected to the same god on the riverbank at Luxor, and smaller temples were built for the other gods of the town. In the midst of these various sanctuaries stood 'the town of the Hundred Gates', that great city which, like all other Egyptian towns, has disappeared. The gigantic ruins of the temples alone remain to mark the site of the old capital of the world, of which even the 'barbarians' in far-off Ionia sang:

'Royal Thebes,
Egyptian treasure house of countless wealth,
Who boasts her hundred gates, through each of which,
With horse and car two hundred warriors march.'

During the course of centuries there arose on the western side of the river a strange city. This 'west end' was very different in character from that of London or Berlin; it was not the quarter of the rich, but the dwelling place of the dead.

The steep sides of the strangely formed western mountains are hollowed out into vaults for the dead, and so numerous did they become that a modern traveller has compared them to the holes in a sponge. In the valley, now called the Bibân el Molûk, were the graves of the kings; immense galleries excavated in the rocks, planned with a boldness and grandeur unlike anything else in Egypt, and which, ever since the time of the Greek travellers, have constituted one of the great sights of Thebes. In Egypt the deceased was honoured as a demigod, and therefore a chapel for his worship was a necessary adjunct of the Egyptian tomb. These chapels were as a rule either close to the tomb or they formed part of it; but in the narrow desert valley of Bibân el Molûk, there was no space to erect funeral temples worthy of the kings, and they therefore stood in the plain. Thus on the edge of the western mountains a series of great buildings arose – the funeral temple of Abt el Qurna (Sety I); Der- el-Bahri (Queen Chnemtamun); Medinet Habu (Ramses III); the Ramesseum (Ramses II) and others to which we shall often refer.

It follows, of course, that these colossal erections, with their dependencies, their gardens, their cattle yards and storehouses, must have given employment to a great number of officials and workmen. If we add to these the crowd of embalmers, coffin manufacturers and priests of the dead, employed in the numberless private tombs, as well as the stonemasons, builders and other artisans always required for the building of new tombs, we shall understand how this realm of the dead gradually became a real city. The tract between the river on the edge of the western hills was doubtless more or less covered with houses, at least along the high roads which led down from each great funeral temple to the Nile.

Strabo reckoned the extent of Thebes, including the western side, as 14 kilometres (nine miles); and even if parts of this gigantic town were taken up with country houses and gardens, yet it may well compare with the great towns of the world of modern times.

Thebes fell like Rome and Nineveh. When the seat of government was removed to Lower Egypt the heart of the city was destroyed and her importance lost, and she became more and more deserted. Those parts of the town which could be used for arable land were cultivated, and gradually the inhabitants who remained withdrew to the sites occupied by the great buildings; and thus the villages of Karnak, Luxor and Medinet Habu nestled round those vast temples, and now constitute the last remains of the great city.

Sailing down the stream from Thebes, we come on the eastern bank to the 'Nome of the two Hawks', important in old and modern days for the same reason. The river here makes a deep bend towards the Red Sea, and is met by a transverse valley of the Arabian desert which forms a natural road from Egypt to the coast. The Egyptian expeditions to the incense country of Punt, the Greek merchantmen travelling to South Arabia, the Indian navigators of the Middle Ages, the modern pilgrims to Mecca, all have used this road; and it is only since the opening of the Suez Canal that traffic has been wholly diverted into another channel. The starting points for the desert, and the harbours, have changed from time to time; Koptos Qobte was the usual starting point in old times; Qus in the Middle Ages; and at the present time it is Keneh, which lies farther to the north.

In old times this road was also important for the great quarries of Rehanu, the modern Hammamat, situated where the limestone meets the older formations. With the exception of granite, all the hard dark-coloured stone used by the Egyptian sculptors came from these quarries; and those who know how much the Egyptians valued these 'eternal stones' can estimate the importance of the road by which alone they could obtain these treasures. Soldiers protected it from the Beduins of the *Ente*, who, like their successors the Troglodytes and the Ababde, would suddenly attack travellers. A higher protection than the soldiers was also at hand, for Koptos was the abode of the great god Min, the Pan of the Egyptians, who, although he was peculiarly the god of nature, took the travellers of the desert under his special protection. The same god had another famous temple in the town of Chemnis, in the ninth nome, which adjoined the fifth nome on the north.

This part of Egypt is the true home of the great gods. In the sixth nome, about 22 kilometres (14 miles) from Koptos, there lay on the western bank the temple of Denderah, the sacred abode of Hathor, the goddess of joy and love. The old sanctuary is now replaced by a Greco-Roman building. Then again, 61 kilometres (38 miles) down the stream in the eighth nome, was the most holy place in Egypt, Abydos, with the grave of Osiris. A blessing was supposed to rest on those buried here, and many who preferred to be interred near their homes put up gravestones here, so that 'Osiris, the lord of Abydos', should receive them into the underworld. Thus Abydos became in the first place a city of the dead, in which, as in western Thebes, the living only dwelt for the sake of the tombs. Politically, the neighbouring town of Thinis, which lay rather nearer to the river, was the more important, at any rate in old times.

Middle Egypt and the Feyum

The 10th and 11th nomes both lay on the western bank; they played but a small part in history; the district belonging to them on the eastern bank, the 'Nome of the two Gods', was of more importance. The chief town of the latter, *Du qau* (high mountain), the modern Qau, lay at the entrance of one of the great desert roads which led to the porphyry quarries in the northern part of the Arabian desert. Traffic also passed along this road, and across the Gulf of Aqabah to the quarries in the peninsula of Sinai; this was an easier route than that by sea from Lower Egypt.

The 12th nome, 'his Mountain', lay on the eastern bank, and was the chief seat of the worship of Anubis, the jackal-headed god of the dead; the same great god was revered in the opposite nome, the 'first sycamore nome', with its chief town of Siut (Saut). This latter fact is significant, for this nome with the two following was governed by a powerful race of rulers during the so-called Middle Empire (about 2100–1900 BCE), and the interesting representations and inscriptions in their rocky tombs are almost all that is left to show us the civilization of this period. In nearly every section of this work we shall have to refer to these tombs of Siut, Bersheh and Beni Hasan.

We next come to the 15th province, probably called the 'Nome of the Hare', with its famous capital of Chmunu (now Ashmunên, the Greek Hermopolis). This town 'of the eight', as Chmunu signifies, was so named from the eight elementary beings of the world, who were honoured here. The chief god of the town was Thoth, the god of wisdom, who was considered to be the guide of these eight elementary beings. The tombs of the princes of this old town lie on the opposite (eastern) side of the river near the modern Bersheh. A little to the south of Bersheh, at a point where the eastern chain of hills retreats somewhat, we find some most remarkable ruins, the remains of the city and tombs of Tell el Amarna. This town was founded (about 1340 BCE) in a peremptory fashion by the so-called heretic king, the strange creature Amenhotep IV. He had broken with the old religion, which had been evolved in the course of centuries, and he wished that the reformation introduced by him should remain untouched by the associations which were bound up with the capital of his fathers. He therefore left Thebes and built a new capital at Tell el Amarna, but this town enjoyed only a short existence, as a few years after the death of this great heretic it was razed to the ground.

We shall often have to speak of Meh, the 16th nome, with the antelope as its coat-of-arms, and of the 'eastern country', connected with that province, and of the town of Men'at Chufu (the nurse of king Chufu). The tombs of the governors of this part of the country are on the east bank, the celebrated tombs of Beni Hasan; they are most precious for the light they throw on the history of Egyptian manners and customs. At other points also in the eastern hills, e.g., at Zawijet el Meïtin and at Qum el ahmar, we find important tombs in the rocks.

The two provinces No. 5 and No. 9, which were contiguous, both served the god Min; No. 12 and No. 13 the jackal-headed god Anubis; the latter god was also worshipped on the opposite side of the Nile in the 17th and 18th nomes. These provinces played little part in political history, least of all the 18th, where there was little arable land, but to which belonged the celebrated alabaster quarries lying in the mountains at the distance of about a day's journey. The 19th nome to the west of the Nile, was one of the few parts of Egypt in which Set or Typhon was revered. The worship of this god, the enemy of all fruitfulness, may have been connected with the calling followed by the inhabitants, who were most of them guides to the desert caravans. The road to the northern oasis, both in old and in more modern times, started from this province.

On the west side there follow the anterior and posterior Nomes of the Date Palm (the 20th and the 21st), both famous in old Egypt. The former for religious reasons, for the sun god Re first appeared, bringing light and order into the world, on the hill of its ancient capital Chenensuten or Chenensu (Herakleopolis, the present Ahnas).

The fertile Feyum belonged to the posterior nome, and the water reservoirs here were most important for the whole country of Egypt. While the other oases lie 20 or 30 miles from the Nile, and are watered by springs, the Feyum is connected with the Nile by a canal, and is close to the edge of the western valley, the traveller in fact can cross the intervening mountainous district in little more than an hour.

A little to the south of the above-mentioned Bersheh, the great canal (the modern Bahr Yusuf, Joseph's river) makes a bend away from the Nile, and flows northwards to the western side of the valley. This is not an artificial canal, as is proved by its many curves and bends, but an old branch of the river like that of Abydos; it is connected with the Bahr Yusuf by a dry watercourse, the remains of the old bed of the Nile, which can easily be traced farther north into the Delta. Herodotus relates that the present eastern channel of the Nile was not the ancient one; the latter formerly flowed close to the western edge of the valley. This great change was probably due to no sudden convulsion of nature; it is well known that a stream left to itself, with no rocky walls to stop it, will slowly shift its bed, and sometimes, after forming a new branch may even for centuries allow its waters to flow through both branches equally before it entirely gives up the old channel, in which the water gradually subsides till the watercourse is left dry.

Thus in ancient Egypt there was probably an older channel to the west of the valley in addition to the present one on the east side; the former, as was related by the priests to Herodotus, was dammed up above Memphis by Menes, the first Egyptian king of human race, in order to make a site for his new capital. It may be that another work as daring was undertaken at the same time that this dam was constructed, that a gorge in the rocks between the Nile valley and the Feyum was deepened and the branch of the river allowed to flow into the Feyum. By these means this barren depression in the ground was changed into one of the most fertile parts of Egypt, and a province of about 2,330 square kilometres (900 square miles) of arable land added to the little country. This was not all. An enterprising king (probably Amenemhat III about 2000 BCE) built dikes some kilometres in length in order to change the south-eastern corner of the Feyum into an immense reservoir in which the water could be regulated by sluices. By this great basin, 170 square kilometres (66 square miles) in area (the Lake Moeris, the wonder of the Greeks), the inundation in the Feyum and in Lower Egypt was regulated; for if the water rose too high, part was retained in this deep lake, if too low, some of the reserve water could be used from it. It was natural that in this *lakeland*, the ancient name of the Feyum, men should revere the crocodile-headed god Subk, whose temple was to be found in the capital Shedet, called in later times Arsinoe. The two nomes of the Date Palm, and the unimportant nome opposite (the 23rd), complete the provinces of 'the South' or Upper Egypt.

Lower Egypt

We now turn to the discussion of the 'North Land', to which the northernmost part of the Nile valley belonged. We shall be able to be the more brief as, with the exception of its southern division, Lower Egypt was of little importance in ancient times. During the course of centuries, in no part of the Nile valley has the river undergone so many changes as in the Delta. There are now but two mouths to the Nile – that of Rosetta and that of Damietta; in Greek times we know there were seven, and of the course of the river in yet earlier periods we really know nothing.

The north of the Delta, as has been said above, was covered with swamps, and our knowledge of the southern part is very scanty. It is therefore difficult to determine the position of individual provinces; indeed it is doubtful whether in the Delta this division was the old national one. We will therefore waive that question entirely, and confine ourselves to the description of certain important towns.

The old capital of Egypt, Memphis (Mennufer), naturally stands first; it was situated a little above the modern Cairo on the west bank of the river. It has entirely disappeared; the mounds overgrown with palms close to the village of Mitrahine alone denote the spot where stood the great temple of Ptah. The famous citadel of the town, the 'White Wall', as well as the other buildings, have utterly vanished, evidently owing to the fact that the inhabitants of the neighbouring Cairo used the ruins of Memphis as a convenient quarry. The long line of pyramids, stretching for kilometres along the western ridge of hills, alone betrays what a powerful city once stood here. Groups of these royal tombs rise from the plateau, which extends past Gizeh, Zawijet el Aryan, Abusir, Sakkarah, Dahshur, and Lisht, to Medum, not far from the entrance to the Feyum. Grouped round each pyramid are the smaller tombs of courtiers; these are the so-called mastabahs – those ancient tombs which teach us so much about the life of the ancient Egyptians in the earliest period, in the same way as those of Thebes picture to us the later times, and those of Beni Hasan the time of the 'Middle Empire'. We are indebted to the private tombs of this Memphite necropolis for almost all contained in this book concerning the 'Old Empire'.

About 19 miles to the north of Memphis, north-east of the bend of the river, was the ancient sacred city of On, better known to us by its Greek name, Heliopolis. This name, 'City of the Sun', shows us which god was revered here; the temple was one of the most splendid in the country, and, according to Herodotus, the priests were considered the wisest in Egypt. A great part of the ancient Egyptian religious literature appears to have been written in this town. At the present day, fields cover the sites both of town and temples, and one obelisk stands alone to point out the spot to visitors.

The west of the Delta was probably inhabited chiefly by Libyans, one town only being frequently mentioned in ancient times, Sais (Sau), the city of the goddess of war, Neith. In the eighth century BCE this town first became of historical importance, the Libyan family reigning there, certain chiefs of the names of Psammetichus and Necho having raised themselves to be kings of Egypt.

The east of the Delta was more thickly populated; at Mendes (*Ded*) the sacred ram was revered; at Busiris was a famous tomb of Osiris; at Bubastis were held the Dionysiac festivals of the cat-headed goddess of pleasure, Bast. To the north-east, on the edge of the swamps, was Tanis (Zoan), an important town even in early ages. Non-Egyptian rulers seem to have reigned there in old times; later kings also resided here and built a great temple to the warrior god Set. Mariette excavated the vast ruins here [in 1860–64], and further work has since been carried on by the Egypt Exploration Fund, the results of which have been published by that society.

The isthmus now cut through by the Suez Canal between the Red Sea and the Mediterranean is intersected by a number of lakes, the remains of the strait which formerly separated Africa from Asia. These lakes are connected with the Delta by a narrow valley, the modern Wadi Tumilat. In old times there was a canal from the Nile into this valley, which fertilized the whole district. This is the well-known Land of Goshen, in which, according to the Hebrew account, the ancestors of the Jews fed their cattle. The towns of Ramses and Pithom, built by the Hebrews when in bondage, must have been situated here. The same king Ramses II, who caused these towns to be built, seems to have undertaken another great work here, the continuation of the canal of the Wadi Tumilat to the Bitter Lakes, and the cutting through of the rising ground between them and the Red Sea. This connection between the Nile and the Red Sea was the true precursor of the Suez Canal. However, this great work seems soon to have been rendered useless by the silting up of the sand; King Pharaoh Necho and King Darius re-opened it, but it was soon filled up again with sand; afterwards Trajan and Hadrian undertook the work, and later the conqueror Amr made the canal navigable for some time. The old course of the canal can still be distinctly traced by the side of the modern one.

The isthmus of Suez was of the greatest consequence also from a military point of view – it was doubtless fortified in very early times. Probably here stood the great fortress T'aru, often spoken of as the starting point for the expeditions into Syria, and also the strongly fortified town of Pelusium, which was situated at the mouth of the eastern branch of the Nile. Close by we must place Hat-uar (Avaris), the fortress which for centuries served as a protection to the power of the barbarian conquerors of Egypt, the Hyksos.

THE PEOPLE OF EGYPT

Origin of the Egyptians

The people who inhabited ancient Egypt still survive in their descendants the modern Egyptians. The vicissitudes of history have changed both language and religion, but invasions and conquests have not been able to alter the features of this ancient people. The hundreds and thousands of Greeks and Arabs who have settled in the country seem to have been absorbed into it; they may have modified the race in the great towns, where their numbers were considerable, but in the open country they scarcely produced any effect. The modern fellah resembles his forefather of 4,000 years ago, except that he speaks Arabic, and has become a Muslim. In a modern Egyptian village, figures meet one which might have walked out of the pictures in an ancient Egyptian tomb. We must not deny that this resemblance is partly due to another reason besides the continuance of the old race. Each country and condition of life stamps the inhabitants with certain characteristics. The nomad of the desert has the same features, whether he wanders through the Sahara or the interior of Arabia; and the Copt, who has maintained his religion through centuries of oppression, might be mistaken at first sight for a Polish Jew, who has suffered in the same way. The Egyptian soil, therefore, with its ever-constant conditions of life, has always stamped the population of the Nile valley with the same seal.

The question of the race-origin of the Egyptians has long been a matter of dispute between ethnologists and philologists, the former maintaining the African theory of descent, the latter the Asiatic. Ethnologists assert that nothing exists in the physical structure of the Egyptian to distinguish him from the native African, and that from the Egyptian to the Black population of tropical Africa, a series of links exist which do not admit of a break. The Egyptians, they maintain, cannot be separated from the Berbers, nor the latter from the Kelowi or the Tibbu, nor these again from the inhabitants round Lake Tsad; all form one race in the mind of the ethnologist, differentiated only by the influence of a dissimilar manner of life and climate. Therefore, they say, many old customs of the ancient Egyptians are now found amongst the people of the Upper Nile. [...] On the other side, philologists maintain that the language of the ancient Egyptians has distinct kinship with that of the so-called Semitic nations.

Spread over anterior Asia, and the east and north of Africa, is found a great root language, which has been called after its chief representatives, the Egypto-Semitic. The Semitic languages of Arabia, Syria and Mesopotamia belong to this group, as well as the allied Ethiopian dialects of east Africa, the languages of the Besharis, Gallas and Somalis. Further removed is the Libyan, spoken by the people of Berber in north Africa, as far as the Atlantic; and still more peculiarly constituted is the ancient Egyptian. Nothing certain has been or probably will be ascertained, for the Libyan and Ethiopian languages are only known to us in their present much-changed forms. But the fact remains that philologists consider that the people who speak these languages belong to one and the same race. Other reasons tend to show us that the Semitic races migrated from one part of Asia to the districts in which they afterwards settled, and therefore the theory has been accepted that the Ethiopian, Libyan and Egyptian people all forsook their Asiatic homes during the dim ages of the past, and seized possession of north and east Africa.

This theory is directly opposed to that of the ethnologists, according to whom these races are purely African. If we free ourselves, however, from the prejudices which have so long held unlimited sway over this domain of science, we shall be able to reconcile these two theories. It seems a very doubtful hypothesis that ancient races should dwell quietly in one inhospitable region until the idea should suddenly seize them to forsake their homes and, with their children and their goods, to seek a better country. Such migrations have certainly taken place amongst the hordes of barbarians (e.g., the old migrations of the Teuton or Scythian races), but they never had much effect. After a few generations all traces of them have disappeared in the countries they conquered, and no one would imagine from the appearance of the inhabitants of modern Italy, Spain or Tunis, that whole tribes of Germanic race had overrun those countries. Neither the language nor the race of the subject nation suffers permanent change from such violent incursions.

On the other hand, if but a few adventurers conquer a country and thus make it possible for their kindred to settle there, the constant influx of immigrants even in small numbers has an immense influence on the people. In the first place, the conquerors succeed in introducing their language to be used officially; the upper classes of the subject race, desiring to belong to the ruling class, then begin ostentatiously to use foreign idioms; at last, perhaps only after 1,000 years, the lower classes begin also to adopt the new language. Thus, in our own days we have seen nations extend their nationality, e.g., a few Spaniards and Portuguese in South America, a few Arabs amongst the Copts and Berbers, a few Anglo-Saxons amongst the Celts in England. In each case we see that in this process the language only of the subject people is changed, the race itself remains unaltered.

In like manner probably, ancient nations underwent transformations. The inhabitants of Libya, Egypt and Ethiopia have probably belonged to the same race since prehistoric times; in physical structure they are still Africans, though in later times they have adopted an Asiatic language. No one can say how long they have used kindred dialects. It may be these proceeded from the one language they originally possessed, or it is quite possible that one of these races imposed their tongue on the others, or they may have been derived from a tribe of which we have never heard. Considering how little we know of the Egypto-Semitic speech, we may suppose that it was to a Libyan invasion that the valley of the Nile owed in the first place its later language; that a similar incursion endowed the inhabitants of Syria and Arabia with the Semitic tongue; and that the latter nations gave the same to the dwellers in east Africa. This is of course pure hypothesis, for the same process may have taken place in many other ways. Probably we shall never have any certainty on the matter, for these events occurred more than 5,000 years ago. [...] How it happened is of small consequence, it is only important to remember that there is no necessity for a great immigration of the Egyptians from some distant corner of Asia. We may conscientiously believe them to be natives of their own country, children of their own soil, even if it should be proved that their old language, like their modern one, was imported from other countries.

It is well known that the Egyptians considered themselves an indigenous people, free from any foreign taint. Were they not the peculiar people, specially loved by the gods? Did not the great gods first manifest themselves in Egypt, where the sun-god ruled and fought as a king, and where his descendants still sat on the throne? Therefore, the Egyptians alone were termed 'men' (romet); other nations were Blacks, Asiatics or Libyans, but not men. According to the myth, these nations were descended from the enemies of the gods, for when the sun-god Re overthrew his opponents at Edfu, a few succeeded in making their escape; those who fled to the south became the Ethiopians, those to the north Asiatics; from the fugitives of the west sprang the Libyans, and from those of the east, the Bedouins.

The Egyptians named their country from the colour of the soil 'the black country' (Qemet), and thus distinguished it from the red country of the barbarians: they also believed themselves to be superior to foreigners by the colour of their skin. The Syrians were light brown, the Libyans white, the Africans black, but the Egyptians had received from the gods their beautiful colour, a deep dark brown for the men, a light yellow for the women.

Circumcision was also practised from early times by the Egyptians, yet probably they did not attach so much importance to this curious custom as the Jews and Muslims. It first became a religious token amongst the Jews, who zealously tried to distinguish themselves in all ways from the surrounding heathen; had the Egyptians also regarded it as a divine institution they would have mentioned it more frequently. [...]

Characteristics of the Egyptian People

Many contrary opinions have been expressed touching the character of the Egyptian people, and their mental faculties. While Herodotus praises the wisdom and the good memory of the Egyptians, and Diodorus declares them to be the most grateful people in the world, the Emperor Hadrian says that, when travelling in Egypt, he found them to be utterly frivolous, vacillating, credulous of every idle tale, hostile, good-for-nothing and slanderous. In the same way many modern scholars represent them as pious folk, who thought more of the future world than of the present, while others praise their cheerful childlike pleasure in the things of this world. The exponents of each of these theories regard the matter too exclusively from one point of view; in truth, the question is one admitting only of a subjective answer. If the character of an individual is complex, that of a nation is still more so, and what Faust says of the 'spirit of the times' is equally true of the 'spirit of the nations', for after all, it is a well-known fact that the mind of the man himself is mirrored in that of the people. [...]

As a nation [the Egyptians] appear to us to have been intelligent, practical and very energetic, but lacking poetical imagination: this is exactly what we should expect from a nation of peasants living in this country of toilsome agriculture. We will quote the words of one, profoundly acquainted with Egypt, referring to the modern lower classes, i.e., to those in whom the characteristics of the nation find their natural expression. He says, 'In his youth the Egyptian peasant is wonderfully docile, sensible and active; in his riper years, owing to want and care, and the continual work of drawing water, he loses the cheerfulness, freshness and elasticity of mind which made him appear so amiable and promising as a boy. He sows and reaps, he works and earns money, but his piastres rarely remain in his own possession, and he sees the fruits of his labour pass into the hands of those above him. His character is therefore like that of a gifted child who has been harshly brought up, and who realizes as he grows older that others are taking advantage of his work.' This picture of a race, cheerful by nature, but losing the happy temperament and becoming selfish and hardened in the severe work of life, represents also the ancient people, as they appear to the eyes of an unprejudiced observer.

Earliest Egyptian History

The earliest monuments that have come down to us represent the Egyptians as possessing, even then, an ancient civilization, also a complete system of writing, a literature, a highly developed art and a well-ordered government. Preceding this first period of Egyptian history, a long time of peaceful development must have elapsed, about which we have no information. The learned men of Egypt imagined the time before their first king Menes to have been a sort of golden age, in which the gods reigned; the learned men of modern times call the same period 'the stone age'; both theories are certainly ingenious, but both are alike difficult to prove. It is but seldom that we can draw any conclusion, as to the life in Egypt in prehistoric times, from customs existing amongst the Egyptians during the historical periods. We may conclude however, from the form of the royal robes, that the dignity of king existed in Egypt at a time when the people, like the [Africans] of today, wore nothing but a kirtle. The royal attire was formerly an apron and a lion's tail, whilst the grandees distinguished themselves from the people by a panther's skin, which they threw over their shoulders. The sportsmen made their way through the swamps on boats made of reeds, and hunted there with throwing sticks. Their knives, in part at least, as well as the tips of their arrows, were made of flint, yet we must not conclude from this fact that they were ignorant of the use of metals. They reckoned their years by notches, reminding us of a time when the art of writing was unknown.

All these customs, which were dying out even in the earliest historical times, are a heritage from that ancient period when the Egyptian civilization may perhaps have equalled that of the modern Somalis or Gallas. [...]

MANNERS AND CUSTOMS OF EGYPTIANS ACCORDING TO HERODOTUS

The Egyptians in agreement with their climate, which is unlike any other, and with the river, which shows a nature different from all other rivers, established for themselves manners and customs in a way opposite to other men in almost all matters: for among them the women frequent the market and carry on trade, while the men remain at home and weave; and whereas others weave pushing the woof upwards, the Egyptians push it downwards: the men carry their burdens upon their heads and the women upon their shoulders: the women make water standing up and the men crouching down: they ease themselves in their houses and they eat without in the streets, alleging as reason for this that it is right to do secretly the things that are unseemly though necessary, but those which are not unseemly, in public: no woman is a minister either of male or female divinity, but men of all, both male and female: to support their parents the sons are in no way compelled, if they do not desire to do so, but the daughters are forced to do so, be they never so unwilling.

The priests of the gods in other lands wear long hair, but in Egypt they shave their heads: among other men the custom is that in mourning those whom the matter concerns most nearly have their hair cut short, but the Egyptians, when deaths occur, let their hair grow long, both that on the head and that on the chin, having before been close shaven: other men have their daily living separated from beasts, but the Egyptians have theirs together with beasts: other men live on wheat and on barley, but to any one of the Egyptians who makes his living on these it is a great reproach; they make their bread of maize, which some call spelt: they knead dough with their feet and clay with their hands, with which also they gather up dung: and whereas other men, except such as have learnt otherwise from the Egyptians, have their members as nature made them, the Egyptians practice circumcision: as to garments, the men wear two each and the women but one: and whereas others make fast the rings and ropes of the sails outside the ship, the Egyptians do this inside: finally in the writing of characters and reckoning with pebbles, while the Hellenes carry the hand from the left to the right, the Egyptians do this from the right to the left; and doing so they say that they do it themselves right-wise and the Hellenes left-wise: and they use two kinds of characters for writing, of which the one kind is called sacred and the other common.

EGYPTIAN ETHICS

Fortunately, we have preserved to us a considerable body of the maxims of conduct from the Pyramid times; and these show very practically what were the ideals and the motives of the early people. [...]

The repudiation of sins before the judgment of Osiris is the earliest code of morals, and it is striking that in this there are no family duties. Such an exclusion points to the family being unimportant in early times, the matriarchate perhaps then excluding the responsibility of the man. In the earliest form the prominence of duties is in the order of those to equals, to inferiors, to gods and to the man's own character. In later times the duties to inferiors have almost vanished, and the inner duties to character are man held up greatly extended, being felt to lie at the root of all else.

The ideal character was drawn in the maxims as being strong, steadfast, commanding, direct, self-respecting, avoiding inferior companionships, active and above all truthful and straightforward. Discretion, quietness and reserve were enforced, and a dignified endurance without pride was to be attained.

In material things energy and self-reliance were held up, and a judicious respect for, and imitation of, successful men. Covetousness was specially reprobated, and luxury and self-indulgence were looked on as a course which ends in bitterness.

The aspect of marriage depended essentially on property. Where a woman had property of her own she was mistress of the house, and her husband was but a kind of permanent boarder. Though in early times, and among the priestesses later, the choice by a woman was scarcely regarded as permanent. Where, however, the household depended on the work of the man, he naturally took the leading part. But the code of abstract morality, and the dictates of common prudence, between men and women, were of as high a standard as in any ancient or modern peoples. No reasonable legislator would wish to add more, although 6,000 years and Christianity have intervened since the Egyptian framed his life. The family sense of duty in training and advancing a man's sons was strongly urged.

In the general interchange of social life, perhaps the main feature was that of consideration for others. A higher standard of good feeling and kindliness existed than any that we know of among ancient peoples, or among most modern nations. The council hall of the local ruler was the main theatre for ability; and the injunctions to be fearless, and at the same time gentle and cautious, would improve the character of any modern assembly. The greater number of precepts however relate to the judicious conduct toward inferiors. Justice and good discipline were the necessary basis, but they were to be always tempered by respect for the feelings and comfort of the servants.

The religious aspect of ethics was almost confined to the respect for the property and offerings of the gods. But the more spiritual side was touched in the precept, 'That which is detestable in the sanctuary of god are noisy feasts; if thou implore him with a loving heart, of which all the words are mysterious, he will do thy matters, he hears thy words, he accepts thine offerings.'

The permanence of the Egyptian character will strike anyone who knows the modern native. The essential mode of justification in the judgment was by the declaration of the deceased that he had not done various crimes [...]. The main fault of character that was condemned was covetousness. [...] The intrusion of scheming underlings between the master and his men is noted as a failing [...] The dominance of the scribe in managing affairs and making profits was familiar in ancient as in modern times.

THE RELIGION OF ANCIENT EGYPT

The purpose of religion to the Egyptian was to secure the favour of the gods. There is but little trace of negative prayer to avert evils or deprecate evil influences, but rather of positive prayer for concrete favours. On the part of kings this is usually of the Jacob type, offering to provide temples and services to the god in return for material prosperity. The Egyptian was essentially self-satisfied, he had no confession to make of sin or wrong, and had no thought of pardon. In the judgment he boldly averred that he was free of the 42 sins that might prevent his entry into the kingdom of Osiris. If he failed to establish his innocence in the weighing of his heart, there was no other plea, but he was consumed by fire and by a hippopotamus, and no hope remained for him.

Religious Customs – According to Herodotus

They are religious excessively beyond all other men, and with regard to this they have customs as follows: they drink from cups of bronze and rinse them out every day, and not some only do this but all: they wear garments of linen always newly washed, and this they make a special point of practice: they circumcise themselves for the sake of cleanliness, preferring to be clean rather than comely. The priests shave themselves all over their body every other day, so that no lice or any other foul thing may come to be upon them when they minister to the gods; and the priests wear garments of linen only and sandals of papyrus, and any other garment they may not take nor other sandals; these wash themselves in cold water twice in a day and twice again in the night; and other religious services they perform (one may almost say) of infinite number. They enjoy also good things not a few, for they do not consume or spend anything of their own substance, but there is sacred bread baked for them and they have each great quantity of flesh of oxen and geese coming in to them each day, and also wine of grapes is given to them; but it is not permitted to them to taste of fish: beans moreover the Egyptians do not at all sow in their land, and those which they grow they neither eat raw nor boil for food; nay the priests do not endure even to look upon them, thinking this to be an unclean kind of pulse: and there is not one priest only for each of the gods but many, and of them one is chief-priest, and whenever a priest dies his son is appointed to his place.

Sacred Animals – According to Herodotus

[...] the Egyptians are excessively careful in their observances, both in other matters which concern the sacred rites and also in those which follow:– Egypt, though it borders upon Libya, does not very much abound in wild animals, but such as they have are one and all accounted by them sacred, some of them living with men and others not. But if I should say for what reasons the sacred animals have been thus dedicated, I should fall into discourse of matters pertaining to the gods, of which I most desire not to speak; and what I have actually said touching slightly upon them, I said because I was constrained by necessity.

About these animals there is a custom of this kind: persons have been appointed of the Egyptians, both men and women, to provide the food for each kind of beast separately, and their office goes down from father to son; and those who dwell in the various cities perform vows to them thus, that is, when they make a vow to the god to whom the animal belongs, they shave the head of their children either the whole or the half or the third part of it, and then set the hair in the balance against silver, and whatever it weighs, this the man gives to the person who provides for the animals, and she cuts up fish of equal value and gives it for food to the animals. Thus food for their support has been appointed and if any one kill any of these animals, the penalty, if he do it with his own will, is death, and if against his will, such penalty as the priests may appoint: but whosoever shall kill an ibis or a hawk, whether it be with his will or against his will, must die.

Of the animals that live with men there are great numbers, and would be many more but for the accidents which befall the cats. For when the females have produced young, they are no longer in the habit of going to the males, and these seeking to be united with them are not able. To this end then they contrive as follows,– they either take away by force or remove secretly the young from the females and kill them (but after killing they do not eat them), and the females being deprived of their young and desiring more, therefore come to the males, for it is a creature that is fond of its young. Moreover, when a fire occurs, the cats seem to be divinely possessed; for while the Egyptians stand at intervals and look after the cats, not taking any care to extinguish the fire, the cats slipping through or leaping over the men, jump into the fire; and when this happens, great mourning comes upon the Egyptians. And in whatever houses a cat has died by a natural death, all those who dwell in this house shave their eyebrows only, but those in which a dog has died shave their whole body and also their head. The cats when they are dead are carried away to sacred buildings in the city of Bubastis, where after being embalmed they are buried; but the dogs they bury each people in their own city in sacred tombs; and the ichneumons are buried just in the same way as the dogs. The shrewmice however and the hawks they carry away to the city of Buto, and the ibises to Hermopolis; the bears (which are not commonly seen) and the wolves, not much larger in size than foxes, they bury on the spot where they are found lying.

Of the crocodile the nature is as follows:– during the four most wintry months this creature eats nothing: she has four feet and is an animal belonging to the land and the water both; for she produces and hatches eggs on the land, and the most part of the day she remains upon dry land, but the whole of the night in the river, for the water in truth is warmer than the unclouded open air and the dew. Of all the mortal creatures of which we have knowledge this grows to the greatest bulk from the smallest beginning; for the eggs which she produces are not much larger than those of geese and the newly hatched young one is in proportion to the egg, but as he grows he becomes as much as 17 cubits long and sometimes yet larger. He has eyes like those of a pig and teeth large and tusky, in proportion to the size of his body; but unlike all other beasts he grows no tongue, neither does he move his lower jaw, but brings the upper jaw towards the lower, being in this too unlike all other beasts. He has moreover strong claws and a scaly hide upon his back which cannot be pierced; and he is blind in the water, but in the air he is of a very keen sight. Since he has his living in the water he keeps his mouth all full within of leeches; and whereas all other birds and beasts fly from him, the trochilus is a creature which is at peace with him, seeing that from her he receives benefit; for the crocodile having come out of the water to the land and then having opened his mouth (this he is wont to do generally towards the West Wind), the trochilus upon that enters into his mouth and swallows down the leeches, and he being benefited is pleased and does no harm to the trochilus.

Now for some of the Egyptians the crocodiles are sacred animals, and for others not so, but they treat them on the contrary as enemies: those however who dwell about Thebes and about the lake of Moiris hold them to be most sacred, and each of these two peoples keeps one crocodile selected from the whole number, which has been trained to tameness, and they put hanging ornaments of molten stone and of gold into the ears of these and anklets round the front feet, and they give them food appointed and victims of sacrifices and treat them as well as possible while they live, and after they are dead they bury them in sacred tombs, embalming them: but those who dwell about the city of Elephantine even eat them, not holding them to be sacred. They are called not crocodiles but *champsai*, and the Ionians gave them the name of crocodile, comparing their form to that of the crocodiles (lizards) which appear in their country in the stone walls.

There are many ways in use of catching them and of various kinds: I shall describe that which to me seems the most worthy of being told. A man puts the back of a pig upon a hook as bait, and lets it go into the middle of the river, while he himself upon the bank of the river has a young live pig, which he beats; and the crocodile hearing its cries makes for the direction of the sound, and when he finds the pig's back he swallows it down: then they pull, and when he is drawn out to land, first of all the hunter forthwith plasters up his eyes with mud, and having done so he very easily gets the mastery of him, but if he does not do so he has much trouble.

The river-horse (hippopotamus) is sacred in the district of Papremis, but for the other Egyptians he is not sacred; and this is the appearance which he presents: he is four-footed, cloven-hoofed like an ox, flat-nosed, with a mane like a horse and showing teeth like tusks, with a tail and voice like a horse and in size as large as the largest ox; and his hide is so exceedingly thick that when it has been dried shafts of javelins are made of it. There are moreover otters in the river, which they consider to be sacred: and of fish also they esteem that which is called the *lepidotos* to be sacred, and also the eel; and these they say are sacred to the Nile: and of birds the fox-goose.

There is also another sacred bird called the phoenix which I did not myself see except in painting, for in truth he comes to them very rarely, at intervals, as the people of Heliopolis say, of 500 years; and these say that he comes regularly when his father dies; and if he be like the painting he is of this size and nature, that is to say, some of his feathers are of gold colour and others red, and in outline and size he is as nearly as possible like an eagle. This bird they say (but I cannot believe the story) contrives as follows:– setting forth from Arabia he conveys his father, they say, to the temple of the Sun (Helios) plastered up in myrrh, and buries him in the temple of the Sun; and he conveys him thus:– he forms first an egg of myrrh as large as he is able to carry, and then he makes trial of carrying it, and when he has made trial sufficiently, then he hollows out the egg and places his father within it and plasters over with other myrrh that part of the egg where he hollowed it out to put his father in, and when his father is laid in it, it proves (they say) to be of the same weight as it was; and after he has plastered it up, he conveys the whole to Egypt to the temple of the Sun. Thus they say that this bird does.

There are also about Thebes sacred serpents, not at all harmful to men, which are small in size and have two horns growing from the top of the head: these they bury when they die in the temple of Zeus, for to this god they say that they are sacred. There is a region moreover in Arabia, situated nearly over against the city of Buto, to which place I came to inquire about the winged serpents: and when I came thither I saw bones of serpents and spines in quantity so great that it is impossible to make report of the number, and there were heaps of spines, some heaps large and others less large and others smaller still than these, and these heaps were many in number. This region in which the spines are scattered upon the ground is of the nature of an entrance from a narrow mountain pass to a great plain, which plain adjoins the plain in Egypt; and the story goes that at the beginning of spring winged serpents from Arabia fly towards Egypt, and the birds called ibises meet them at the entrance to this country and do not suffer the serpents to go by but kill them.

On account of this deed it is (say the Arabians) that the ibis has come to be greatly honoured by the Egyptians, and the Egyptians also agree that it is for this reason that they honour these birds. The outward form of the ibis is this:– it is a deep black all over, and has legs like those of a crane and a very curved beak, and in size it is about equal to a rail: this is the appearance of the black kind which fight with the serpents, but of those which most crowd round men's feet (for there are two kinds of ibises) the head is bare and also the whole of the throat, and it is white in feathering except the head and neck and the extremities of the wings and the rump (in all these parts of which I have spoken it is a deep black), while in legs and in the form of the head it resembles the other. As for the serpent its form is like that of the water snake; and it has wings not feathered but most nearly resembling the wings of the bat.

Animal Worship

The worship of animals has been known in many countries; but in Egypt it was maintained to a later pitch of civilization than elsewhere, and the mixture of such a primitive system with more elevated beliefs seemed as strange to the Greek as it does to us. The original motive was a kinship of animals with man, much like that underlying the system of totems. Each place or tribe had its sacred species that was linked with the tribe; the life of the species was carefully preserved, excepting in the one example selected for worship, which after a given time was killed and sacramentally eaten by the tribe. This was certainly the case with the bull at Memphis and the ram at Thebes. That it was the whole species that was sacred, at one place or another, is shown by the penalties for killing any animal of the species, by the wholesale burial and even mummifying of every example, and by the plural form of the names of the gods later connected with the animals, Heru, hawks, Khnumu, rams, etc.

In the prehistoric times the serpent was sacred; figures of the coiled serpent were hung up in the house and worn as an amulet; similarly in historic times a figure of the agathodaemon serpent was placed in a temple of Amenhotep III at Benha. In the first dynasty the serpent was figured in pottery, as a fender round the hearth. The hawk also appears in many predynastic figures, large and small, both worn on the person and carried as standards. The lion is found both in life-size temple figures, lesser objects of worship and personal amulets. The scorpion was similarly honoured in the prehistoric ages.

It is difficult to separate now between animals which were worshipped quite independently, and those which were associated as emblems of anthropomorphic gods. Probably we shall be right in regarding both classes of animals as having been sacred at a remote time, and the connection with the human form as being subsequent. The ideas connected with the animals were those of their most prominent characteristics; hence it appears that it was for the sake of the character that each animal was worshipped, and not because of any fortuitous association with a tribe.

The baboon was regarded as the emblem of Tahuti, the god of wisdom; the serious expression and human ways of the large baboons are an obvious cause for their being regarded as the wisest of animals. Tahuti is represented as a baboon from the first dynasty down to late times; and four baboons were sacred in his temple at Hermopolis. These four baboons were often portrayed as adoring the sun; this idea is due to their habit of chattering at sunrise.

The lioness appears in the compound figures of the goddesses Sekhet, Bast, Mahes and Tefnut. In the form of Sekhet, the lioness is the destructive power of Ra, the sun: it is Sekhet who, in the legend, destroys mankind from Herakleopolis to Heliopolis at the bidding of Ra. The other lioness goddesses are probably likewise destructive or hunting deities. The lesser Felidae also appear; the cheetah and serval are sacred to Hathor in Sinai; the small cats are sacred to Bast, especially at Speos Artemidos and Bubastis.

The bull was sacred in many places, and his worship underlay that of the human gods, who were said to be incarnated in him. The idea is that of the fighting power, as when the king is figured as a bull trampling on his enemies, and the reproductive power, as in the title of the self-renewing gods, 'bull of his mother'.

The most renowned was the Hapi or Apis bull of Memphis, in whom Ptah was said to be incarnate, and who was Osirified and became the Osir-hapi. This appears to have originated the great Ptolemaic god Serapis, as certainly the mausoleum of the bulls was the Serapeum of the Greeks. Another bull of a more massive breed was the Mnevis of Heliopolis, in whom Ra was incarnate. A third bull was Bakh or Bakis of Hermonthis the incarnation of Mentu. And a fourth bull, Ka-nub or Kanobos, was worshipped at the city of that name. The cow was identified with Hathor, who appears with cow's ears and horns, and who is probably the cow goddess Ashtaroth or Istar of Asia. Isis, as identified with Hathor, is also joined in this connection.

The ram was also worshipped as a procreative god; at Mendes in the Delta identified with Osiris, at Herakleopolis identified with Hershefi, at Thebes as Amon, and at the cataract as Khnumu the creator. The association of the ram with Amon was strongly held by the Ethiopians; and in the Greek tale of Nektanebo, the last Pharaoh, having by magic visited Olympias and become the father of Alexander, he came as the incarnation of Amon wearing the ram's skin.

The hippopotamus was the goddess Ta-urt, 'the great one', the patroness of pregnancy, who is never shown in any other form. Rarely this animal appears as the emblem of the god Set.

The jackal haunted the cemeteries on the edge of the desert, and so came to be taken as the guardian of the dead, and identified with Anubis, the god of departing souls. Another aspect of the jackal was as the maker of tracks in the desert; the jackal paths are the best guides to practicable courses, avoiding the valleys and precipices, and so the animal was known as Upuat, 'the opener of ways', who showed the way for the dead across the western desert. Species of dogs seem to have been held sacred and mummified on merely the general ground of confusion with the jackal. The ichneumon and the shrewmouse were also held sacred, though not identified with a human god.

The hawk was the principal sacred bird, and was identified with Horus and Ra, the sun-god. It was mainly worshipped at Edfu and Hierakon polis. The souls of kings were supposed to fly up to heaven in the form of hawks, perhaps due to the kingship originating in the hawk district in Upper Egypt. Seker, the god of the dead, appears as a mummified hawk, and on his boat are many small hawks, perhaps the souls of kings who have joined him. The mummy hawk is also Sopdu, the god of the east.

The vulture was the emblem of maternity, as being supposed to care especially for her young. Hence, she is identified with Mut, the mother goddess of Thebes. The queen-mothers have vulture headdresses; the vulture is shown hovering over kings to protect them, and a row of spread-out vultures are figured on the roofs of the tomb passages to protect the soul. The ibis was identified with Tahuti, the god of Hermopolis. The goose is connected with Amon of Thebes. The swallow was also sacred.

The crocodile was worshipped especially in the Fayum, where it frequented the marshy levels of the great lake, and Strabo's description of the feeding of the sacred crocodile there is familiar. It was also worshipped at Onuphis; and at Nubti or Ombos it was identified with Set, and held sacred. Beside the name of Sebek or Soukhos in Fayum, it was there identified with Osiris as the western god of the dead. The frog was an emblem of the goddess Heqt, but was not worshipped.

The cobra serpent was sacred from the earliest times to the present day. It was never identified with any of the great deities, but three goddesses appear in serpent form: Uazet, the Delta goddess of Buto; Mert-seger, 'the lover of silence', the goddess of the Theban necropolis; and Rannut, the harvest goddess. The memory of great pythons of the prehistoric days appears in the serpent-necked monsters on the slate palettes at the beginning of the monarchy, and the immense serpent Apap of the underworld in the later mythology. The serpent has however been a popular object of worship apart from specific gods. We have already noted it on prehistoric amulets, and coiled round the hearths of the early dynasties. Serpents were mummified; and when we reach the full evidences of popular worship, in the terracotta figures and jewellery of later times, the serpent is very prominent. There were usually two represented together, one often with the head of Serapis, the other of Isis, so therefore male and female. Down to modern times a serpent is worshipped at Sheykh Heridy, and miraculous cures attributed to it.

Various fishes were sacred, as the Oxyrhynkhos, Phagros, Lepidotos, Latos and others; but they were not identified with gods, and we do not know of their being worshipped. The scorpion was the emblem of the goddess Selk, and is found in prehistoric amulets; but it is not known to have been adored, and most usually it represents evil, where Horus is shown overcoming noxious creatures.

It will be observed that nearly all the animals which were worshipped had qualities for which they were noted, and in connection with which they were venerated. If the animal worship were due to totemism, or a sense of animal brotherhood in certain tribes, we must also assume that that was due to these qualities of the animal; whereas totemism in other countries does not seem to be due to veneration of special qualities of the animals. It is therefore more likely that the animal worship simply arose from the nature of the animals, and not from any true totemism, although each animal came to be associated with the worship of a particular tribe or district.

The Cosmogony

Man in all times and places has speculated on the nature and origin of the world, and connected such questions with his theology. In Egypt there are not many primitive theories of creation, though some have various elaborated forms. Of the formation of the earth there were two views. (1) That it had been brought into being by the word of a god, who when he uttered any name caused the object thereby to exist. Thoth is the principal creator by this means, and this idea probably belongs to a period soon after the age of the animal gods. (2) The other view is that Ptah framed the world as an artificer, with the aid of eight Khnumu, or earth-gnomes. This belongs to the theology of the abstract gods. The primitive people seem to have been content with the eternity of matter, and only personified nature when they described space (Shu) as separating the sky (Nut) from the earth (Seb). This is akin to the separation of chaos into sky and sea in Genesis.

The sun is called the egg laid by the primeval goose; and in later time this was said to be laid by a god, or modelled by Ptah. Evidently this goose egg is a primitive tale which was adapted to later theology.

The sky is said to be upheld by four pillars. These were later connected with the gods of the four quarters; but the primitive four pillars were represented together, with the capitals one over the other, in the sign *dad* [*djed*], the emblem of stability. These may have belonged to the Osiris cycle, as he is 'lord of the pillars' (*daddu*), and his centre in the Delta was named Daddu from the pillars. The setting up of the pillars or *dad* emblem was a great festival in which the kings took part, and which is often represented.

The creation of life was variously attributed to different great gods where they were worshipped. Khnumu, Osiris, Amen or Atmu, each are stated to be the creator. The mode was only defined by the theorists of Heliopolis; they imagined that Atmu self-produced Shu and Tefnut, they produced Seb and Nut, and they in turn other gods, from whom at last sprang mankind. But this is merely later theorising to fit a theology in being.

The cosmogonic theories, therefore, were by no means important articles of belief, but rather assumptions of what the gods were likely to have done similar to the acts of men. The creation by the word is the most elevated idea, and is parallel to the creation in Genesis.

The conception of the nature of the world was that of a great plain, over which the sun passed by day, and beneath which it travelled through the hours of night. The movement of the sun was supposed to be that of floating on the heavenly ocean, figured by its being in a boat, which was probably an expression for its flotation. The elaboration of the nature of the regions through which the sun passed at night essentially belongs to the Ra theology, and only recognizes the kingdom of Osiris by placing it in one of the hours of night. The old conception of the dim realm of the cemetery-god Seker occupies the fourth and fifth hours; the sixth hour is an approach to the Osiride region, and the seventh hour is the kingdom of Osiris. Each hour was separated by gates, which were guarded by demons who needed to be controlled by magic formulae.

THE DAWN OF HISTORY

Traditions Concerning M'na, or Menes

The Egyptians themselves taught that the first man of whom they had any record was a king called M'na, a name which the Greeks represented by Mên or Menes [probably Narmer]. M'na was born at Tena (This or Thinis) in Upper Egypt, where his ancestors had borne sway before him. He was the first to master the Lower country, and thus to unite under a single sceptre the 'two Egypts' – the long narrow Nile valley and the broad Delta plain. Having placed on his head the double crown which thenceforth symbolized dominion over both tracts, his first thought was that a new capital was needed. Egypt could not, he felt, be ruled conveniently from the latitude of Thebes, or from any site in the Upper country; it required a capital which should abut on both regions, and so command both. Nature pointed out only one fit locality, the junction of the plain with the vale – 'the balance of the two regions', as the Egyptians called it; the place where the narrow 'Upper Country' terminates, and Egypt opens out into the wide smiling plain that thence spreads itself on every side to the sea. Hence there would be easy access to both regions; both would be, in a way, commanded; here, too, was a readily defensible position, one assailable only in front. Experience has shown that the instinct of the first founder was right, or that his political and strategic foresight was extraordinary. Though circumstances, once and again, transferred the seat of government to Thebes or Alexandria, yet such removals were short-lived. The force of geographic fact was too strong to be permanently overcome, and after a few centuries power gravitated back to the centre pointed out by nature.

Site of Memphis

If we may believe the tradition, there was, when the idea of building the new capital arose, a difficulty in obtaining a site in all respects advantageous. The Nile, before debouching upon the plain, hugged for many miles the base of the Libyan hills, and was thus on the wrong side of the valley. It was wanted on the other side, in order to be a water-bulwark against an Asiatic invader. The founder, therefore, before building his city, undertook a gigantic work. He raised a great embankment across the natural course of the river; and, forcing it from its bed, made it enter a new channel and run midway down the valley, or, if anything, rather towards its eastern side. He thus obtained the bulwark against invasion that he required, and he had an ample site for his capital between the new channel of the stream and the foot of the western hills.

It is undoubtedly strange to hear of such a work being constructed at the very dawn of history, by a population that was just becoming a people. But in Egypt precocity is the rule – a Minerva starts full-grown from the head of Jove. The pyramids themselves cannot be placed very long after the supposed reign of Menes; and the engineering skill implied in the pyramids is simply of a piece with that attributed to the founder of Memphis.

Great Temple of Phthah at Memphis

In ancient times a city was nothing without a temple; and the capital city of the most religious people in the world could not by any possibility lack that centre of civic life which its chief temple always was to every ancient town. Philosophy must settle the question how it came to pass that religious ideas were in ancient times so universally prevalent and so strongly pronounced. History is only bound to note the fact. Coeval, then, with the foundation of the city of Menes was, according to the tradition, the erection of a great temple to Phthah – 'the Revealer', the Divine artificer, by whom the world and man were created, and the hidden thought of the remote Supreme Being was made manifest to His creatures, Phthah's temple lay within the town, and was originally a *naos* or 'cell', a single building probably not unlike that between the Sphinx's paws at Giza, situated within a *temenos*, or 'sacred enclosure', watered from the river, and no doubt planted with trees.

Like the medieval cathedrals, the building grew with the lapse of centuries, great kings continually adding new structures to the main edifice, and enriching it with statuary and painting. Herodotus saw it in its full glory, and called it 'a vast edifice, very worthy of commemoration'. Abd-el-Latif saw it in its decline, and noted the beauty of its remains: 'the great monolithic shrine of breccia verde, nine cubits high, eight long, and seven broad, the doors which swung on hinges of stone, the well-carven statues, and the lions terrific in their aspect.' At the present day scarcely a trace remains. One broken colossus of the Great Ramesses, till very recently prostrate, and a few nondescript fragments, alone continue on the spot, to attest to moderns the position of that antique fane, which the Egyptians themselves regarded as the oldest in their land.

Names of Memphis

The new city received from its founder the name of Men-nefer – 'the Good Abode'. It was also known as Ei-Ptah – 'the House of Phthah'. From the former name came the prevailing appellations – the 'Memphis' of the Greeks and Romans, the 'Moph' of the Hebrews, the 'Mimpi' of the Assyrians, and the name still given to the ruins, 'Tel-Monf'. It was indeed a 'good abode' – watered by an unfailing stream, navigable from the sea, which at once brought it supplies and afforded it a strong protection, surrounded on three sides by the richest and most productive alluvium, close to quarries of excellent stone, warm in winter, fanned by the cool northern breezes in the summertime, within easy reach of the sea, yet not so near as to attract the cupidity of pirates. Few capitals have been more favourably placed. It was inevitable that when the old town went to ruins, a new one should spring up in its stead. Memphis still exists, in a certain sense, in the glories of the modern Cairo, which occupies an adjacent site, and is composed largely of the same materials.

The Egyptians knew no more of their first king than that he turned the course of the Nile, founded Memphis, built the nucleus of the great temple of Phthah and 'was devoured by a hippopotamus'. This last fact is related with all due gravity by

Manetho [an Egyptian priest *c*. 300 BCE who wrote a history of Egypt in Greek], notwithstanding that the hippopotamus is a graminivorous animal, one that 'eats grass like an ox'. Probably the old Egyptian writer whom he followed meant that M'na at last fell a victim to Taourt, the Goddess of Evil, to whom the hippopotamus was sacred, and who was herself figured as a hippopotamus erect. This would be merely equivalent to relating that he succumbed to death. Manetho gave him a reign of 62 years.

Question of the Existence of M'na

The question is asked by the modern critics, who will take nothing on trust, 'Have we in Menes a real Egyptian, a being of flesh and blood, one who truly lived, breathed, fought, built, ruled and at last died? Or are we still dealing with a phantom, as much as when we spoke of Seb, and Thoth, and Osiris, and Set and Horus?' The answer seems to be, that we cannot tell. The Egyptians believed in Menes as a man; they placed him at the head of their dynastic lists; but they had no contemporary monument to show inscribed with his name. A name like that of Menes is found at the beginning of things in so many nations, that on that account alone the word would be suspicious; in Greece it is Minos, in Phrygia Manis, in Lydia Manes, in India Menu, in Germany Mannus. And again, the name of the founder is so like that of the city which he founded, that another suspicion arises – Have we not here one of the many instances of a personal name made out of a local one, as Nin or Ninus from Nineveh (Ninua), Romulus from Roma, and the like? Probably we shall do best to acquiesce in the judgment of Dr. [Samuel] Birch [British Egyptologist]: 'Menes must be placed among those founders of monarchies whose personal existence a severe and enlightened criticism doubts or denies.'

The city was, however, a reality, the embankment was a reality, the temple of Phthah was a reality, and the founding of a kingdom in Egypt, which included both the Upper and the Lower country some considerable time before the date of Abraham, was a reality, which the sternest criticism need not – nay, cannot – doubt. All antiquity attests that the valley of the Nile was one of the first seats of civilization. Abraham found a settled government established there when he visited the country, and a consecutive series of monuments carries the date of the first civilization at least as far back as 2,700 BCE – probably further.

[illegible]

THE OLD KINGDOM

The Old Kingdom is often referred to as the age of The Pyramid Builders, as throughout the period we see the development, rise and decline of pyramids. This starts with the first step pyramid of Djoser at Saqqara (third dynasty), culminating in the Great Pyramid at Giza of Khufu (fourth dynasty), then advances to the first pyramid bearing the Pyramid Texts (Unas of the fifth dynasty) and ends with the poorly built pyramids of the sixth dynasty. The text presented here shows the accumulation of knowledge from classical resources about the pyramids and the kings who built them.

The Old Kingdom was also a time where the civilization had become centralized under a dual king, following the unification of Dynasty 0. This means that many aspects we associate with 'ancient Egypt', such as gods, kingship and temple design, were now firmly in place, providing a foundation for following generations.

AFTER MENES

Supposed successors of M'na

If the great Menes, then, notwithstanding all that we are told of his doings, be a mere shadowy personage, little more than *magni nominis umbra*, what shall we say of his 20 or 30 successors of the first, second and third dynasties? What but that they are shadows of shadows? The native monuments of the early Ramesside period (about 1,400–1,300 BCE) assign to this time some 25 names of kings; but they do not agree in their order, nor do they altogether agree in the names. The kings, if they were kings, have left no history – we can only by conjecture attach to them any particular buildings, we can give no account of their actions, we can assign no chronology to their reigns. They are of no more importance in the 'story of Egypt' than the Alban kings in the 'story of Rome'. 'Non ragionam di loro, ma guarda e passi.'

First Historical Egyptian, Sneferu

The first living, breathing, acting, flesh-and-blood personage, whom so-called histories of Egypt present to us, is a certain Sneferu, or Seneferu, whom the Egyptians seem to have regarded as the first monarch of their fourth dynasty. Sneferu – called by Manetho, we know not why, Soris – has left us a representation of himself, and an inscription. On the rocks of Wadi Maghara, in the Sinaitic peninsula, may be seen to this day an incised tablet representing the monarch in the act of smiting an enemy, whom he holds by the hair of his head, with a mace. The action is apparently emblematic, for at the side we see the words *Ta satu*, 'Smiter of the nations'; and it is a fair explanation of the tablet, that its intention was to signify that the pharaoh in question had reduced to subjection the tribes which in his time inhabited the Sinaitic regions.

The motive of the attack was not mere lust of conquest, but rather the desire of gain. The Wadi Maghara contained mines of copper and of turquoise, which the Egyptians desired to work;

and for this purpose it was necessary to hold the country by a set of military posts, in order that the miners might pursue their labours without molestation. Some ruins of the fortifications are still to be seen; and the mines themselves, now exhausted, pierce the sides of the rocks, and bear in many places traces of hieroglyphical inscriptions The remains of temples show that the expatriated colonists were not left without the consolations of religion, while a deep well indicates the care that was taken to supply their temporal needs. Thousands of stone arrowheads give evidence of the presence of a strong garrison, and make us acquainted with the weapon which they found most effectual against their enemies.

Sneferu calls himself *Neter aa*, 'the Great God', and *Neb mat*, 'the Lord of Justice'. He is also 'the Golden Horus', or 'the Conqueror'. *Neb mat* is not a usual title with Egyptian monarchs; and its assumption by Sneferu would seem to mark, at any rate, his appreciation of the excellence of justice, and his desire to have the reputation of a just ruler. Later ages give him the title of 'the beneficent king', so that he would seem to have been a really unselfish and kindly sovereign. His form, however, only just emerges from the mists of the period to be again concealed from our view, and we vainly ask ourselves what exactly were the benefits that he conferred on Egypt, so as to attain his high reputation.

The Egypt of His Time

Still, the monuments of his time are sufficient to tell us something of the Egypt of his day, and of the amount and character of the civilization so early attained by the Egyptian people. Besides his own tablet in the Wadi Maghara, there are in the neighbourhood of the pyramids of Giza a number of tombs which belong to the officials of his court and the members of his family. These tombs contain both sculptures and inscriptions, and throw considerable light on the condition of the country.

Hieroglyphics

In the first place, it is apparent that the style of writing has been invented which is called hieroglyphical, and which has the appearance of a picture writing, though it is almost as absolutely phonetic as any other. Setting apart a certain small number of 'determinatives', each sign stands for a sound – the greater part for those elementary sounds which we express by letters. An eagle is *a*, a leg and foot *b*, a horned serpent *f*, a hand *t*, an owl *m*, a chicken *u* and the like. It is true that there are signs which express a compound sound, a whole word, even a word of two syllables. A bowl or basin represents the sound of *neb*, a hatchet that of *neter*, a guitar that of *nefer*, a crescent that of *aah* and so on. Secondly, it is clear that artistic power is considerable. The animal forms used in the hieroglyphics – the bee, the vulture, the uraeus, the hawk, the chicken, the eagle – are well drawn. In the human forms there is less merit, but still they are fairly well proportioned and have spirit. No rudeness or want of finish attaches either to the writing or to the drawing of Sneferu's time; the artists do not attempt much, but what they attempt they accomplish.

Tombs

Next, we may notice the character of the tombs. Already the tomb was more important than the house; and while every habitation constructed for the living men of the time has utterly perished, scores of the dwellings assigned to the departed still exist, many in an excellent condition. They are stone buildings resembling small houses, each with its door of entrance, but with no windows, and forming internally a small chamber generally decorated with sculptures. The walls slope at an angle of 75 or 80 degrees externally, but in the interior are perpendicular. The roof is composed of large flat stones.

Strictly speaking, the chambers are not actual tombs, but mortuary chapels. The embalmed body of the deceased, encased in its wooden coffin, was not deposited in the chamber, but in an excavation under one of the walls, which was carefully closed up after the coffin had been placed inside it. The chamber was used by the relations for sacred rites, sacrificial feasts and the like, held in honour of the deceased, especially on the anniversary of his death and entrance into Amenti. The early Egyptians indulged, like the Chinese, in a worship of ancestors. The members of a family met from time to time in the sepulchral chamber of their father or their grandfather and went through various ceremonies, sang hymns, poured libations and made offerings, which were regarded as pleasing to the departed, and which secured their protection and help to such of their descendants as took part in the pious practices.

Incipient Pyramids

Sometimes a tomb was more pretentious than those above described. There is an edifice at Meydoum, improperly termed a pyramid, which is thought to be older than Sneferu, and was probably erected by one of the 'shadowy kings' who preceded him on the throne. Situated on a natural rocky knoll of some considerable height, it rises in three stages at an angle of 74 degrees to an elevation of 38 metres (125 feet). It is built of a compact limestone, which must have been brought from some distance. The first stage has a height a little short of 21 metres (70 feet); the next exceeds 10 metres (32 feet); the third is a little over 6.5 metres (22 feet). It is possible that originally there were more stages, and probable that the present highest stage has in part crumbled away; so that we may fairly reckon the original height to have been between 42 and 45 metres (140 and 150 feet). The monument is generally regarded as a tomb, from its situation in the Memphian necropolis and its remote resemblance to the pyramids; but as yet it has not been penetrated, and consequently has not been proved to have been sepulchral.

A construction, which has even a greater appearance of antiquity than the Meydoum tower, exists at Saqqara. Here the architect carried up a monument to the height of 60 metres (200 feet), by constructing it in six or seven sloping stages, having an angle of 73 degrees. The core of his building was composed of rubble, but this was protected on every side by a thick casing of limestone roughly hewn, and apparently quarried on the spot. The sepulchral intention of the construction is unquestionable. It covered a spacious chamber excavated in the rock, whereon the monument was built, which, when first discovered, contained a sarcophagus and was lined with slabs of granite. Carefully concealed passages connected the chamber with the outer world, and allowed of its being entered by those in possession of the 'secrets of the prison-house'. In this structure we have, no doubt, the tomb of a king more ancient than Sneferu – though for our own part we should hesitate to assign the monument to one king rather than another.

Social Condition of the People

If we pass from the architecture of the period to its social condition, we remark that grades of society already existed, and were as pronounced as in later times. The kings were already deities and treated with superstitious regard. The state officials were a highly privileged class, generally more or less connected with the royal family. The land was partly owned by the king, who employed his own labourers and herdsmen upon it; partly, mainly perhaps, it was in the hands of great landed proprietors – nobles, who lived in country houses upon their estates, maintaining large households, and giving employment to scores of peasants, herdsmen, artisans, huntsmen and fishermen. The 'lower orders' were of very little account. They were at the beck and call of the landed aristocracy in the country districts, of the state officials in the towns. Above all, the monarch had the right of impressing them into his service whenever he pleased, and employing them in the 'great works' by which he strove to perpetuate his name.

Manners

There prevailed, however, a great simplicity of manners. The dress of the upper classes was wonderfully plain and unpretending, presenting little variety and scarcely any ornament. The grandee wore, indeed, an elaborate wig, it being imperative on all men to shave the head for the sake of cleanliness. But otherwise, his costume was of the simplest and the scantiest. Ordinarily, when he was employed in the common duties of life, a short tunic, probably of white linen, reaching from the waist to a little above the knee, was his sole garment. His arms, chest, legs, even his feet, were naked; for sandals, not to speak of stockings or shoes, were unknown. The only decoration which he wore was a chain or riband round the neck, to which was suspended an ornament like a locket – probably an amulet. In his right hand he carried a long staff or wand, either for the purpose of belabouring his inferiors, or else to use it as a walking stick. On special occasions he made, however, a more elaborate toilet. Doffing his linen tunic, he clothed himself in a single, somewhat scanty, robe, which reached from the neck to the ankles; and having exchanged his chain and locket for a broad collar, and adorned his wrists with bracelets, he was ready to pay visits or to receive company. He had no carriage, so far as appears, not even a palanquin; no horse to ride, nor even a mule or a donkey. The great men of the East rode, in later times, on 'white asses'; the Egyptian of Sneferu's age had to trudge to court, or to make calls upon his friends, by the sole aid of those means of locomotion which nature had given him.

Position of Women

Women, who in most civilized countries claim to themselves far more elaboration in dress and variety of ornament than men, were content, in the Egypt of which we are here speaking, with a costume, and a personal decoration, scarcely less simple than that of their husbands. The Egyptian *materfamilias* of the time wore her hair long, and gathered into three masses, one behind the head, and the other two in front of either shoulder. Like her spouse, she had but a single garment – a short gown or petticoat reaching from just below the breasts to halfway down the calf of the leg, and supported by two broad straps passed over the two shoulders. She exposed her arms and bosom to sight, and her feet were bare, like her husband's. Her only ornaments were bracelets.

There was no seclusion of women at any time among the ancient Egyptians. The figure of the wife on the early monuments constantly accompanies that of her husband. She is his associate in all his occupations. Her subordination is indicated by her representation being on an unduly smaller scale, and by her ordinary position, which is behind the figure of her 'lord and master'. In statuary, however, she appears seated with him on the same seat or chair. There is no appearance of her having been either a drudge or a plaything. She was regarded as man's true 'helpmate', shared his thoughts, ruled his family, and during their early years had the charge of his children. Polygamy was unknown in Egypt during the primitive period; even the kings had then but one wife. Sneferu's wife was a certain Mertitefs, who bore him a son, Nefer-mat, and after his death became the wife of his successor. Women were entombed with as much care, and almost with as much pomp, as men. Their right to ascend the throne is said to have been asserted by one of the kings who preceded Sneferu; and from time to time women actually exercised in Egypt the royal authority.

THE KINGDOM OF MEMPHIS, CAPITAL OF THE OLD KINGDOM

Recap

As we have seen, the lists of the Egyptians place Menes (Mena) at the head of their series of kings. They describe him as a native of This, a place in the neighbourhood of

Abydus, below Thebes, a district which Diodorus considers the oldest part of Egypt. Menes passes for the founder of the kingdom and the builder of Memphis (Mennefer); he is said to have taught the Egyptians the worship of the gods and the offering of sacrifice. Herodotus informs us that he learnt from the Egyptian priests that Menes had thrown a dam across the Nile about 100 stades [1 stade measured about 185 metres or 606.9 feet] above Memphis, and thus forced the stream which previously flowed at the foot of the Libyan chain of hills to leave its ancient channel, and flow at an equal distance between the two ranges. When the land thus gained by the dam had become firm, he built upon it the city, now called Memphis, and still situated in the narrow part of Egypt. Towards the north and west sides of the city, Menes had excavated a lake, and filled it with water from the river – which was itself a protection to the city on the east, – and in the city he built the greatest and most remarkable temple of Hephaestus (Ptah).

Diodorus observes: 'The founder of Memphis, the most splendid city in Egypt, selected the most suitable site by founding the city in the place where the Nile separates into several arms, so that the city, lying on the pass, commanded the navigation up the Nile. He also obtained for the place a wonderful advantage and security by throwing a huge dam in front of it towards the south, as the Nile at the time of inundation overflows the district. This dam was a protection against the rising water, and at the same time served as an acropolis and defence from the attack of enemies. On all the other sides of the city he caused a large and deep lake to be excavated, which received the overflow of the water and afforded the strongest protection for the city. The circuit of the city he placed at 150 stades, and owing to the excellence of the situation, Memphis was generally chosen by the kings as their place of residence.' The situation, just a little above the place where the river valley, hitherto enclosed between the two ranges of hills, opens out into the Delta, was certainly the best adapted to form the centre of an empire extending over the narrow valley of the upper river and the broader district of the Delta, with its wealth of cornland and meadows, and to check the entrance of enemies who came from the north-west or the north-east into the upper valley, even when it was no longer possible to maintain the Delta against them. About 24 kilometres (15 miles) above Memphis, at Kafr-el-Yat, the Nile makes a considerable bend to the east, and modern investigations claim to have discovered traces showing that this curve is due to the hand of man.

Menes, whose accession, according to the arrangement of [Egyptologist Karl Richard] Lepsius, would fall in the year 3892 BCE, was followed on the throne by King Athotis (Ateta) [Hor-Aha], who was said to have built the citadel at Memphis. Next came Kenkenes, whose successor was Uenephes [Djet], to whom is ascribed the erection of the pyramids. We have seen what care and labour the Egyptians devoted to their tombs, their 'everlasting houses'. The west, where the sun sets, and the desert spreads out in boundless expanse beyond the Libyan range, belonged in their minds to the gods of night, of the underworld and of death. About 16 kilometres (10 miles) to the west of Memphis there rises a desolate and barren plateau of rock, which for many miles runs parallel to the river, about 30 metres (100 feet) above the blooming and animated valley through which the Nile takes its course. In that rocky soil, which separates the fruitful land from the desert, the bodies of the dead were placed in chambers, either hewn in the solid stone, or, where the soil was less firm, built of masonry, and thus secured even from the overflow of the river. Even the kings sought their resting places on this plateau of rock. They, above all, gave attention to the solidity and durability of their tombs; and in death, as in life, they wished to be kings.

Evolution of the Pyraminds

The place where a king rested must be marked as royal, and visible from a distance; the grave of a king must tower over the rest; his chamber must be of all most difficult to open. Thus, at first blocks of stone were rolled upon the closed burial place of a king, or a mound of earth was raised over it, if sand and soil were to be obtained in the neighbourhood. The strong winds which blew from the desert made it, however, necessary to secure these mounds, and cover them with stone. Hence by degrees the sepulchral heaps acquired a definite shape: they were rectangular structures, lessening toward the apex; then, by extending the base and sharpening the gradient, they were brought into the form of pyramids, and thus obtained the greatest possible firmness and solidity. For a similar reason the core, or central part, was no longer made of earth, but of brick; where blocks of stone could be obtained they were fitted into the core with more and more regularity, until at last these structures were completed within and without of rectangular hewn blocks of stone in regular layers, and artificial mountains of stone towered over the sepulchral chambers of the kings.

'At a distance of 40 stades from Memphis,' Strabo tells us, 'is a range of hills, on which stand the pyramids, or sepulchres of the kings. Among these, three are especially deserving of notice. Rectangular in shape, they are about one stadium high; and the height is slightly less than the length of either side. The sides are not equal, one is a little longer than the other, and near the middle of the longer side is a stone, which can be taken out. Behind this a winding, hollow passage leads to the tomb. Two of these pyramids stand close to each other on the same level; at a distance, on a higher level, rises the third, which, though much smaller, has been erected at much greater cost.' 'Like mountains,' says Tacitus, 'the pyramids have been raised amid impassable quicksands by the emulation and power of the kings.'

About 70 of these structures, which rise in a long line on the plateau of Memphis, from Abu Roash to Dahshur, remain as witnesses of the rulers of the old kingdom of Memphis and their dependants, of the artistic skill and laborious industry of their nation. Of some only the bases and a few fragments are in existence; of the largest, the points, and at least a part of the casing, are either decayed, fallen down or broken off; for at a later time the Arabs used these monuments as quarries. Three pyramids which stand in the neighbourhood of the modern Abusir are formed of rough blocks of stone, both in the cores and in the passages to the sepulchral chambers; and these blocks are fastened together by mud from the Nile poured in between them; their casings, now decayed, were of limestone blocks, and in height they extended from 45 to 60 metres (150 to 200 feet). Others, originally at least, of an equal height, of which the core was regularly built of brick, are found farther to the south near Dahshur. The architecture of these remains shows that the kings of Memphis commenced building their tombs soon after their accession. They began, it would seem, with a core of moderate size, and in this they probably constructed a sort of temporary chamber. If time sufficed, the first plan was overlaid with new strata, and thus it gradually increased in size. Should the builder die before the whole was completed, the casing of the structure thus raised in the form of steps was left to the successor.

The Three Pyramids of Giza

Between seven smaller pyramids, built regularly of stone blocks, which are about 45 metres (150 feet) in height, and of similar plan and structure, rise the three largest at Giza; the highest was originally 146 metres (480 feet) in height, though now it measures only 137 metres (450 feet); the next greatest, standing south-west of the highest, is now 136 metres (447 feet), and was originally 139 metres (457 feet) in height; the third measures but 66 metres (218 feet). The second largest, originally seven metres (23 feet) lower than the largest, is on a slightly higher level, the masonry is inferior to the largest, and the chamber lies immediately under the area of the structure. The largest measures 218 metres (716 feet), or 500 Egyptian cubits, on each side of the area; the height along the slope is 175 metres (574 feet), and the structure contains about 90 million cubic feet of masonry.

Fifteen metres (50 feet) above the original area, now covered with the sand of the desert, in the middle of the north side, there commences a gradually descending passage, about one metre (three feet) broad and 1.2 metres (four feet) high, leading to a chamber hewn deep in the foundation rock. This chamber lies more than 30 metres (100 feet) below the level of the pyramid, exactly 183 metres (600 feet) under the apex, and in a perpendicular line with it; it is 11 metres (36 feet) above the level of the Nile. From this passage to the chamber there branches off, just behind the entrance, a horizontal shaft, and from this rises an ascending passage leading to two chambers, one over the other, which, like the sepulchral chamber below, lie in the axis of the pyramid.

The third and smaller pyramid – its sides measure 101 metres (333 feet), and the height of the slope is 80 metres (262 feet) – being built upon looser soil, required a greater substructure, on which it rose in five or six perpendicular and gradually diminishing stories, the spaces between being filled up with bevelled masonry. Up to a considerable height the casing consists of polished slabs of granite. Under this structure in the native rock lies a larger chamber, and behind this the sepulchral chamber.

When Herodotus visited Egypt about the middle of the fifth century BCE, and questioned his interpreter and guide about the builders of these three pyramids, he was told in answer that they were built by Cheops [also known as Khufu], Chephren [also known as Khafre], and Mycerinus [also known as Menkaure]. He was told that Cheops first caused a road to be made from the stone quarries in the Arabian chain of hills – the range east of the Nile – down to the river, and again from the west side of the river to the high ground above Memphis. The road was built of smoothed stones five stades in length, 10 fathoms broad, and at the highest places 32 fathoms high; and it was intended to convey the materials from the Arabian side of the river. In making this road and building the subterranean chamber for the grave of Cheops 10 years were consumed, although 100,000 men were constantly employed upon it by spaces of three months, when they were relieved by an equal number of fresh workmen.

Twenty years were then spent upon the pyramid, of which each side and the height measured 244 metres (800 feet); it was built in such a manner that the structure was carried out by landings and steps, like a staircase. When the proper height was reached, the landings were covered from top to bottom with smoothed and carefully fitted stones, and no stone is less than nine metres (30 feet). Under the surface was a canal carried in masonry from the Nile round the subterranean chamber. When Cheops had reigned 50 years, he was succeeded by his brother Chephren, who also built a pyramid, though not equal in size to the other, and without any chamber or subterranean canal. When Chephren had reigned 56 years, he was followed by Mycerinus, the son of Cheops. This king also left a pyramid behind him.

The account of Diodorus is as follows: King Chemmis of Memphis reigned 50 years, and built the largest of the three pyramids, which in height measures more than six plethra [one plethra equals 30 metres or 100 feet], and along the sides more than seven plethra. It is entirely constructed of solid stone, very difficult to work, and therefore of endless durability. Even now, although not less than 1,000, or as some say even more than 3,400, years have passed, the structure is uninjured, and the joints of the stones unloosened. Besides, we are told that these stones were brought from a considerable distance out of Arabia, and the structure was carried to its present height by means of mounds of earth. Most wonderful of all, no traces of these mounds, no fragments from the hewing and smoothing of the stones remain; so that it would seem that this work was not accomplished gradually by the hand of man, but was planted complete by a god in the midst of the surrounding sand. Though it is said that 360,000 men bestowed their labour on the structure, the work can hardly have been finished in 20 years, and the number of men who erected it must also have removed the mounds of earth and excavated material, and put everything in its original condition. Chemmis was followed by his brother Kephren, who reigned 56 years.

Other accounts tell us that the kingdom descended on his son, Chabryes, and not on his brother. But all agree that he built the second pyramid, which resembles the first in the art of the execution, though much inferior in size, since on the sides it measures only one stadium (or, according to recent measurement, exactly 700½ Greek feet). And while the money spent in radishes and garden herbs for the builders is inscribed on the larger one, the smaller remains without any inscription. Though both these kings had destined these tombs for their place of burial, neither is buried there. Roused by the burden of their labours, the cruelty and violence of these kings – and in Herodotus also Cheops and Chephren appear as wicked and godless kings – the people threatened to take their bodies out of their graves and insult them. Terrified by this threat, each of the kings in his last moments bade his relations bury him privately in a secret place.

After Kephren reigned Mycerinus, whom others call Mencherinus, the son of Chemmis. He built the smallest pyramid. Though less in size, it surpasses the others in the excellence of the work and the beauty of the stone; up to the 15th layer it consists of black stone resembling the stone of

Thebes; from thence to the top the stone is the same as in the other pyramids. On the north side is written the name of the builder, Mycerinus. Abhorring the cruelty of his predecessors, Mycerinus, as we learn, sought to make his rule moderate and beneficent to his subjects, and did everything to gain the affections of the nation. He paid great attention to the administration of justice; and to the common people who had not received from the tribunals such a sentence as seemed just to him, he made presents. 'But as to the building of the pyramids, there is no agreement either among the Egyptians or their historians; some ascribe them to the kings I have mentioned; some to other kings.'

The accounts given by Herodotus and Diodorus of the structure of the largest pyramid are completely confirmed by modern research. Even now it is thought that traces can be recognized of the causeway which served for the transport of the materials from the left bank of the Nile to the plateau. The pyramid itself is built in large regular steps constructed of squares of granite. The yellow limestone of the casing must also have been really brought from the Arabian side of the Nile, because better stone of that kind was found there. On the other hand, the account of a subterranean canal round the grave chamber is merely a legend of the people, who desired to adorn with new marvels the structure already so marvellous; it is impossible, simply because the lower chamber, and not only the area of the pyramid, is above the lower level of the Nile.

The 100,000 workmen of Herodotus changed every three months, and the 360,000 of Diodorus – a number formed from the days in the old Egyptian year – have arisen out of the free invention of later times, although the building must certainly have occupied more than a decade of years. Inscriptions are not found now on the external side of the pyramid. If such were in existence at the time of Herodotus, they certainly contained other things than those which the interpreter pretended to read there. The interpreters who served as guides to the travellers of that day in Egypt, as the dragoman does now, could hardly have read the hieroglyphics; they contented themselves with narrating the traditions and stories popularly connected with the great monuments of past time, not without certain exaggerations and additions.

But the names of the builders of the three largest pyramids, which these interpreters mentioned to the Greeks, are confirmed by the monuments. In the deep chamber of the largest pyramid there is no sarcophagus; in the upper of the two chambers which lie in the axis of the pyramid there has been found, it is true, a simple sarcophagus of red granite, but it bears no inscription. Above these chambers, however, there are certain small spaces left open, with a view no doubt of diminishing the pressure of the stonework upon them, and on the walls of these spaces is written the name, Chufu, Chnemu Chufu, in hieratic characters. The same name frequently recurs in the tombs surrounding this pyramid, in which, according to the inscriptions, the wives, sons, officers and priests of Chufu were buried; and among them the scribe of the buildings of the kings and the priest of Apis, who was at the same time keeper of the gates and of the palace. In this inscription the pyramid of Chufu is called 'Chut'.

On a monumental stone found in the Apis tombs – now in Cairo – we read, 'The living Horus, the King of Egypt, Chufu, has built a temple to Isis near the temple of the Sphinx, north of the temple of Osiris, and has erected his pyramid beside the temple of Isis.' Chufu himself is not found in Egypt, but in the peninsula of Sinai he is pictured in relief on the rocks in the Wadi Maghara. He is represented as lifting his war club against an enemy whom he has forced upon his knee and seized by the headdress with the left hand. In an inscription in the same valley, the oldest which we possess, his predecessor Snefru claims to have subjugated these regions.

In the second pyramid, in the chamber under the surface, a sarcophagus of granite has been discovered on the floor without any inscription. But in the inscriptions on the graves, especially on the grave of the architect of King Chafra, his pyramid is mentioned as 'the great pyramid'. Between the paws of the Sphinx which stands to the north of the second pyramid, hewn out of the living rock, is a monumental stone, on which is read the name Chafra, and in the ruins of a temple lying near the Sphinx – the same without doubt which is mentioned in the stone at Cairo – seven statues have been exhumed, the inscriptions on which prove that they represent 'the Master and Gold Horus, Chafra, the good god, the lord of the crown', i.e., King Chafra himself. And lastly, the inscriptions on the tomb of a woman whose name is read as Mertitef, prove that she was the chief favourite of Snefru and of Chufu, and had been united to Chafra. Hence Chafra must have succeeded Chufu, and the 'great' pyramid built by him can hardly have been any other than that which now holds the second place.

In the sepulchral chamber of the third pyramid, it is known in the inscriptions as 'Har', i.e., 'the supreme', the sarcophagus of King Menkera with his mummy has been discovered. It is made of blue basalt, and bears the following inscription: 'O

Osiris, King Menkera, ever living one; begotten of the sky, carried in the bosom of Nut, scion of Seb. Thy mother Nut is outstretched over thee, in her name of the mystery of the sky may she deify thee and destroy thy enemies, King Menkera, ever living one.'

It is therefore an ascertained fact that Chufu, Chafra, and Menkera were the builders of the three great pyramids. In the mouth of the Greeks the name Chufu passed into Cheops, and by a farther change into Suphis. The name Chemmis in Diodorus has arisen out of the name Chnemu in the form Chnemu Chufu; from Chafra naturally arose Chephren, Kephren and Chabryes.

In the list of kings in Eratosthenes [a Greek scholar], the 14th successor of Menes is Saophis; Eratosthenes allows him a reign of 29 years. His successor, who has a reign of 27 years, bears the same name. The second Saophis is followed by Moscheres with a reign of 31 years. Manetho's list gives the name Suphis to the 27th king after Menes, and he is said to have reigned 63 years. Then follows a second Suphis, with a reign of 66 years, and this king is succeeded by Menchres, who reigned 63 years. On the first Suphis in Manetho's list the excerpt of Africanus remarks: 'This king built the largest pyramid, which Herodotus assigns to the time of Cheops'; in the excerpt of Eusebius, both in the Greek text and the Armenian translation, this remark is made on the second Suphis. Hence, we can have no hesitation in identifying the Cheops and Chephren of Herodotus, the Chemmis and Kephren of Diodorus, with the first and second Saophis and Sufis of the lists, the Chufu and Chafra of the inscriptions; and the Mycerinus of Herodotus and Diodorus is beyond doubt the same as the Moscheres of Eratosthenes, the

Mencheres of Manetho and the Menkera of the sarcophagus in the third pyramid.

In the national tradition of the Egyptians, as received by the Greeks, Cheops and Chephren were called brothers, and this is no doubt mainly due to the fact that the monuments of these two kings surpassed all the other pyramids, and were of nearly the same height and size. It is impossible that Cheops should have reigned 50 years, and his brother Chephren who succeeded him, 56 years, as Herodotus and Diodorus tell us – the inscription quoted above makes the same woman the favourite of the predecessor of Chufu, of Chufu, and Chafra also; even more impossible is it that the first Suphis should have reigned 63 years, and the second 66, as given in the list of Manetho, if they were brothers; or that Mycerinus, whom Herodotus as well as Diodorus calls the son of Cheops, should have succeeded Chephren with a reign of 63 years, as Manetho tells us.

Like their brotherhood, the wickedness of Cheops and Chephren is due to the popular legends of later times. The sight of the enormous structures forced on later generations the reflection what labour, what stupendous efforts must have been necessary for their erection. This reflection united with certain dim memories, and gathered round the rule of the strangers, the shepherd tribes, which for a long time afflicted Egypt, as is clear enough from a trait in the narrative of Herodotus. He assures us that the Egyptians could scarcely be induced to mention the names of the kings who built the great pyramids: they spoke of them as the works of the shepherd Philitis. In the eyes of the Egyptians of the olden time, tombs would never have appeared to be works of impiety and wickedness, realizing as they did in such an extraordinary degree the object most eagerly desired, a secure and indestructible resting place for the dead: with them they would rather pass as works of singular piety. Without doubt it is the older tradition, that of the priests, which meets us in the observation appended in the list of Manetho and the excerpt of Africanus to the first Suphis, and in the excerpt of Eusebius, both in the Greek text and Armenian translation, to the second Suphis, in which we are told that this king had composed a sacred book, and the Egyptians regarded it as a very great treasure.

According to the inscription, Chufu had erected a temple to Isis by the side of the temple of the Sphinx, and therefore the latter temple must have been already in existence. And as a fact the ruins still found beside the great Sphinx give evidence of very ancient workmanship. There was a court, the ante-court of the temple, which surrounded a portico supported on 12 square pillars; next came a hall supported on monoliths, the temple itself, and finally the Holy of Holies, surrounded by small chambers. The material used in building was limestone and granite. The symbolic form of the deity, to whom the temple belonged, was the enormous Sphinx, 58 metres (190 feet) in length, hewn out of the rock, with the body of a lion and the head of a man.

From the memorial stone before it we learn that it symbolized the god Harmachu (Armachis of the Greeks), i.e. Horus in Splendour (*har-em-chu*). From the inscription on this stone, which dates from the time of Tuthmosis IV, it seems to follow that it was Chafra who caused this shape to be hewn out of the rock and consecrated it to the god. Other inscriptions inform us that the pyramids were regarded as sepulchral temples, and that there were priests for the service of the princes who were buried there, and had attained to a divine nature, and these services were still in existence at the time of the Ptolemies. One of the tombs at Giza belongs to a priest, a relation of Chafra, whose duty it was to 'honour the pyramid Uer (the Great) of king Chafra'; another is found at Saqqara belonging to 'a priest of Chufu, and Chafra'. On a monumental stone of the time of the Ptolemies (found in the Serapeum, and now in the Louvre) mention is made of the temple of Harmachu on the south of the house of Isis, and of a certain Psamtik, the prophet of Isis, of Osarhapi, of Harmachu, of Chufu and Chafra.

The temples of Osiris and Isis, near the three great pyramids, and the inscription on the sarcophagus of king Menkera are evidence that the cult of Osiris, the belief in his rule in the next world, in the return of the soul to its divine origin, and its deification after death, was already in existence at the time when these monuments were erected. The use not of hieroglyphics only, but also of the hieratic alphabet, in red and black colours, in the pyramid of Chufu, and the graves around it, in the sculptures of which writing materials and rolls of papyrus are frequently engraved, the forms of domestic and household life, of agriculture and the cultivation of the vine, of hunting and fishing, preserved on the tombs of Giza, are evidence of the long existence and manifold development of civilization, no less than those great monuments, or even the graves themselves with their artistic mode of construction, their severe and simple style of execution, and the pleasing forms of their ornaments.

Of the seven statues of Chafra, discovered in the temple of the Sphinx, one, chiselled out of hard green and yellow basalt, has been preserved uninjured. The king is represented sitting, and naked, with the exception of a covering on the head and a girdle round the loins. The lower arms rest on the thighs, the left hand is outstretched, the right holds a fillet. The sides of the cube, on which Chafra is seated, are formed by lions, between the feet of which are stems of papyrus. On the high back of the chair, behind the head of the king, sits the hawk of Horus, whose wings are spread forwards in an attitude of protection. The execution of the statue of the king is a proof of long practice in sculpture. The natural form is truly and accurately rendered, and though even here Egyptian art displays its characteristic inclination to severity, and correctness in the proportions of the body, to repose and dignity, yet in the head there is an unmistakable attempt to individualize an outline already fixed – an attempt not without success. Still more distinctly individual are two statues found near the pyramids of Meidum, from the reign of the predecessor of Chufu, a wooden statue, and certain pictures in relief from the tombs near the great pyramids. The architecture, no less than the sculpture, of these most ancient monuments, displays a high degree of experience and a knowledge of the principles of art, a conscious purpose and effort existing together with a fixed obedience to rule.

We learnt from Diodorus that the great pyramids were erected 1,000, or, according to some, 3,400 years before his time. According to the list of Manetho, Cheops, Chephren and Mycerinus belonged to the fourth dynasty. If we accept the incredible reigns of 63, 66, and again, 63 years, which Manetho allows to those three kings, they reigned over Egypt, according to Lepsius' dates, from the year 3095 BCE to 2903 BCE.

THE MIDDLE KINGDOM

The Middle Kingdom comprises two dynasties: the eleventh and the twelfth. This period was considered a stable one during which the language was established, meaning that Middle Egyptian is considered the classic form of hieroglyphics for scholars to learn today, and the artistic cannon was formed, creating a benchmark from which later adaptations were made.

The kings of the Middle Kingdom started building at Deir el Bahri (Mentuhotep I) and Karnak (Senusret I). They continued with pyramid construction (Senusret II at Lahun) and built the so-called labyrinth at Hawara, a pyramid and associated funerary complex made famous in classical texts. The Middle Kingdom is an understated era of Egyptian history but one that is important.

The end of the Middle Kingdom saw the Hyksos kings take control of the Delta town of Tell el-Dab'a/Avaris and rule Egypt for more than a century. When Duncker wrote this text about the Hyksos in 1877, he was only able to draw upon classical texts. The site of their capital city, and all the information it would provide, was not to be discovered for nearly a century.

THE RISE OF THEBES TO POWER, AND THE EARLY THEBAN KINGS

Hitherto Egypt had been ruled from a site at the junction of the narrow Nile valley with the broad plain of the Delta – a site sufficiently represented by the modern Cairo. But now there was a shift of the seat of power. There is reason to believe that something like a disruption of Egypt into separate kingdoms took place, and that for a while several distinct dynasties bore sway in different parts of the country. Disruption was naturally accompanied by weakness and decline. The old order ceased, and opportunity was offered for some new order – some new power – to assert itself.

Site of Thebes

The site on which it arose was one 563 kilometres (350 miles) distant from the ancient capital, or 643 kilometres (400 miles) and more by the river. Here, about latitude 26 degrees, the usually narrow valley of the Nile opens into a sort of plain or basin. The mountains on either side of the river recede, as though by common consent, and leave between themselves and the river's bank a broad amphitheatre, which in each case is a rich green plain – an alluvium of the most productive character – dotted with *dom* and date palms, sometimes growing single, sometimes collected into clumps or groves. On the western side the Libyan range gathers itself up into a single considerable peak, which has an elevation of 365 metres (1,200 feet). On the east the desert-wall maintains its usual level character, but is pierced by valleys conducting to the coast of the Red Sea. The situation was one favourable for commerce. On the one side was the nearest route through the sandy desert to the Lesser Oasis, which commanded the trade of the African interior; on the other the way led through the valley of Hammamat, rich with *breccia verde* and other valuable and rare stones, to a district abounding in mines of gold, silver and lead, and thence to the Red Sea coast, from which, even in very early times, there was communication with the opposite coast of Arabia, the region of gums and spices.

Origin of the Name of Thebes

In this position there had existed, probably from the very beginnings of Egypt, a provincial city of some repute, called by its inhabitants Apé or Apiu, and, with the feminine article prefixed, Tapé, or Tapiu, which some interpret 'The city of thrones'. To the Greeks the name 'Tapé' seemed to resemble their own well-known 'Thebai', whence they transferred the familiar appellation from the Baeotian to the Mid-Egyptian town, which has thus come to be known to Englishmen and Anglo-Americans as 'Thebes'. Thebes had been from the first the capital of a 'nome'. It lay so far from the court that it acquired a character of its own – a special cast of religion, manners, speech, nomenclature, mode of writing and the like – which helped to detach it from Lower or Northern Egypt more even than its isolation. Still, it was not until the northern kingdom sank into decay from internal weakness and exhaustion, and disintegration supervened in the Delta and elsewhere, that Thebes resolved to assert herself and claim independent sovereignty. Apparently, she achieved her purpose without having recourse to arms. The kingdoms of the north were content to let her go. They recognized their own weakness, and allowed the nascent power to develop itself unchecked and unhindered.

Earliest Known Theban King, Antef I

The first known Theban monarch is a certain Antef or Enantef, whose coffin was discovered in the year 1827 by some Arabs near Qurnah, to the west of Thebes. The mummy bore the royal diadem, and the epigraph on the lid of the coffin declared the body which it contained to be that of 'Antef, king of *the two Egypts*'. The phrase implied a claim to dominion over the whole country, but a claim as purely nominal as that of the kings of England from Edward IV to George III to be monarchs of France and Navarre. Antef's rule may possibly have reached to Elephantine on the one hand, but is not likely to have extended much beyond Coptos on the other. He was a local chieftain posing as a great sovereign, but probably with no intention to deceive either his own contemporaries or posterity. His name appears in some of the later Egyptian dynastic lists; but no monument of his time has come down to us except the one that has been mentioned.

His Successors, Mentuhotep I and Antef the Great

Antef I is thought to have been succeeded by Mentuhotep I, a monarch even more shadowy, known to us only from the 'Table of Karnak'. This prince, however, is followed by one who possesses a greater amount of substance – Antefaa, or 'Antef the Great', grandson, as it would seem, of the first Antef – a sort of Egyptian Nimrod, who delighted above all things in the chase. Antefaa's sepulchral monument shows him to us standing in the midst of his dogs, who wear collars, and have their names engraved over them.

The dogs are four in number, and are of distinct types. The first, which is called *Mahut* or 'Antelope', has drooping ears, and long but somewhat heavy legs; it resembles a foxhound, and was no doubt both swift and strong, though it can scarcely have been so swift as its namesake. The second was called *Abakaru*, a name of unknown meaning; it has pricked up, pointed ears, a pointed nose and a curly tail. Some have compared it with the German *Spitz* dog, but it seems rather to be the original dog of nature, a near congener of the jackal, and the type to which all dogs revert when allowed to run wild and breed indiscriminately. The third, named *Pahats* or *Kamu*, i.e. 'Blacky', is a heavy animal, not unlike a mastiff; it has a small, rounded, drooping ear, a square, blunt nose, a deep chest and thick limbs. The late Dr. Birch supposed that it might have been employed by Antefaa in 'the chase of the lion'; but we should rather regard it as a watchdog, the terror of thieves, and we suspect that the artist gave it the sitting attitude to indicate that its business was not to hunt, but to keep watch and ward at its master's gate. The fourth dog, who bears the name of *Tekal*, and walks between his master's legs, has ears that seem to have been cropped. He has been said to resemble 'the Dalmatian hound': but this is questionable. His peculiarities are not marked; but, on the whole, it seems most probable that he is 'a pet housedog' of the terrier class, the special favourite of his master. Antefaa's dogs had their appointed keeper, the master of his kennel, who is figured on the sepulchral tablet behind the monarch, and bears the name of Tekenru.

The hunter king was buried in a tomb marked only by a pyramid of unbaked brick, very humble in its character, but containing a mortuary chapel in which the monument above described was set up. An inscription on the tablet declared that it was erected to the memory of Antef the Great, Son of the Sun, King of Upper and Lower Egypt, in the 50th year of his reign.

Other Antefs and Mentuhoteps

Other Mentuhoteps and other Antefs continued on the line of Theban kings, reigning quietly and ingloriously, and leaving no mark upon the scroll of time, yet probably advancing the material prosperity of their country, and preparing the way for that rise to greatness which gives Thebes, on the whole, the foremost place in Egyptian history. Useful projects occupied the attention of these monarchs. One of them sank wells in the valley of Hammamat, to provide water for the caravans which plied between Coptos and the Red Sea. Another established military posts in the valley to protect the traffic and the Egyptian quarrymen.

Sankh-ka-ra and His Fleet

Later on, a king called Sankh-ka-ra (Mentuhotep III) launched a fleet upon the Red Sea waters, and opened direct communications with the sacred land of Punt, the region of odoriferous gums and of strange animals, as giraffes, panthers, hunting leopards, cynocephalus apes [baboons] and long-tailed monkeys. There is some doubt whether 'Punt' was Arabia Felix, or the Somali country. In any case, it lay far down the gulf, and could only be reached after a voyage of many days.

Dynasty of Usurtasens and Amenemhats: Spirit of Their Civilization

The dynasty of the Antefs and Mentuhoteps, which terminated with Sankh-ka-ra, was followed by one in which the prevailing names were Usurtasen and Amenemhat. This dynasty is Manetho's 12th, and the time of its rule has been characterized as 'the happiest age of Egyptian history?' The second phase of Egyptian civilization now set in – a phase which is regarded by many as outshining the glories of the first. The first civilization had subordinated the people to the monarch, and had aimed especially at eternizing the memory and setting forth the power and greatness of king after king. The second had the benefit and advantage of the people for its primary object; it was utilitarian, beneficent, appealing less to the eye than to the mind, far-sighted in its aims and most successful in the results which it effected. The wise rulers of the time devoted their energies and their resources, not, as the earlier kings, to piling up undying memorials of themselves in the shape of monuments that 'reached to heaven', but to useful works, to the excavation of wells and reservoirs, the making of roads, the encouragement of commerce and the development of the vast agricultural wealth of the country. They also diligently guarded the frontiers, chastised aggressive tribes and checked invasion by the establishment of strong fortresses in positions of importance. They patronized art, employing themselves in building temples rather than tombs, and adorned their temples not only with reliefs and statues, but also with the novel architectural embellishment of the obelisk, a delicate form, and one especially suited to the country.

Reign of Amenemhat I

The founder of the 12th dynasty, Amenemhat I, deserves a few words of description. He found Thebes in a state of anarchy; civil war raged on every side; all the traditions of the past were forgotten; noble fought against noble; the poor were oppressed; life and property were alike insecure; 'there was stability of fortune neither for the ignorant nor for the learned man'. One night, after he had lain down to sleep, he found himself attacked in his bedchamber; the clang of arms sounded near at hand. Starting from his couch, he seized his own weapons and struck out; when lo! his assailants fled; detected in their attempt to assassinate him, they dared not offer any resistance, thus showing themselves alike treacherous and cowardly. Amenemhat, having once taken arms, did not lay them down till he had defeated every rival, and so fought his way to the crown. Once acknowledged as king, he ruled with moderation and equity; he 'gave to the humble, and made the weak to live'; he 'caused the afflicted to cease from their afflictions, and their cries to be heard no more'; he brought it to pass that none hungered or thirsted in the land; he gave such orders to his servants as continually increased the love of his people towards him. At the same time, he was an energetic warrior. He 'stood on the boundaries of the land, to keep watch on its borders', personally leading his soldiers to battle, armed with the *khopesh* or falchion. He carried on wars with the Petti, or bowmen of the Libyan interior, with the Sakti or Asiatics, with the Maxyes or Mazyes of the north-west, and with the Ua-uat and other Black tribes of the south; not, however, as it would seem, with any desire of making conquests, but simply for the protection of his own frontier. With the same object he constructed on his north-eastern frontier a wall or fortress 'to keep out the Sakti', who continually harassed the people of the Eastern Delta by their incursions.

His Wars and Hunting Expeditions

The wars of Amenemhat I make it evident that by his time Thebes had advanced from the position of a petty kingdom situated in a remote part of Egypt, and held in check by two or more rival kingdoms in the lower Nile valley and the Delta, to that of a power which bore sway over the whole land from Elephantine to the Mediterranean. 'I sent my messengers up to Abu (Elephantine) and my couriers down to Athu' (the coast lakes), says the monarch in his 'Instructions' to his son – the earliest literary production from a royal pen that has come down to our days; and there is no reason to doubt the truth of his statement. In the Delta alone could he come into contact with either the Mazyes or the Sakti, and a king of Thebes could not hold the Delta without being master also of the lower Nile valley from Coptos to Memphis. We must regard Egypt, then, under the 12th dynasty, as once more consolidated into a single state – a state ruled, however, not from Memphis, but from Thebes, a decidedly inferior position.

Amenemhat I is the only Egyptian king who makes a boast of his hunting prowess. 'I hunted the lion,' he says, 'and brought back the crocodile a prisoner.' Lions do not at the present time frequent Egypt, and, indeed, are not found lower down the Nile valley than the point where the Great Stream receives its last tributary, the Atbara. But anciently they seem to have haunted the entire desert tracts on either side of the river. The Roman Emperor Hadrian is said to have hunted one near Alexandria, and the monuments represent lions as tamed and used in the chase by the ancient inhabitants. Sometimes they even accompanied their masters to the battlefield. We know nothing of Amenemhat's mode of hunting the king of beasts, but may assume that it was not very different from that which prevailed at a later date in Assyria. There, dogs and beaters were employed to rouse the animals from their lairs, while the king and his fellow sportsmen either plied them with flights of arrows, or withstood their onset with swords and spears. The crocodile was certainly sometimes attacked while he was in the water, the hunters using a boat, and endeavouring to spear him at the point where the head joins the spine; but this could not have been the mode adopted by Amenemhat, since it would have resulted in instant death, whereas he tells us that he 'brought the crocodile home a prisoner'. Possibly, therefore, he employed the method which Herodotus says was in common use in his day. This was to bait a hook with a joint of pork and throw it into the water at a point where the current would carry it out into mid-stream; then to take a live pig to the riverside, and belabour him well with a stick till he set up the squeal familiar to most ears. Any crocodile within hearing was sure to come to the sound, and falling in with the pork on the way, would instantly swallow it down. Upon this the hunters hauled at the rope to which the hook was attached, and, notwithstanding his struggles, drew 'leviathan' to shore. Amenemhat, having thus 'made the crocodile a prisoner', may have carried his captive in triumph to his capital, and exhibited him before the eyes of the people.

Usurtasen I: His Wars

Amenemhat, having reigned as sole king for 20 years, was induced to raise his eldest son, Usurtasen (Senusret I), to the royal dignity, and associate him with himself in the government of the empire. Usurtasen was a prince of much promise, he 'brought prosperity to the affairs of his father. He was, as a god, without fears; before him was never one like to him. Most skilful in affairs, beneficent in his mandates, both in his going out and in his coming in he made Egypt flourish.' His courage and his warlike capacity were great. Already, in the lifetime of his father, he had distinguished himself in combats with the Petti and the Sakti. When he was settled upon the throne, he made war upon the Cushite tribes who bordered Egypt upon the south, employing the services of a general named Ameni, but also taking a part personally in the campaign. The Cushites or Ethiopians, who in later times became such dangerous neighbours to Egypt, were at this early period weak and insignificant. After the king had made his expedition, Ameni was able with a mere handful of 400 troops to penetrate into their country, to 'conduct the golden treasures' which it contained to the presence of his master, and to capture and carry off a herd of 3,000 cattle.

His Sculptures and Architectural Works

It was through his sculptures and his architectural works that the first Usurtasen made himself chiefly conspicuous. Thebes, Abydos, Heliopolis or On, the Fayoum and the Delta, were equally the scenes of his constructive activity, and still show traces of his presence. At Thebes, he carried to its completion the cell, or *naos*, of the great temple of Ammon, in later times the innermost sanctuary of the building, and reckoned so sacred, that when Tuthmosis III rebuilt and enlarged the entire edifice he reproduced the structure of Usurtasen, unchanged in form, and merely turned from limestone into granite. At Abydos and other cities of Middle Egypt, he constructed temples adorned with sculptures, inscriptions and colossal statues. At Tanis, he set up his own statue, exhibiting himself as seated upon his throne. In the Fayoum he erected an obelisk 12 metres (41 feet) high to the honour of Ammon, Phthah, and Mentu, which now lies prone upon the ground near the Arab village of Begig.

Indications of his ubiquitous activity are found also at the Wadi Maghara, in the Sinaitic peninsula, and at Wady Haifa in Nubia, a little above the Second Cataract; but his grandest and most elaborate work was his construction of the great temple of the Sun at Heliopolis, and his best memorial is that tall finger pointing to the sky which greets the traveller approaching Egypt from the east as the first sample of its strange and mystic wonders. This temple the king began in his third year. After a consultation with his lords and counsellors, he issued the solemn decree: 'It is determined to execute the work; his majesty chooses to have it made. Let the superintendent carry it on in the way that is desired; let all those employed upon it be vigilant; let them see that it is made without weariness; let every due ceremony be performed; let the beloved place arise.' Then the king rose up, wearing a diadem, and holding the double pen; and all present followed him. The scribe read the holy book, and extended the measuring cord, and laid the foundations on the spot which the temple was to occupy. A grand building arose; but it has been wholly demolished by the ruthless hand of time and the barbarity of conquerors. Of all its glories nothing now remains but the one taper obelisk of pink granite, which rises into the soft sleepy air above the green cornfields of Matariyeh, no longer tipped with gold, but still catching on its summit the earliest and latest sunrays, while wild bees nestle in the crannies of the weird characters cut into the stone.

Reign of Amenemhat II: Tablet Belonging to His Time

Usurtasen, after reigning 10 years in conjunction with his father and 32 years alone, associated his son, Amenemhat II, who became sole king about three years later. His reign, though long, was undistinguished, and need not occupy our attention. He followed the example of his predecessors in associating a son in the government; and this son succeeded him, and is known as Usurtasen II (Senusret II).

One event of interest alone belongs to this time. It is the reception by one of his great officials of a large family or tribe of Semitic immigrants from Asia, who beg permission to settle permanently in the fertile Egypt under the protection of its powerful king. Thirty-seven Amu, men, women and children, present themselves at the court which the great noble holds near the eastern border, and offer him their homage, while they solicit a favourable hearing. The men are represented draped in long garments of various colours, and wearing sandals unlike the Egyptian – more resembling, in fact, open shoes with many straps. Their arms are bows, arrows, spears and clubs. One plays on a seven-stringed lyre by means of a plectrum. Four women, wearing fillets round their heads, with garments reaching below the knee, and wearing anklets but no sandals, accompany them. A boy, armed with a spear, walks at the side of the women; and two children, seated in a kind of pannier placed on the back of an ass, ride on in front. Another ass, carrying a spear, a shield and a pannier, precedes the man who plays on the lyre.

The great official, who is named Khnumhotep, receives the foreigners, accompanied by an attendant who carries his sandals and a staff, and who is followed by three dogs. A scribe, named Neferhotep, unrolls before his master a strip of papyrus, on which are inscribed the words, 'The sixth year of the reign of King Usurtasen Sha-khepr-ra: account rendered of the Amu who in the lifetime of the chief, Khnumhotep, brought to him the mineral, *mastemut*, from the country of Pit-shu – they are in all 37 persons.' The mineral *mastemut* is thought to be a species of stibium or antimony, used for dying the skin around the eyes, and so increasing their beauty. Besides this offering, the head of the tribe, who is entitled *khak*, or 'prince', and named Abusha, presents to Khnumhotep a magnificent wild goat, of the kind which at the present day frequents the rocky mountain tract of Sinai. He wears a richer dress than his companions, one which is ornamented with a fringe, and has a wavy border round the neck.

The scene has been generally recognized as strikingly illustrating the coming of Jacob's family into Egypt, and was at one time thought by some to represent that occurrence; but the date of Abusha's coming is long anterior to the arrival in

Egypt of Jacob's family, the number is little more than half that of the Hebrew immigrants, the names do not accord; and it is now agreed on all hands, that the interest of the representation is confined to its illustrative force.

Usurtasen III and His Conquests

Usurtasen II reigned for 19 years. He does not seem to have associated a son, but was succeeded by another Usurtasen, most probably a nephew. The third Usurtasen (Senusret III) was a conquering monarch, and advanced the power and glory of Egypt far more than any other ruler belonging to the Old Kingdom. He began his military operations in his eighth year, and starting from Elephantine in the month Epiphi, or May, moved southward, like another Lord Wolseley, with a fixed intention, which he expressed in writing upon the rocks of the Elephantine island, of permanently reducing to subjection 'the miserable land of Cush'. His expedition was so far successful that in the same year he established two forts, one on either side of the Nile, and set up two pillars with inscriptions warning the black races that they were not to proceed further northward, except with the object of importing into Egypt cattle, oxen, goats or asses. The forts are still visible on either bank of the river a little above the Second Cataract, and bear the names of Koommeh and Semneh. They are massive constructions, built of numerous squared blocks of granite and sandstone, and perched upon two steep rocks which rise up perpendicularly from the river. Usurtasen, having made this beginning, proceeded, from his eighth to his 16th year, to carry on the war with perseverance and ferocity in the district between the Nile and the Red

Sea – to kill the men, fire the crops and carry off the women and children. The memory of his razzias was perpetuated upon stone columns set up to record his successes. Later on, in his 19th year he made a last expedition, to complete the conquest of 'the miserable Kashi', and recorded his victory at Abydos.

The effect of these inroads was to advance the Egyptian frontier 150 miles to the south, to carry it, in fact, from the First to above the Second Cataract. Usurtasen drew the line between Egypt and Ethiopia at this period, very much where the British Government drew it between Egypt and the Soudan in 1885. The boundary is a somewhat artificial one, as any boundary must be on the course of a great river; but it is probably as convenient a point as can be found between Assouan (Syene) and Khartoum. The conquest was regarded as redounding greatly to Usurtasen's glory, and made him the hero of the [Middle] Kingdom. Myths gathered about his name, which, softened into Sesostris, became a favourite one in the mouths of Egyptian minstrels and minnesingers. Usurtasen grew to be a giant more than seven feet high, who conquered, not only all Ethiopia, but also Europe and Asia; his columns were said to be found in Palestine, Asia Minor, Scythia and Thrace; he left a colony at Colchis, the city of the golden fleece; he dug all the canals by which Egypt was intersected; he invented geometry; he set up colossi above 50 feet high; he was the greatest monarch that had ruled Egypt since the days of Osiris!

No doubt these tales were, in the main, imaginary; but they marked the fact that in Usurtasen III the military glories of the [Middle] Kingdom culminated.

THE GOOD AMENEMHAT AND HIS WORKS

Dangers Connected With the Inundation of the Nile, Twofold

The great river to which Egypt owes her being, is at once the source of all her blessings and her chiefest danger. Swelling with a uniformity, well calculated to call forth man's gratitude and admiration, almost from a fixed day in each year, and continuing to rise steadily for months, it gradually spreads over the lands, covering the entire soil with a fresh coating of the richest possible alluvium, and thus securing to the country a perpetual and inexhaustible fertility. Nature's mechanism is so perfect, that the rise year after year scarcely varies a foot, and is almost exactly the same now as it was when the first pharaoh poured his libation to the river-god from the embankment which he had made at Memphis; but though this uniformity is great, and remarkable, and astonishing, it is not absolute.

An Excessive Inundation...

There are occasions, once in two or three centuries, when the rainfall in Abyssinia is excessive. The Blue Nile and the Atbara pour into the deep and steady stream of the White Nile torrents of turbid water for months together. The windows of heaven seem to have been opened, and the rain pours down as if it would never cease. Then the river of the Egyptians assumes a threatening character; faster and faster it rises, and higher and higher; and further and further it spreads, until it begins to creep up the sides of the two ranges of hills. Calamitous results ensue. The mounds erected to protect the cities, the villages and the pasture lands, are surmounted, or undermined or washed away; the houses, built often of mud, and seldom of any better material than crude brick, collapse; cattle are drowned by hundreds; human life is itself imperilled; the population has to betake itself to boats, and to fly to the desert regions which enclose the Nile valley to the east and west, regions of frightful sterility, which with difficulty support the few wandering tribes that are their normal inhabitants. If the excessive rise continues long, thousands or millions starve; if it passes off rapidly, then the inhabitants return to find their homes desolated, their cattle drowned, their household goods washed away, and themselves dependent on the few rich men who may have stored their corn in stone granaries which the waters have not been able to penetrate. Disasters of this kind are, however, exceedingly rare, though, when they occur, their results are terrible to contemplate.

...A Defective One

The more usual form of calamity is of the opposite kind. Once or twice in a century the Abyssinian rainfall is deficient. The rise of the Nile is deferred beyond the proper date. Anxious eyes gaze daily on the sluggish stream, or consult the 'Nilometers' which kings and princes have constructed along its course to measure the increase of the waters. Hopes and fears alternate as good or bad news reaches the inhabitants of the lower valley from those who dwell higher up the stream. Each little rise is expected to herald a greater one, and the agony of suspense is prolonged until the 'hundred days', traditionally assigned to the increase, have gone by, and there is no longer a doubt that the river has begun to fall. Then hope is swallowed up in despair. Only the lands lying nearest to the river have been inundated; those at a greater distance from it lie parched and arid during the entire summertime, and fail to produce a single blade of grass or spike of corn. Famine stares the poorer classes in the face, and unless large supplies of grain have been laid up in store previously, or can be readily imported from abroad, the actual starvation of large numbers is the inevitable consequence.

There is reason to believe that, under the 12th dynasty, some derangement of meteoric or atmospheric conditions passed over Abyssinia and Upper Egypt, either in both the directions above noticed, or, at any rate, in the latter and more ordinary one. An official belonging to the later part of this period, in enumerating his merits upon his tomb, tells us, 'There was no poverty in my days, no starvation in my time, even when there were years of famine. I ploughed all the fields of Mah to its southern and northern boundaries; I gave life to its inhabitants, making its food; no one was starved in it. I gave to the widow as to the married woman.' As the late Dr. Birch observes, 'Egypt was occasionally subject to famines; and these, at the time of the 12th dynasty, were so important, that they attracted great attention, and were considered worthy of record by the princes or hereditary lords who were buried at Beni-Hassan. Under the 12th dynasty, also, the tombs of Abydos show the creation of superintendents, or storekeepers of the public granaries, a class of functionaries apparently created to meet the contingency.'

Sufferings from These Causes Under Amenemhat III

The distress of his subjects under these circumstances seems to have drawn the thoughts of 'the good Amenemhat' to the devising of some system which should effectually remedy these evils, by preventing their occurrence. In all countries where the supply of water is liable to be deficient, it is of the utmost importance to utilize to the full that amount of the life-giving fluid, be it more or be it less, which the bounty of nature furnishes. Rarely, indeed, is nature absolutely a niggard. Mostly she gives far more than is needed, but the improvidence or the apathy of man allows her gifts to run to waste.

Possible Storage of Water

Careful and provident husbanding of her store will generally make it suffice for all man's needs and requirements. Sometimes this has been affected in a thirsty land by conducting all the rills and brooks that flow from the highlands or hills into subterranean conduits, where they are shielded from the sun's rays, and prolonging these ducts for miles upon miles, till every drop of the precious fluid has been utilized for irrigation. Such is the *kareez* or *kanat* system of Persia. In other places vast efforts have been made to detain the abundant supply of rain which nature commonly provides in the spring of the year, to store it, and prevent it from flowing off down the river courses to the sea, where it is absolutely lost. For this purpose, either huge reservoirs must be constructed by the hand of man, or else advantage must be taken of some facility which nature offers for storing the water in convenient situations. Valleys may be blocked by massive dams, and millions of gallons thus imprisoned for future use, as is done in many parts of the North of England, but for manufacturing and not for irrigation purposes. Or naturally land-locked basins may be found, and the overflow of streams at their flood time turned into them and arrested, to be made use of later in the year.

In Egypt the one and only valley was that of the Nile, and the one and only stream that which had formed it, and flowed along it, at a lower or higher level, ceaselessly. It might perhaps have been possible for Egyptian engineering skill to have blocked the valley at Silsilis, or at the Gebelein, and to have thus turned Upper Egypt into a huge reservoir always full, and always capable of supplying Lower Egypt with enough water to eke out a deficient inundation. But this could only have been done by an enormous work, very difficult to construct, and at the sacrifice of several hundred square kilometres of fertile territory, thickly inhabited, which would have been covered permanently by the artificial lake. Moreover, the Egyptians would have known that such an embankment can under no circumstances be absolutely secure, and may have foreseen that its rupture would spread destruction over the whole of the lower country.

Amenemhat's Reservoir, the 'Lake Moeris'

Amenemhat, at any rate, did not venture to adopt so bold a design. He sought for a natural depression, and found one in the Libyan range of hills to the west of the Nile valley, about a degree south of the latitude of Memphis – a depression of great depth and of ample expanse, 80 kilometres (50 miles) or more in length by 48 kilometres (30 miles) in breadth, and containing an area of 1,550 to 1,800 square kilometres (600 or 700 square miles). It was separated from the Nile valley by a narrow ridge of hills about 60 metres (200 feet) high, through which ran from south-east to north-west a narrow rocky gorge, giving access to the depression. It is possible that in very high floods some of the water of the inundation passed naturally into the basin through this gorge; but whether this were so or no, it was plain that by the employment of no very large amount of labour a canal or cutting might be carried along the gorge, and the Nile water given free access into the depression, not only in very high floods, but annually when the inundation reached a certain moderate height.

This is, accordingly, what Amenemhat did. He dug a canal from the western branch of the Nile – the modern Bahr Yousuf – leaving it at El-Lahoun, carried his canal through the gorge, in places cutting deep into its rocky bottom, and by a system of sluices and floodgates retained such an absolute control over the water that he could either admit or exclude the inundation at his will, as it rose; and when it fell, could either allow the water that had flowed in to return, or imprison it and keep it back. Within the gorge he had thus at all times a copious store of the invaluable fluid, banked up to the height of high Nile, and capable of being applied to purposes of cultivation both within and without the depression by the opening and shutting of the sluices.

Doubts as to Its Dimensions

So much appears to be certain. The exact size and position of Amenemhat's reservoir within the depression, which a

French *savant* was supposed to have discovered, are now called in question, and must be admitted to be still *sub judice*. M. Linant de Bellefonds [Louis Maurice Adolphe Linant de Bellefonds, also known as Linant Pasha, was an explorer of Egypt and the chief engineer of Egypt's public works from 1831–69] regarded the reservoir as occupying the south-eastern or upper portion of the depression only, as extending from north to south a distance of 22 kilometres (14 miles) only, and from east to west a distance varying from nine to 17 kilometres (six to 11 miles). He regarded it as artificially confined towards the west and north by two long lines of embankment, which he considered that he had traced, and gave the area of the lake as 405 million square metres, or about 480 million square yards.

Mr. [Frederic] Cope Whitehouse [American archaeologist, Egyptologist and engineer, who surveyed Lake Moeris in Egypt] believes that the water was freely admitted into the whole of the depression, which it filled, with the exception of certain parts, which stood up out of the water as islands, from 45 to 60 metres (150 to 200 feet) high. He believes that it was in places 91 metres (300 feet) deep, and that the circuit of its shores was from (300 to 500 miles). Whatever may be the truth regarding 'Lake Moeris', as this great reservoir was called, it is certain that it furnished the ancients one of the least explicable of all the many problems that the remarkable land of the Nile presented to them. Herodotus added to the other marvels of the place a story about two sitting statues based upon pyramids, which stood 91 metres (300 feet) above the level of the lake, and a famous labyrinth, of which we shall soon speak.

Whether the reservoir of Amenemhat had the larger or the smaller dimensions ascribed to it, there can be no doubt that it was a grand construction, undertaken mainly for the benefit of his people, and greatly conducing to their advantage. Even if the reservoir had only the dimensions assigned to it by M. de Bellefonds, it would, according to his calculations, have contained water sufficient, not only for irrigating the northern and western portions of the Fayoum throughout the year, but also for the supply of the whole western bank of the Nile from Beni-Souef to the embouchure at Canopus for six months. This alone would in dry seasons have been a sensible relief to a large portion of the population. If the dimensions exceeded those of De Bellefonds, the relief would have been proportionately greater.

Amenemhat's 'Labyrinth'

The good king was not, however, content merely to benefit his people by increasing the productiveness of Egypt and warding off the calamities that occasionally befell the land; he further gave employment to large numbers, which was not of a severe or oppressive kind, but promoted their comfort and welfare. In connection with his hydraulic works in the Fayoum he constructed a novel species of building, which after ages admired even above the constructions of the pyramid builders, and regarded as the most wonderful edifice in all the world. 'I visited the place,' says Herodotus, 'and found it to surpass description; for if all the walls and other great works of the Greeks could be put together in one, they would not equal, either for labour or expense, this Labyrinth; and yet the temple of

Ephesus is a building worthy of note, and so is the temple of Samos. The pyramids likewise surpass description, and are severally equal to a number of the greatest works of the Greeks; but the Labyrinth surpasses the pyramids. It has 12 courts, all of them roofed, with gates exactly opposite one another, six looking to the north, and six to the south. A single wall surrounds the whole building. It contains two different sorts of chambers, half of them underground, and half above-ground, the latter built upon the former; the whole number is 3,000, of each kind 1,500.

The upper chambers I myself passed through and saw, and what I say of them is from my own observation; of the underground chambers I can only speak from report, for the keepers of the building could not be induced to show them, since they contained (they said) the sepulchres of the kings who built the Labyrinth, and also those of the sacred crocodiles. Thus it is from hearsay only that I can speak of them; but the upper chambers I saw with my own eyes, and found them to excel all other human productions; for the passages through the houses, and the varied windings of the paths across the courts, excited in me infinite admiration, as I passed from the courts into chambers, and from the chambers into colonnades, and from the colonnades into fresh houses, and again from these into courts unseen before. The roof was, throughout, of stone, like the walls; and the walls were carved all over with figures; every court was surrounded with a colonnade, which was built of white stones, exquisitely fitted together. At the corner of the Labyrinth stands a pyramid, 40 fathoms high, with large figures engraved upon it, which is entered by a subterranean passage.'

His Pyramid, and Name of Ra-n-mat

The pyramid intended is probably that examined by [John S.] Perring and [Karl Richard] Lepsius [today known as Lepsius Number One at Abu Rowash], which had a base of 91 metres (300 feet), and an elevation, probably, of about 56 metres (185 feet). It was built of crude brick mixed with a good deal of straw, and cased with a white silicious limestone. The same material was employed for the greater part of the so-called 'Labyrinth', but many of the columns were of red granite, and some perhaps of porphyry. Most likely the edifice was intended as a mausoleum for the sacred crocodiles, and was gradually enlarged for their accommodation – Amenemhat, whose praenomen was found on the pyramid, being merely the first founder. The number of the pillared courts, and their similarity, made the edifice confusing to foreigners, and got it the name of 'The Labyrinth'; but it is not likely the designers of the building had any intention to mislead or to confuse.

Amenemhat's praenomen, or throne-name, assumed (according to ordinary custom) on his accession, was Ra-n-mat, 'Sun of Justice' or 'Sun of Righteousness'. The assumption of the title indicates his desire to leave behind him a character for justice and equity. It is perhaps noticeable that the name by which the Greeks knew him was Moeris, which may mean 'the beloved'. With him closes the first period of Theban greatness. A cloud was impending, and darker days about to follow; but as yet Egypt enjoyed a time of progressive, and in the main peaceful, development. Commerce, art, religion, agriculture, occupied her. She did not covet other men's lands, nor did other men covet hers. The world beyond her borders knew little of her, except that she was a fertile and well-ordered land, whereto, in time of dearth, the needy of other countries might resort with confidence.

THE HYKSOS AND THE RESTORATION OF THE EGYPTIAN KINGDOM

In spite of the union of Upper and Lower Egypt, and the extension of the Egyptian dominion up the Nile as far as Semne and Kumne, the kingdom of the pyramids, of the lake of Moeris, and the labyrinth succumbed to the attack of a foreign enemy. According to Josephus, Manetho, in the second book of his Egyptian history, gave the following account: 'There was a king Amyntimaeus. In his reign the divine power, I know not why, was ungracious. From the East came an unexpected swarm of men belonging to a tribe of no great reputation, with a bold resolution of taking the country. This they succeeded in doing without much trouble. They made themselves masters of the ruling princes, ruthlessly set fire to the cities and destroyed the shrines of the gods. Towards the inhabitants they behaved in a most hostile manner; some they put to the sword, from others they carried away their wives and children into slavery.

'At last they made one of their own number, by name Salatis, their king. He took up his abode at Memphis, collected tribute from the Upper and Lower country, and placed garrisons in the most suitable places. The eastern districts were fortified most strongly, since he foresaw that the Assyrians, who were then growing in power, would be seized with the desire of invading his country. In the Saitic

(Sethroitic) province he found a city excellently adapted for his purpose, lying eastwards of the river from Bubastis, and called Avaris, from some old legend or another. This he surrounded with the strongest walls, filled it with inhabitants, and placed there the bulk of his armed soldiers, 240,000 men, as a garrison. In the summer he visited this stronghold to measure the corn, pay his soldiers and exercise his troops in order to strike fear in those who dwelt beyond the fortress.

'After a reign of 19 years Salatis died. After him reigned a king of the name of Beon, for 44 years, then Apachnas for 36 years and seven months, then Apophis for 61 years, and Annas for 50 years and one month, and finally Assis for 49 years and two months. These six were their first rulers, and they sought more and more to destroy Egypt to the very root. The whole tribe was called Hyksos, i.e. shepherd kings. For in the sacred language *hyk* means 'king', and *sos* in the ordinary dialect is 'a shepherd', and from composition of the two comes the word Hyksos. Some authorities say that they were Arabs.'

'The shepherd kings named above and their descendants are supposed by Manetho to have ruled over Egypt for 511 years. Yet he afterwards tells us that kings arose in the district of Thebes and the rest of Egypt, between whom and the shepherds there was a long and severe struggle. In the reign of a king named Misphragmuthosis the shepherds were defeated by the king, driven out of Egypt and confined in one place, 10,000 arourae [an ancient Egyptian unit of land measure equal to 0.677 acres] in extent, the name of which was Avaris. This space, as Manetho tells us, the shepherds surrounded with a great and strong wall, in order to preserve their possessions and their booty in security. But Tuthmosis, the son of Misphragmuthosis, attempted to take Avaris by force, and led out 480,000 men before the walls. When he found that the investment made but little way, he came to terms with the shepherds, permitting them to leave Egypt uninjured and go whither they would. On these terms they departed from Egypt with their families, and goods, not less than 240,000 strong, and went into the Syrian desert, and through fear of the Assyrians, who were then the great power in Asia, they built a city in the land now called Judea, large enough to contain their numbers, and named it Jerusalem.'

The short excerpts made by Africanus and Eusebius from the Egyptian history of Manetho only tell that 'there were certain foreign kings, Phoenicians, who took Memphis, and built a city in the Sethroitic province, from which they went forth and subdued the Egyptians'. Africanus gives six, Eusebius four, names of these foreign kings, which are somewhat the same in sound as those in Josephus, only in Africanus Apophis is the last in the list, not last but two.

If Josephus has transcribed and reproduced Manetho correctly there is an obvious contradiction in his narrative. The first shepherd king, Salatis, fortified and peopled Avaris, and placed there a garrison of 240,000 men, for protection against the Assyrians. Then after a lapse of 511 (or according to the excerpt of Africanus of 953) years, when the shepherds had lost Egypt, they were shut up in a place containing 10,000 arourae, i.e. a square of 40 kilometres (25 miles), of the name of Avaris, which they surrounded with a strong wall in order to keep their possessions and booty in security. At last they were compelled to retire even from this, and march out in just the same strength as the garrison which Salatis had placed so long before at Avaris, towards Judea, and here they founded a second city of Jerusalem, also for protection against the Assyrians.

We may leave the Assyrians out of the question, and assume that the reference to them has been transferred by Manetho from the later position which Assyria took up towards Syria and Egypt in the eighth and seventh centuries BCE to those earlier times; we may also regard the turn of the narrative, which makes the shepherds the ancestors of the Jews and builders of Jerusalem, as a combination invented by Manetho, for in the tradition of the Hebrews there is no hint that their ancestors had once ruled over Egypt for centuries, and Jerusalem down to the time of David was merely the stronghold of a small tribe, the Jebusites. Still, it remains inexplicable that these shepherds, who, after they had taken Egypt, or, in order to take it, fortified Avaris, and garrisoned it with 240,000 men, should fortify Avaris a second time centuries later, in order to maintain their last possession in Egypt, and at last march out of Avaris in exactly the same numbers as the garrison originally settled there. Shepherds, i.e. nomads, do not make war by building fortresses as a base of operations for extending their conquests; they had nothing to gain by conquering Egypt for the mere purpose of shutting up the whole or the greater part of their numbers with their flocks in a fortified place. On the other hand, it might have seemed advisable to them, when they had subjugated Egypt, to possess a fortified place on the eastern border, in order to keep up a connection with their tribe; and it was natural that the shepherds, when the Egyptians had risen against them with success, and they were no longer able to hold the Delta, should attempt to maintain themselves in the flats and swamps of the Eastern Delta; and when forced to act on the defensive should fortify their camp at Avaris in this district.

In the narrative of Manetho we can accept no more than the facts that Egypt succumbed to the attack of the shepherds, and that they, to take the lower estimate, ruled over Egypt for five centuries. Herodotus also learnt in Egypt that the shepherd Philitis had once pastured his flocks at Memphis. There is nothing wonderful in such an occurrence. Nomad tribes dwelt in the deserts on the east and west of Egypt, to whose poverty and scanty means of subsistence the abundance and cultivation of Egypt must have presented a continual temptation. That temptation would increase in force when the tribes became more numerous, when unusual heat diminished the springs in the oases, and robbed these shepherds of the produce of their scanty agriculture. The tradition of the Hebrews tells us that their ancestor Abraham went to Egypt when 'there was a famine in the land', and the sons of Jacob bought corn in Egypt.

According to Manetho's account, the tribes from whom the attack proceeded were not famous, and he regarded the invaders as coming from the east. The peninsula of Sinai, Northern Arabia and the Syrian desert sheltered in the Amalekites, Horites, Edomites and Midianites, tribes who were rendered hardy and warlike by life in the desert, tribal feuds and raids for plunder; and these may very well have united in considerable number under some leader of military genius, and attempted the invasion of the rich river valley in their neighbourhood. According to Manetho, the invaders were Phoenicians or Arabians. The name of the shepherd Philitis, given by Herodotus, points to a Semitic tribe, and one immediately bordering on Egypt on the Syrian coast – the Philistines (Pelischtim), from whom the whole Syrian coast was called by the Greeks Palestina. The name of the stronghold of the shepherds, Avaris, or Abaris, recurs in Hauara, a town of Arabia on the shore of the Red Sea. If the shepherds who conquered Egypt had not been Semitic, and closely related to the Hebrews, Manetho would not have made them the ancestors of the Hebrews and founders of Jerusalem after their expulsion from Egypt.

After the conquest, the chiefs of the shepherds ruled over Egypt. The inscriptions on the monuments repeatedly denote certain tribes in the east of Egypt by the name Schasu, which in the later language is contracted into Sôs. *Schasu* means shepherds. Moreover, in old Egyptian, the head of a family, a tribe and a province is called *hak*, and Hyksos thus can be explained by *Haku-schasu*, chiefs of the shepherds, shepherd kings, as Josephus, Eusebius and Africanus render it. What Manetho tells us of the destruction of the cities and shrines, the slaughter and enslaving of the Egyptians may be correct for the time of the war and conquest. But this hostility and destruction cannot, as he intimates, have gone on for centuries, for, on the restoration of the pharaohs, we find ancient Egypt unimpaired in population, unchanged in language, customs and manners, in civilization and art. If the national development was interrupted and repressed by the Hyksos, it still remained uninjured at the core, so far as we have the means of judging.

When at a subsequent period the kings of Ethiopia subjugated Egypt, the warrior caste, the soldiers settled in the country by the pharaohs, were deprived of their lands. The same thing may have taken place on the irruption of the shepherds. The warriors of the pharaohs fell in battle, were carried away as prisoners, or deprived of their weapons; and in their place came the victorious army of the shepherds. Of these many would soon return home laden with the booty of Egypt, others pitched their tents in the conquered land, and settled in the greenest meadows, more especially in the eastern provinces of the Delta, nearest their own home, on the Tanitic and Pelusiac arms of the Nile, and Lake Menzaleh. The chief of the immigrants became the head of the conquerors and the conquered. The latter would render the same abject homage to their new masters as they rendered before and after to their native kings; and the power which the conquered willingly acknowledged in the chief would exalt his position even among the conquerors. As time went on, the culture and civilization of Egypt had their natural effect on the barbarous invaders, and when the storm of conquest was over, we may assume that Egypt was no worse off under the rule of the shepherd kings than at later periods under the rule of the Persians, the Ptolemies and the Romans.

That the new princes, soon after the conquest, attempted to approximate their position as much as possible to that of the ancient pharaohs may be concluded from the mere fact that Manetho was in a position to give a catalogue of their reigns by years and months. But this is proved more definitely still by certain monuments. In the neighbourhood of Lake Menzaleh, among the ruins of the ancient Tanis, the modern San, two old statues have been discovered, the forms and lineaments of which exhibit a physique different from the Egyptian. In the heads of four sphinxes, discovered in the same place, it is thought that we may recognize the portraits of four shepherd kings, and a colossus discovered at Tel Mokdam is said to bear the following inscription: 'The good god, the star of both worlds, the child of the sun, Sel Salati, beloved by Sutech, the lord of Hauar.'

The six shepherd kings enumerated by Josephus from the Egyptian history of Manetho reigned, according to the dates given by the latter, for 260 years, i.e. from the year 2101 BCE, in which, on Lepsius's arrangement, the irruption of the shepherds took place, till the year 1842 BCE. Their successors must therefore have ruled over Egypt for 251 years more, i.e., down to the year 1591 BCE. But in the time of the later shepherd kings, native princes again arose in Upper Egypt, although subject to tribute. A papyrus of the British Museum tells us: 'It so happened that the land of Egypt became the possession of her enemies, and when this took place there was no king. And behold Raskenen became king of the country in the south. The enemy were in possession of the fortress of Aamu, and their chief, Ra Apepi was at Hauar. The whole land paid tribute to him, and rendered service of all kinds, and brought to him the produce of Lower Egypt. King Apepi chose Sutech as his lord, and served no other god, and built him a temple of firm and lasting structure.'

The power of the native princes at Thebes must have been gradually strengthened till the successors of Raskenen were in a position to press forward towards Lower Egypt, and place limits on the sway of the shepherd kings, and finally to drive them entirely out of Egypt. Josephus has already told us from Manetho that the princes of Thebes and the rest of Egypt rose up against the shepherds, and in consequence a long and severe struggle took place between them.

For the period of the actual expulsion of the Hyksos there are but two documents, Manetho as recorded by Josephus, and the tomb of the warrior Aahmes at El Kab. We see in the tale of Apepa that during the Seqenenra period, somewhere between 1660 and 1600 BCE, the Theban princedom was completely in the power of the Hyksos, and open war had not yet broken out, or become continuous. But the last Seqenenra died in battle, probably at some distance away, and yet was buried properly at Thebes. This points to the Theban powers having become independent by 1597 BCE, and having a fighting frontier some way to the north, so that ceremonials at Thebes were uninterrupted. During the reign of Kames further advance was probably made by 'the valiant prince', as we see that king Aahmes was able to besiege the stronghold of the Hyksos down in the Delta at the beginning of his reign, about 1585 BCE. So probably the Thebans had been gradually pushing their way north, and claiming independence, during perhaps 20 years before the country gathered itself together and made the grand effort of the expulsion under Aahmes; and it was that effort which placed Aahmes on the throne as a victorious conqueror, and founded the 28th dynasty.

Manetho summarized the story, according to Josephus, in this form: 'The kings of the Thebaid and of the rest of Egypt made insurrection against the Shepherds, and a long and mighty war was carried on between them, until the Shepherds were overcome by a king whose name was Alisphragmouthosis (var. Mis-phra-gmu-thosis, "Aahmes, the golden Horus binding together the two lands", a title of his referring to the united action in the war, and recovery of the Delta), and they were by him driven out of the other parts of Egypt, and hemmed up in a place containing about 10,000 arouras, which was called Auaris. All this tract the Shepherds surrounded with a vast and strong wall, that they might retain all their property and their prey within a hold of their strength.

'And Thummosis the son of Alisphragmouthosis tried to force them by a siege, and beleaguered the place with a body of 480,000 men; but at the moment when he despaired of reducing them by siege, they agreed to a capitulation, that they would leave Egypt, and should be permitted to go out without molestation wheresoever they pleased. And, according to this stipulation, they departed from Egypt with all their families and effects, in number not less than 240,000, and bent their way through the desert towards Syria. But as they stood in fear of the Assyrians, who then had dominion over Asia, they built a city in that country which is now called Judea, of sufficient size to contain this multitude of men, and named it Jerusalem. [...]'

Aahmes concluded the Hyksos war within five years, and then turned his arms to the south. Two separate attempts were made apparently by the defeated Hyksos subsequently: Aata arose during the absence of Aahmes in his southern campaign, and overran the land as far as the south country; but he was soon crushed. Again, another flicker of the conquered force seems to have arisen under Teta'an, which was likewise soon crushed.

The history of the war of independence then seems to have been, that perhaps for 20 or 30 years before 1600 BCE the Nubian princes of Thebes had been pushing their way northward against the decaying power of the Hyksos. Active warfare was going on at about 1600 BCE; and a sudden outburst of energy, under the active young leader Aahmes, concluded the expulsion of the foreigners, and the capture of their stronghold, within a few years, ending in 1582 BCE. A couple of last flickers of the war were crushed during the succeeding years, and the rest of his reign Aahmes was able to devote to the reorganization of the whole country.

One question remains, What effect had the Hyksos occupation upon the people? That there were large numbers of the race is evident; only a considerable mass of people could have thus held down a whole country for some centuries, while yet remaining so distinct that they could be expelled as a separate body. The number reported to have left Egypt – a quarter of a million – from a land which very probably only held then about two million, as at the beginning of this century, shows how large their numbers were after they had become intermingled with the natives during some 20 generations. It was not merely the upsetting of a government [...] but it was the thrusting out of a large part of the population, probably the greater part of the inhabitants of the Delta. We cannot doubt, then, that from such a large body of a ruling race there must have been a great amount of mixture with the earlier occupiers of the land. The Semitising of Egypt took place largely then, so far as race was concerned; and bore full effect when the fashions, ideas and manners of Syria were implanted after the Asiatic conquests of Thutmose III.

The great event of the reign of Aahmes was the war by which he established his power at the beginning of his reign, that great war of independence which was the most glorious page of Egyptian history. Within four or five years, Aahmes succeeded not only in finally throwing off the suzerainty of the Hyksos kings, but also in driving them out of the Nile valley, in seizing on their great centre of Hauar in the eastern Delta (probably Tanis) and in chasing them across the desert into Palestine, where, in the fifth year, he captured Sharhana, or Sharuhen, upon the southern border, some miles south of Lachish. He also pushed on into Zahi (Phoenicia), where Pennekheb states that he took 10 hands. Having then slaughtered the Mentiu of Setet, or the Bedawin of the hill country, he turned back, and found the need of his presence on the opposite frontier in the south. The southern races appear to have pushed forward in the rear of the Egyptians on their advance northward, and to have needed repelling, as in the time of Usertesen III. Going, therefore, up the Nile, he made a great slaughter of the Anu Khenti, and is mentioned at Semneh by Thutmose II.

His triumphant return, however, was greeted with the news of outbreaks among the remains of the Hyksos people. The expulsion of a race as a whole cannot be affected after several centuries of occupation; and though the foreign army might be driven out, there must have been a large part of the population of mixed race, ready to tolerate the Egyptians if they were the conquerors, but preferring an independent life. From such a source were, doubtless, the two last outbursts of the war. Aata seems to have been of a branch of the Hyksos party who tried to make headway up the country in the absence of Aahmes; and Teta'an afterwards was the head of a rising of the half-breed race, who refused to accept as yet the new power of the Egyptians. Both were, however, defeated summarily; and after that there seems to have been no further trouble with the Asiatic people.

THE NEW KINGDOM

The New Kingdom, covering the eighteenth to the twentieth dynasties, is considered the high point of Egyptian culture, with more international trade, building works and well-known pharaohs than any other point in Egyptian history. The period starts with Ahmose I overthrowing the Hyksos rulers of the Second Intermediate Period, and progresses with a Who's Who of Egyptian royalty, including Thutmosis III, Hatshepsut, Amenhotep III, Akhenaten, Tutankhamun and Ramses II. The era ends with the Ramesside dynasty (twentieth dynasty) during which there were nine kings called Ramses (III–XI).

In this chapter you will read about the military gains of Thutmosis I as he helped restore Egypt to glory following the Second Intermediate Period; the female pharaoh Hatshepsut, who decided that the role of queen was not enough and adopted the role of king; the military prowess shown by Thutmosis III; and the glory of the reign of Amenhotep III.

In the nineteenth century Akhenaten was incredibly popular as his new religion, the primary god of which was Aten, gave the appearance of monotheism. This appealed to scholars with a strong theological background such as Rawlinson (1886). This period has generated a lot of research and understanding of Akhenaten and the Aten cult, and Budge provides an insight into where the research was at the end of the nineteenth/beginning of the twentieth centuries. Following the collapse of the Aten cult and a return to tradition, this chapter ends with a discussion of the power of Ramses II, the third king of the nineteenth dynasty.

THE RISE OF THE EIGHTEENTH DYNASTY

With the conclusive triumph of the Theban royal line, represented by Aahmes I, over the Hyksos, the history of Egypt enters upon a new phase, and assumes an entirely new character [...].

The new Egypt which had arisen out of the flames of the War of Independence had been, by her trying experiences, thoroughly attuned to the spirit of the new age, and was eager to take her place on the wider stage which circumstances now offered her. War, continued for more than a generation, had created in her people that restlessness which a great war never fails to leave behind it; and along with that state of mind, there went the conviction that in the lands which had sent forth the oppressors of Egypt and equipped them with the strange weapons which had helped them to success, there must be much that was worth the getting, now that the tide had turned, and the comfortable assurance that the strength of Egypt was such as to enable her to put in her claim for possession with every prospect of its being honoured.

Behind all the rest was the spirit of revenge, which made every Egyptian, from Pharaoh downwards, feel that in invading and ravaging the lands of the hated Asiatics he was really waging a holy war, a kind of crusade against the lands that had sent forth the men who had dishonoured the sacred soil of Egypt, and committed sacrilege against her gods. Our old friend Aahmes, son of Abana, uses a phrase in describing the great Syrian invasion of Thutmose I, which exactly expresses the light in which these repeated campaigns of the early pharaohs of the 18th dynasty were regarded, both by themselves and by their people. 'One (i.e., Pharaoh) journeyed to the Retenu,' he says, 'to wash his heart among the foreign countries.' To wash the heart was to obtain satisfaction for past injuries, such as would cleanse away all the feeling of bitterness and humiliation which the past had left. It was such a desire which sharpened the swords of the Egyptian soldiers, and urged on their chariots, as they pressed up through Palestine and Syria into the Land of Rivers. They felt that they were getting their own back, and wiping out forever the stain which had been left upon the escutcheon of their national renown [...].

Meanwhile, however, after the first rush of the victorious Egyptians had carried them as far as Sharuhen, and through the long siege of that city, King Aahmes found that he had to attend to affairs on his southern frontier. Here the Nubian chieftains, among whom one A'ata was apparently conspicuous, had been taking advantage of Egypt's weakness and her preoccupation with the Hyksos danger, to undo the work of the great pharaohs of the Middle Kingdom.

Aahmes was now to show them that Egypt meant to reassert her ancient claims to dominion over Nubia. Aahmes, son of Abana, tells us the story of the double campaign which followed with his usual dry terseness and his usual little bit of personal detail and self-glorification:

'Now when His Majesty had slain the Mentiu of Asia, he fared southwards to Khenthennofer to destroy the Nubian Beduin; and His Majesty proceeded to make a great slaughter among them. Then I brought away spoil thence: two living men and three hands. Then I was rewarded with the gold anew, and behold two female slaves were given unto me. And His Majesty sailed downstream, with glad heart in valour and victory, having taken possession of both Southerners and Northerners [...].'

'Then,' says our chronicler, 'there came A'ata of the South, whose fate drew him to doom. For the gods of Upper Egypt laid hold upon him; His Majesty found him in Tentta'a. And His Majesty brought him a living prisoner, and all his people as an easy spoil. Then I captured two bowmen from the ship of A'ata. And one gave me five heads, and a parcel of land, three and a half acres in my city; and the like was done to all the navy [...].'

Be that as it may, there was no question to the native character of the last revolt with which King Aahmes was called to deal. It was stirred up and led by an Egyptian of the name Teta'an (a common name at this period), and it met with no better success than its predecessors had done.

Our sailor of El Kab dismisses the business with scant notice: 'then came that wretch, whose name was Teta'an; he had gathered rebels unto himself. His Majesty slew him, and annihilated his gang [...].'

With the slaying of Teta'an, Aahmes seems to have fairly completed his domination of the discontented element of his kingdom. One result of the disaffection shown by some of the native nobility seems to have been the adoption of a policy on the part of the Crown by which the administration of local affairs, and even of the family estates of the great barons, was largely taken out of the hands of the great families, whose power, once the buttress of the state, had now proved to be a danger to it, and was carried on by the central government. The great families, instead of being the local providences of their districts, as under the Middle Kingdom, now became courtiers of the regular type, who resided at Thebes and were buried there, instead of occupying the ancient tombs of their lines. Thus the entire control of the land passed into the hands of the pharaoh himself, and Egypt, as [American Egyptologist James Henry] Breasted has pointed out, 'became the personal estate of the pharaoh [...].'

The deprivation of the aristocracy of their former local powers is not to be looked on as being generally punishment for disaffection, but rather as part of a fixed policy designed to remove forever such a risk as even the partial rebellions had shown to exist. Under this policy, no doubt, the innocent suffered with the guilty, if, indeed, the local magnates reckoned their summons to court, with the consequent abnegation of their administrative functions in their own provinces, as a grievance, and not rather, as is quite possible, a resumption of the old honour, which had been theirs under the Old Kingdom, and being in personal association with and attendance on the Good God the land.

However this may be, there can be little doubt that the new policy, however much it may have appeared to strengthen the power of the Crown for the time being, actually tended to the ultimate weakening of the Egyptian state, as undue centralization always does. The new aristocracy, divorced from local interest which had formerly given each local magnate a personal pride in his country and his own share of its work, must inevitably have become a much less healthy body than the old; and its tendency to luxury and corruption must have been vastly increased by the constant influx of captured treasure and foreign slaves and immigrants which was the result of the continual campaigns of the conquering pharaohs of the 18th dynasty [...].

One more warlike adventure the founder of the dynasty had to undertake, before he was finally able to rest from external strife. This took the shape of another Asiatic campaign, in the course of which he penetrated into Phoenicia – Zahi, as the Egyptians called it – to drive the Hyksos so far back from the Egyptian frontiers that there should be no further danger of trouble from them [...].

So, with the Hyksos enemy humbled and pushed far from the borders of Egypt, the Nubian attempt to regain independence frustrated, and all internal disaffection quelled, King Aahmes was able to turn his attention to the huge task of restoring his country to order, and of bringing it back to some semblance of decency with regard to its great public and religious works, which had suffered at the hands of the Semitic tyrants. It was a task which neither he nor his immediate successors saw completed, for we find it still going on in the reign of Queen Hetshetsup, after Aahmes, Amenhotep I, Thutmose I and Thutmose II had passed away; but at all events he made a beginning [...].

The king to whom Egypt owed her final liberation from Hyksos, and the establishment of the most world famous, if not the greatest, of her dynasties, and who therefore deserves to rank as one of the greatest kings of Egyptian history, died, apparently, in the prime of his life, at an age probably between

40 and 50. His mummy, which was one of those found at Der el-Bahri, was that of a string, broad-shouldered man of about five feet, six inches in height, his hair of a dark brown colour, thick and curly, his front teeth somewhat prominent – a family trait. Around his neck he wore a wreath of delphinium orientele. In addition to his 'Great Royal Wife', he had married several secondary wives, of whom the most prominent was the Princess Inhapi, whose daughter, the Princess Aahmes Hent-Temehu, was the mother, by Thutmosis I, of the famous Queen Hetshetsup. Another was the lady Sensenb, who became the mother of Thutmosis I; so that King Aahmes was not only the founder of the 18th dynasty, but had a direct and considerable share in providing it with some of its most famous members.

He was succeeded by Amenhotep I, who was his son by Queen Aahmes-Nefertari.

TUTHMOSIS I, THE FIRST GREAT EGYPTIAN CONQUEROR

Early Wars of Tuthmosis in Ethiopia and Nubia

Tuthmosis I was the grandson of the Aahmes who drove out the Hyksos. He had thus hereditary claims to valour and military distinction. The Ethiopian blood which flowed in his veins through his grandmother, Aahmes-Nefertaris, may have given him an additional touch of audacity, and certainly showed itself in his countenance, where the short, depressed nose and the unduly thick lips are of the Cushite rather than of the Egyptian type. His father, Amenhotep I, was a somewhat undistinguished prince; so that here, as so often, where superior talent runs in a family, it seems to have skipped a generation, and to have leapt from the grandsire to the grandson.

Tuthmosis began his military career by an invasion of the countries upon the Upper Nile, which were still in an unsettled state, notwithstanding the campaigns which had been carried on, and the victories which had been gained in them, during the two preceding reigns, by King Aahmes, and by the generals of Amenhotep. He placed a flotilla of ships upon the Nile above the Second Cataract, and supporting it with his land forces on either side of the river, advanced from Semneh, the boundary established by Usurtasen III, to Tombos, conquering the tribes, Nubian and Cushite, as he proceeded, and from time to time distinguishing himself in personal combats with his enemies. On one occasion, we are told, 'his majesty became more furious than a panther', and placing an arrow on his bowstring, directed it against the Nubian chief so surely that it struck him, and remained fixed in his knee, whereupon the chief 'fell fainting down before the royal diadem'. He was at once seized and made a prisoner; his followers were defeated and dispersed; and he himself, together with others, was carried off on board the royal ship, hanging with his head downwards, to the royal palace at the capital. This victory was the precursor of others; everywhere 'the Petti of Nubia were hewed in pieces, and scattered all over their lands', till 'their stench filled the valleys'.

At last a general submission was made, and a large tract of territory was ceded. The Egyptian terminus was pushed on from the 22nd parallel to the 19th, and at Tombos, beyond Dongola, an inscription was set up, at once to mark the new frontier, and to hand down to posterity the glory of the conquering monarch.

The inscription still remains, and is couched in inflated terms, which show a departure from the old official style. Tuthmosis declares that 'he has taken tribute from the nations of the North, and from the nations of the South, as well as from *those of the whole earth*; he has laid hold of the barbarians; he has not let a single one of them escape his gripe upon their hair; the Petti of Nubia have fallen beneath his blows; he has made their waters to flow backwards; he has overflowed their valleys like a deluge, like waters which mount and mount. He has resembled Horus, when he took possession of his eternal kingdom; all the countries included within the circumference of the entire earth are prostrate under his feet'. Having affected his conquest, Tuthmosis sought to secure it by the appointment of a new officer, who was to govern the newly annexed country under the title of 'Prince of Cush', and was to have his ordinary residence at Semneh.

His Desire to Avenge the Hyksos Invasion

Flushed with his victories in this quarter, and intoxicated with the delight of conquest, Tuthmosis, on his return to Thebes, raised his thoughts to a still grander and more adventurous enterprise. Egypt had a great wrong to avenge, a huge disgrace to wipe out. She had been invaded, conquered, plundered, by an enemy whom she had not provoked by any aggression; she had seen her cities laid in ashes, her temples torn down and demolished, the images of her gods broken to pieces, her soil dyed with her children's blood; she had been trampled under the iron heel of the conqueror for centuries; she had been exhausted by the payment of taxes and tribute; she had had to bow the knee, and lick the dust under the conqueror's feet

– was not retribution needed for all this? True, she had at last risen up and expelled her enemy, she had driven him beyond her borders, and he seemed content to acquiesce in his defeat, and to trouble her no more; but was this enough? Did not the law of eternal justice require something more:

'Nec lex justior ulla est,
Quàm necis artifices arte perire sua.'

Was it not proper, fitting, requisite for the honour of Egypt, that there should be retaliation, that the aggressor should suffer what he had inflicted, should be attacked in his own country, should be made to feel the grief, the despair, the rage, the shame, that he had forced Egypt to feel for so many years; should expiate his guilt by a penalty, not only proportioned to the offence, but its exact counterpart? Such thoughts, we may be sure, burned in the mind of the young warrior, when, having secured Egypt on the south, he turned his attention to the north, and asked himself the question how he should next employ the power that he had inherited, and the talents with which nature had endowed him.

Condition of Western Asia at this Period

It is uncertain what amount of knowledge the Egyptians of the time possessed concerning the internal condition, population and resources, of the continent which adjoined them on the north-east. We cannot say whether Tuthmosis and his counsellors could, or could not, bring before their mind's eye a fairly correct view of the general position of Asiatic affairs, and form a reasonable estimate of the probabilities of success or discomfiture, if a great expedition were led into the heart of Asia. Whatever may have been their knowledge or ignorance, it will be necessary for the historical student of the present day to have some general ideas on the subject, if he is to form an adequate conception either of the dangers which Tuthmosis affronted, or of the amount of credit due to him for his victories. We propose, therefore, in the present place, to glance our eye over the previous history of Western Asia, and to describe, so far as is possible, its condition at the time when Tuthmosis began to contemplate the invasion which it is his great glory to have accomplished.

Western Asia is generally allowed to have been the cradle of the human race. Its more fertile portions were thickly peopled at a very early date. Monarchy, it is probable, first grew up in Babylonia, towards the mouths of the Tigris and Euphrates. But it was not long ere a sister kingdom established itself in Susiana, or Elam, the fertile tract between the Lower Tigris and the Zagros mountains. The ambition of conquest first showed itself in this latter country, whence Kudur-Nakhunta, about 2300 BCE, made an attack on Erech, and Chedorlaomer (about 2000 BCE) established an empire which extended from the Zagros mountains on the one hand to the shores of the Mediterranean on the other. Shortly after this, a third power, that of the Hittites, grew up towards the north, chiefly perhaps in Asia Minor, but with a tendency to project itself southward into the Mesopotamian region.

Upper Mesopotamia, Syria and Palestine were at this time inhabited by weak tribes, each under its own chief, with no coherence, and no great military spirit. The chief of these tribes, at the time when Tuthmosis I ascended the Egyptian throne, were the Rutennu in Syria, and the Nahari or Naïri in Upper Mesopotamia. The two monarchies of the south, Elam and Babylon were not in a flourishing condition, and exercised no suzerainty beyond their own natural limits. They were, in fact, a check upon each other, constantly engaged in feuds and quarrels, which prevented either from maintaining an extended sway for more than a few years. Assyria had not yet acquired any great distinction, though it was probably independent, and ruled by monarchs who dwelt at Asshur (Kileh-Sherghat). The Hittites, about 1900 BCE, had received a severe check from the Babylonian monarch, Sargon, and had withdrawn themselves into their northern fortresses.

Thus the circumstances of the time were, on the whole, favourable to the enterprise of Tuthmosis. No great organized monarchy was likely to take the field against him, or to regard itself as concerned to interfere with the execution of his projects, unless they assumed extraordinary dimensions. So long as he did not proceed further north than Taurus, or further east than the western Khabour, the great affluent of the Euphrates, he would come into contact with none of the 'great powers' of the time; he would, at the worst, have to contend with loose confederacies of tribes, distrustful of each other, unaccustomed to act together, and, though brave, possessing no discipline or settled military organization. At the same time, his adversaries must not be regarded as altogether contemptible. The Philistines and Canaanites in Palestine, the Arabs of the Sinaitic and Syrian deserts, the Rutennu of the Lebanon and of Upper Syria, the Naïri of the western Mesopotamian region, were individually brave men, were inured to warfare, had a strong love of independence and were likely to resist with energy any attempt to bring them under subjection. They were also, most of them, well acquainted with the value of the horse for military service, and could bring into the field a number of war chariots, with riders well accustomed to their management Egypt had only recently added the horse to the list of its domesticated animals, and followed the example of the Asiatics by organizing a chariot force. It was open to doubt whether this new and almost untried corps would be able to cope with the experienced chariot troops of Asia.

Geographical Sketch of the Countries to be Attacked

The country also in which military operations were to be carried on was a difficult one. It consisted mainly of alternate mountain and desert. First, the sandy waste called El Tij – the 'Wilderness of the Wanderings' – had to be passed, a tract almost wholly without water, where an army must carry its own supply. Next, the high upland of the Negeb would present itself, a region wherein water may be procured from wells, and which in some periods of the world's history has been highly cultivated, but which in the time of Tuthmosis was probably almost as unproductive as the desert itself. Then would come the green rounded hills, the lofty ridges and the deep gorges of Palestine, untraversed by any road, in places thickly wooded, and offering continually greater obstacles to the advance of an army, as it stretched further and further towards the north. From Palestine the Lebanon region would have to be entered on, where, though the Coele-Syrian valley presents a comparatively easy line of march to the latitude of Antioch, the country on either side of the valley is almost untraversable, while the valley itself contains many points where it can be easily blocked by a small force. The Orontes, moreover, and the Litany, are difficult to cross, and in the time of Tuthmosis I would be unbridged, and form no contemptible obstacles. From the lower valley of the Orontes, first mountains and then a chalky desert had to be crossed in order to reach the Euphrates, which could only be passed in boats, or else by swimming. Beyond the Euphrates was another dreary and infertile region, the tract about Haran, where Crassus lost his army and his life.

Probable Information of Tuthmosis on These Matters

How far Tuthmosis and his counsellors were aware of these topographical difficulties, or of the general condition of Western Asia, it is, as already observed, impossible to determine. But, on the whole, there are reasons for believing that intercourse between nation and nation was, even in very early times, kept up, and that each important country had its 'intelligence department', which was not badly served. Merchants, refugees, spies, adventurers desirous of bettering their condition, were continually moving, singly or in bodies, from one land to another, and through them a considerable acquaintance with mundane affairs generally was spread abroad. The knowledge was, of course, very inexact. No surveys were made, no plans of cities or fortresses, no maps; the military force that could be brought into the field by the several nations was very roughly estimated; but still, ancient conquerors did not start off on their expeditions wholly in the dark as to the forces which they might have to encounter, or the difficulties which were likely to beset their march.

His Great Expedition into Syria and Mesopotamia

Tuthmosis probably set out on his expedition into Asia in about his sixth or seventh year. He was accompanied by two officers, who had served his father and his grandfather, known respectively as 'Aahmes, son of Abana', and 'Aahmes Pennishem'. Both of them had been engaged in the war which he had conducted against the Petti of Nubia and their Ethiopian allies, and both had greatly distinguished themselves. Aahmes, the son of Abana, boasts that he seven times received the prize of valour – a collar of gold – for his conduct in the field; and Aahmes Pennishem gives a list of 29 presents given to him as military rewards by three kings. It does not appear that any resistance was offered to the invading force as it passed through Palestine; but in Syria Tuthmosis engaged the Rutennu, and 'exacted satisfaction' from them, probably on account of the part which they had taken in the Hyksos struggle; after which he crossed the Euphrates and fell upon the far more powerful nation of the Naïri.

The Naïri, when first attacked by the Assyrians, had 23 cities, and as many kings; they were rich in horses and mules, and had so large a chariot force that we hear of 120 chariots being taken from them in a single battle. At this time the number of the chariots was probably much smaller, for each of the two officers named Ahmes takes great credit to himself on account of the capture of one such vehicle. It is uncertain whether more than a single battle was fought. All that we are told is, that 'His Majesty, having arrived in Naharina' (i.e. the Naïri country), 'encountered the enemy, and organized an attack. His Majesty made a great slaughter of them; an immense number of live captives was carried off by His Majesty.' These words would apply equally to a single battle and to a series of battles. All that can be said is, that Tuthmosis returned victorious from his Asiatic expedition, having defeated the Rutennu and the Naïri, and brought with him into Egypt a goodly booty, and a vast number of Asiatic prisoners.

His Buildings

The warlike ambition of Tuthmosis I was satisfied by his Nubian and Asiatic victories. On his return to Egypt at the close of his Mesopotamian campaign, he engaged in the peaceful work of adorning and beautifying his capital cities. At Thebes he greatly enlarged the temple of Ammon, begun by Amenemhat I, and continued under his son, the first Usurtasen, by adding to it the cloistered court in front of the central cell – a court 73 metres (240 feet) long by 19 metres (62 broad), surrounded by a colonnade, of which the supports were Osirid pillars, or square piers with a statue of Osiris in front. This is the first known example of the cloistered court, which became afterwards so common; though it is possible that constructions of a similar character may have been made by the 'Shepherd Kings' at Tanis, Tuthmosis also adorned this temple with obelisks. In front of the main entrance to his court he erected two vast monoliths of granite, each of them 23 metres (75 feet) in height, and bearing dedicatory inscriptions, which indicated his piety and his devotion to all the chief deities of Egypt.

Further, at Memphis he built a new royal palace, which he called 'The Abode of Aa-khepr-ka-ra', a grand building, afterwards converted into a magazine for the storage of grain.

His Greatness Insufficiently Appreciated

The greatness of Tuthmosis I has scarcely been sufficiently recognized by historians. It may be true that he did not affect much; but he broke ground in a new direction; he set an example which led on to grand results. To him it was due that Egypt ceased to be the isolated, unaggressive power that she had remained for perhaps 10 centuries, that she came boldly to the front and aspired to bring Asia into subjection. Henceforth she exercised a potent influence beyond her borders – an influence which affected, more or less, all the western Asiatic powers. She had forced her way into the comity of the great nations. Henceforth whether it was for good or for evil, she had to take her place among them, to reckon with them, as they reckoned with her, to be a factor in the problem which the ages had to work out – What should be the general march of events, and what states and nations should most affect the destiny of the world.

HATSHEPSUT

With Hatshepsut, or Hatsu, some 1600 BCE, we come to the most celebrated of all the Egyptian queens, not perhaps excluding the world-renowned Cleopatra, and her reign bears also a noteworthy feature, an especial ornament to a woman's brow – it was a reign of peace. Her father and brothers, especially the younger, were warriors, but she was not. To the male of all species the fighting instinct more particularly and rightfully belongs. No wars of defence, none of aggression and conquest, disturbed the peaceful course of her rule. The arts flourished, and friendly expeditions sought distant shores to gain fresh knowledge of the outer world, to extend the hand of fellowship, and to exchange in the ordinary channels of commerce the products and manufactures of one land for those of the other.

No such lengthened gap exists between Hatshepsut and the previous kings. She was in direct descent, being the great-grand-daughter of Aahmes and Aahmes-Nefertari, and the grand-daughter of Amenhotep or Amenophis I. Her father was Tutmes or Tahutmes [Tuthmosis] I, 'Thut's child', and her mother, probably his sister, Aahmes, A'mose or Amensi. Some things suggest that the mother of Queen Amensi was of different and higher birth than the mother of Tuthmosis, and this may account for the position which seemed at once accorded to Hatshepsut. Another legend states that the god Amen was Hatshepsut's father, and being of divine origin, a sort of Minerva sprung from the brain of Jupiter, she took unquestioned the first place; but she was evidently of the blood royal and the arrangement which gave her precedence of her brothers and claim to the crown did not seem to be disputed. Every princess at her birth received the title of 'royal consort'. A son and daughter of Tuthmosis, probably older than Hatshepsut, died in childhood, the former named Uatmes (who by some is believed to be brother rather than son of Tuthmosis) and a daughter Kheb-no-fru-ra or Nefer'kebt. Tuthmosis himself is considered the son of Amenhotep I and Queen Sen-semb.

Tuthmosis I, like his predecessors, was a warrior. He fought in the north, made conquests in Palestine and Syria and penetrated into Mesopotamia. A stele, erected east of the Euphrates, bore record of his victories, but his daughter adopted a different policy. She and her brother regarded many of these conquests as empty possessions, difficult to retain and of no real value to the kingdom, so preferred to abandon them.

Hatshepsut rejoiced in the usual wealth of names, in addition to or instead of that by which she is most generally known, Hatasu, each writer selecting a different one for his own reasons. These were Hatshopsitou, Hasheps, Hatshepsut, which seems to be generally used by [British Egyptologist Flinders] Petrie, Khnumt-Amen, Chuemtamun, the throne name Ra-ma-ka, Maat-ka-ra, etc., as derived from different languages and given by different authorities.

The Egyptian's awe of and respect for his monarch was usually so great that he hesitated to speak of him directly, but used some circumlocution or descriptive phrase. The name of the god Ra seems to have been frequently, though not invariably, introduced. This was the principal solar deity of Egypt, the 'sun-god', the 'father of gods and men', the chief seat of this very ancient worship being Heliopolis. The sun's disk was his emblem, and he was pictured as hawk-headed.

The tie between Tuthmosis I and his daughter, admirable wherever seen, was one of close affection, and the former doubtless recognized and took pride in the ability of his gifted child. The male historians, with one or two exceptions, seem rather grudgingly to admit Hatasu's claims, pass somewhat slightingly over her achievements and attribute to her successors what may really be her due. Miss Edwards [Amelia Ann Blanford Edwards, also known as Amelia B. Edwards, an English novelist, journalist, traveller and Egyptologist], on the contrary, is fired with enthusiasm, encircles this queenly figure with the halo of her own poetic imagination and claims for her certain engineering works which others believe to be the performance of her successors.

Hatshepsut has been called the Semiramis, the Catharine and the Elizabeth of Egyptian history. Bold and clever, no ideal womanly soul was this, but the masculine grasp, the masculine intellect was hers. Strong but centred on a few, her love was probably not given to the many; her attachment to her father cannot be doubted. Her ambition and determination to keep the royal power is evident, but it was not the ambition of the soldier and the conqueror. She loved power, she wished to rule, but the belongings of others did not excite her cupidity. Her desire was to build up her own kingdom, and the way to that was not, in her eyes, through annexation and conquest. No claims of posterity, no pleas for 'the cause of humanity' stained her pathway with blood. One of her boasts was that she had imported and caused to grow a great variety of trees. Some philosopher has said that he who can make two blades of grass grow where one grew before is the greatest benefactor of his race, and some such credit as this seems rightfully to belong to Queen Hatshepsut.

In the latter part of his reign, Tuthmosis I associated his daughter with him in the imperial power, as he had probably taken her into his counsel previously in matters of state policy and shared with her all the pleasures of his daily life. Their mutual devotion and his high appreciation of her great abilities is evident, even after the lapse of centuries.

The two half-brothers of Hatshepsut were Tuthmosis II and Tuthmosis III, or as later authorities say Tuthmosis III was son of Tuthmosis II, the latter proved to be a ruler of great ability, but neither seemed to hold the place in the father's regard that she did, and being much younger were naturally not equally companionable to him. The limestone statue of Queen Mutnefert, mother of Tuthmosis II, before referred to, was found at Thebes in 1886 and is now at Giza. Her son had it carved and it was in the ruins of a little temple. She is seated, in a long white robe, which shows the form and the flesh is coloured yellow. The whole is refined and well proportioned, and despite the mutilation of the nose one notices the sweetness of expression, lightened by large eyes. To this day one sees the type near Thebes. The mother of Tuthmosis III was more truly a concubine and was called the Lady As't, she was a royal mother but not a royal wife.

Shortly before her father's death, according to the Egyptian custom, Hatshepsut married her brother Tuthmosis II, who shared the throne with her or she with him, but it is evident she was the ruling spirit. There is little doubt that she was the elder of the two; it is estimated that at this time she was about 24 and Tuthmosis 17. A somewhat similar instance to this is narrated by the African traveller, Captain A.St.H. Gibbons, who describes an ancient custom which he found prevailing at Nalolo, whereby the eldest surviving sister of the ruling king was invested with the prerogatives of a queen, without whose advice and consent her brother could not arrange matters of state. She was absolute in her own district, held the power of life and death over her subjects and wedded or deposed a husband at will.

A statue of Tuthmosis II exists at Giza, which bears some resemblance to the ancient King Chafre (Khafre). He is not of large size, has fine pathetic eyes, a gentle expression and perhaps resembles his mother. That no love was lost between the consorts is evident from the fact that Hatshepsut conferred such special marks of favour upon her architect Semut, and after the death of Tuthmosis II (in which old historians, some of them, though perhaps unfairly, were disposed to implicate her) she erased his name from many of the monuments, giving all honour, where possible, to her father or keeping it for herself, to the great bewilderment of later students. She is said to have detained Tuthmosis II, in his younger days, in Buto, away from her palace and the seat of power, and doubtless relegated him to the background wherever she could. No more than Queen Elizabeth perhaps had custom and conventionality permitted her to stand quite alone, would she have accepted a consort.

Dress, which had for many reigns and centuries remained unchanged, began somewhat to alter at the time of the 18th dynasty and more rapidly later. The highest orders of women wore petticoats or gowns secured at the waist by a coloured sash, or a strap over the shoulder and over this a large loose robe of the finest linen and tied in front and under the breast, the right arm was left exposed at religious ceremonies and funerals. Another description says that the long tunic, called a basui, was suspended by straps or bracers over the shoulders or a short petticoat with the body strapped over the shoulder and a loose upper garment, which exposed the breast and which could be easily laid aside. There also came changes in the patterns of beads, mode of glazing, hair dressing, furniture and the painting of tombs. The network of beads was of course largely used for the decoration of mummies.

The admixture of blood with Syrian and other captives, as wives and concubines, seemed to introduce a new ideal type, with small features and fascinating, graceful figures. The ends of the braided hair were fringed during the Middle Kingdom, and during the New the face was framed with wonderful plaits and short tresses, which were secured with combs. Or, more naturally, it hung loose or was bound with a fillet. Female servants wore their hair fastened at the back of the head with loops or plaits. They had a plain garment with short sleeves, but threw off the upper part when working. In the earliest times, as has before been said, men seemed to care for dress more than women. From the queen to the peasant female attire was similar, and from the Fourth to the 18th dynasty there was little change. About the time of Hatshepsut it assumed a new character, and the upper part of the body was also clothed. At one period colour and pattern had been almost excluded and the higher classes wore linen so fine that the figure showed through. Bands woven or embroidered were later added, but their neighbours, the Syrians, always wore more elaborate embroidery than the Egyptians. Shend'ot was the name of the royal dress under the Old Kingdom. Men wore a short skirt round the hips, and a second was added during the Middle Kingdom; in one century this was short and narrow, in another wide and shapeless, and in a third, peculiarly folded; the breast was also covered, and the apron, now chiefly a female appanage, was then exclusively the property of men.

Costumes differed with classes, yet, as with us, a fashion initiated by the upper end would sometimes descend and spread. The lords and the priests and priestesses in offering sacrifices bore a panther skin thrown over the shoulder, the small head and forepaws hanging down. To the hind paws long ribbons were attached, which were drawn forward, and it was the fashion to play with them when sitting idle. Perhaps it was an aid to conversation thus to trifle, as with Madame de Stael's well-known sprig of poplar. Soldiers and merchants wore white garments bordered with coloured fringes. Policemen carried staves, and priests went about in long white robes with aprons and jewelled collars.

The woman's short petticoat under the tunic, called a basni, was white, red, yellow and sometimes, in the Middle Kingdom, green. The higher orders sometimes secured the petticoat at the waist with a coloured sash. Occasionally there was only one sleeve for the left arm. The cloak of the 19th and 20th Dynasties fell over the arms with a short sleeve added and at the end of the 20th dynasty there was a thick underdress. The bare foot of the earliest times, as has been shown, was later sandalled and shod.

As time went on the tendency seemed to be more and more to vary from the fashions of the Garden of Eden and to add to the amount of clothing. The more civilized the nation the more elaborate the covering. The primitive Egyptian thought more of painting and rouging the face and oiling the limbs, of both living and dead, than he did of dress. Two colours were chiefly used, green, with which under the Old Kingdom they put a line below the eye, and black for brows and lids, to make the eyes look larger and more brilliant. The eyelids were dyed with mestem, the fingernails made red with henna. For this, of course, many kohl pots and mirrors were needed. The latter were of burnished metal, chiefly of copper, round, with wooden or ivory handles and ornamented with carved lotus buds. Necklaces and bracelets on the upper arm and wrist were worn by both men and women, but the latter only used anklets.

Earrings were round, single loops of gold, and rings, especially on the third finger and thumb, were numerous.

Of the daily life of a queen we have no detailed account, but various pictures and inscriptions make a sort of outline which study and imagination may fill up and not be utterly astray. One writer has sketched some such programme as this, of course that of a queen who was herself regent, or ruled in her own right. After the first meal of the day the queen would go to the throne room and listen to reports, petitions, etc., doubtless attended by scribes, who were more ubiquitous than even the modern reporter, to note down everything and extol her majesty's power, clemency and charm. Before the heat grew excessive she might walk in the garden or among the colonnades of the palace or ride out to take the air and view the public works which were in process of building.

Neither horses nor camels are represented on the monuments in the earliest times. Persons of distinction were borne in chariots or chairs carried by bands of slaves, and the ass or mule was the beast of burden. A royal chariot was sometimes adorned by a burnished shield rising above the back, carved with open work and lined with silk. It had two wheels, and a pair of horses were attached to the car by a single trace, their heads held up by a bridle made fast to a hook in front of the saddle. The long reins passed through a loop at the side; the horses' heads were adorned with plumes, and the harness and housings ornamented with the royal devices in gold, silver and brass. Sometimes for ladies there was a seat, one in each chariot, but the usual rule was not to have any, a man stood. Says one writer, 'When the queen rides she stands on a dais borne at speed by six horses abreast, and looks like a flying goddess.' Thus perhaps our fancy may paint Queen Hatshepsut.

The throne room was probably a magnificent apartment of immense size with a polished floor, on which were laid the skins of beasts. Enormous statues of the gods, chief among them, Osiris and Isis, were ranged on either side, between tall granite columns with lotus capitals, looking like a forest of great trees. The throne of ivory stood on a raised platform, to which one ascended by steps, guarded on either side by carven figures of sphinxes and crouching animals. Behind were again immense statues of Justice and Truth. The steps were of valuable marbles, and the throne itself inlaid with jewels, all the numbers and designs were symbolic, the footstool was of precious marbles, in a gold frame, and above the throne was a canopy of silk upheld by slender white and gold columns and embroidered with the stars and constellations. Bands of soldiers and officers, richly attired, waited upon the queen. She, on all solemn occasions, wore the double crown of Egypt, which one writer describes as a graceful conical bonnet of white silk, ending in a knob like a pomegranate, the colour white, of Upper, as the outer band of gold lined with red silk, was of Lower Egypt, the vulture wings and the raised asp. Her garments were of finest linen with silk robe of white and green and a girdle adorned with diamonds and precious stones. With these or similar surroundings we imagine Queen Hatshepsut.

There is a picture in [Adolf] Erman [German Egyptologist] of King 'Tuet-anch-amun' giving audience to a governor of Ethiopia. The king wears his war helmet and carries a whip and sceptre, while the governor bears a sceptre and fan as sign of rank. The king is called 'Lord of Hermothis'. Sceptre and whip doubtless Hatshepsut could wield right royally, but the war bonnet she probably had little occasion for. Some writers claim that it was her father's conquests which gave her immunity from warfare and that it was her peaceful reign and neglect to keep the wild tribes in orderly submission that paved the way for the career of bloodshed which distinguished her great successor, Tuthmosis III, so that on this question, as on most, there will always remain a wide difference of opinion. But that a peaceful reign is in many respects a great blessing and a justifiable cause of pride to its successful promoter, and that peace and not war is the ideal state, cannot be denied.

The coronation of Hatshepsut, the building of her great temple at Deir el Bahri and the expedition to Punt are events of such moment that they deserve a volume rather than the narrow space of a single chapter to do them justice.

An inscription in the temple of Karnak reads thus, it is as it were the deed of gift of the royal father Tuthmosis I to his favourite child, and addressed to the god Amen: 'I bestow the Black Land and the Red Land upon my daughter, the queen of Lower and Upper Egypt Ma-Ka-ra, living eternally. Thou hast transmitted the world into her power, thou hast chosen her as king.' Hatshepsut claimed divine origin in that the god Amen had taken upon him the person of her father and in an especial manner considered herself the daughter of the god. Hatshepset spelled with the e means 'the first among the favourite women', but the queen changed the e to u and later called herself Hatshepsut, which signifies 'the first among the great and honourable nobles of the kingdom', which she considered more befitting her exalted position.

The 18th dynasty is included in the Golden Age of Egyptian history, and in no period was its power more widely felt, its individual monarchs more remarkable or its architectural and literary remains grander or more impressive.

Before his death, Tuthmosis I seems to have had celebrated the marriage of his two children, his daughter of 24 and his son of 17. All things combined to put Hatshepsut in the first place, her more royal heritage, by the mother's side, her father's devotion to her, her superiority in years and her more striking talents, while Tuthmosis II was perhaps both physically and mentally her inferior. Death at last had severed the tie which bound father and daughter together, but no such tender feeling seems to have existed between the two now occupying the throne, hers was the dominant will, hers is the prominent figure. After this she frequently wore male attire and the dress and ornaments belonging to a king, and doubtless, had it been a matter of choice, she would have been a man.

She styles herself 'King Horus abounding in divine gifts, mistress of diadems, rich in years (not a claim the modern lady is ever anxious to establish), the golden Horus, goddess of diadems, queen of Upper and Lower Egypt, daughter of the sun, consort of Ammon, daughter of Ammon, living forever and dwelling in his breast.' Another inscription reads, speaking of her by her name Cheremtamun, 'He has created (her) in order to exalt his splendour. She who creates beings like the god Chefr'a. She whose diadems shine like those of the god of the horizon.'

She used both the male and female sign and the title, 'daughter of the sun'. As the sphinx bore sometimes a male, sometimes a female head, so this strange and wonderful woman assumed now the one, now the other character. A curious life this old Egyptian history brings before us, so permeated as it was with the constant thought of death and its belief, real or assumed, in the actual intercourse with a race of superior beings, gods, and yet set forth in the lowest images of the brute creation. To the poor and uneducated doubtless as in all idolatrous countries, the semblance seemed the reality and their thought did not pierce beyond the image before them, but the more intellectual and spiritual minds must have rent the veil of sense and stretched out longingly to the infinite beyond, if peradventure they might 'feel after and find' the truly godlike.

Hatshepsut did not at once set to work, like the early kings, to build a pyramid in which she might herself be interred. Mundane subjects at first occupied her, and later she built a memorial to her father in the form of an obelisk which described his powers and virtues, and temples for the worship and to the glory of the gods.

Probably the regulation of the country and the administration of internal affairs occupied the earliest years of Hatshepsut's rule, after the death of Tuthmosis I, but in them she was also preparing for the expedition which was one of the great features of her reign and took place in its ninth year. Punt, a country on the eastern bank of the Red Sea, had been, to some extent, known to the Egyptians in the earliest times, those of Chafre of the fourth dynasty. 'Under the name of Punt,' says one writer, 'the old inhabitants of Kemi meant a distant land washed by the great ocean, full of valleys and hills, abounding in ebony and other rich woods, balsams, spices, precious metals and stones and of animals, hunting-leopards, panthers, dog-headed apes, etc.' It was the Ophir of the Egyptians, the present coast of Somali, perhaps the land in sight of Arabia, but separated by the Red Sea.

Old traditions said that it was the original seat of the gods, and from it had travelled the holy ones to the Nile valley, at their head Amen, called Kak, as king of Punt, Horus and Hathor. This last was the queen and ruler of Punt, Hor, the holy morning star, which rose to the west of the land. The god Bes also was peculiarly associated with the country. Under the last king of the 11th dynasty is said to have taken place the first journey to Ophir and Punt, and the envoys sent were attended by 3,000 men and brought back spices and precious stones. After that it seemed to relapse in the popular imagination into a sort of fairyland which was inhabited by strange serpents.

Like a new Columbus the great queen decided to attempt the rediscovery and exploration of these distant shores. Amen of Thebes, the lord of gods, it is said, had suggested the thought to her, 'because he held this ruler so dear, dearer than any other king who had been in this country'. Pictures and accounts of this expedition were afterwards placed in illustration on the walls of the temple of Deir-el-Bahari, built by the queen, and the inscription concludes with the statement that nothing like it had been done under any king before. 'And,' says an authority on these subjects, 'it speaks the truth. Hatasu showed her people the way to the land whose products were later to fill the treasuries not only of the pharaohs, but also of the Phoenicians and the Jews.'

It was a peaceful expedition, perhaps the only one that had ever been sent forth, this voyage of discovery, nearly 1,600 years before the Christian Era; but of course great preparations and even some military ones had to be made that in case of unexpected attack they might be prepared. Ships were built for the expedition, and doubtless years passed between the time of the first conception of the enterprise and its execution.

An inscription by the picture of the squadron thus describes it. 'Departure of the squadron of the Lord of the two Worlds, traversing the great sea on the Good Way to the Land of the gods, in obedience to the will of the King of the gods, Amen of Thebes. He commanded that there should be brought to him the marvellous products of the Land of Punt, for he loveth the Queen Hatasu above all other kings that have ruled this land.'

A canal connecting the Nile with the Red Sea which has been attributed to Seti I, Miss Edwards claims as an engineering feat of Hatasu, as it would shorten the length of the voyage rather than to take the almost inconceivably long trip around the west coast of Africa, the Cape of Good Hope, the Mozambique Channel and the coast of Zanzibar.

The ships, five in number, were large and stately for the time. They are described as having a narrow keel with stern and prow high above the water, 21 metres (70 feet) in length and with no cabin accommodations. A raised platform at either end, with a balustrade, probably afforded some shelter to the officers. A single mast supported the spreading sail, there were no decks and the hull was fitted with seats for the rowers. After the Old Kingdom all large boats were adapted for sailing, as well as rowing. Other vessels of this or a little later time were one-decked galleys with 30 oars, with seats and shrines and the stern ornamented with figures of animals. The cabin of those of royal or high rank was a stately house, with roof and pillars, sides brightly coloured, in the fore, large paintings and the stern a gigantic lotus. The blade of the oar was like a bouquet of flowers with the head of the king at top, the sails the richest cloth of gay colours. A royal vessel of this description belonged to King Tuthmosis III, Hatasu's successor and was called 'Star of the two countries'.

Another description speaks of war ships having the poop twisted, with armed mariners in helmets of brass, with four short masts and on each a large castle containing bowmen with steel-headed arrows. Upon the prow a sort of fortress, the soldiers carrying long spears and oval shields decorated with hieroglyphics in brilliant colours. Above the rowers large black Ethiopians in steel cuirasses and long swords. The captains in variegated armour and accompanied by 1,000 soldiers and 300 rowers. The prow ornamented with a lion's head and colossal shoulders across a broad gilded image of the feathered globe of the sun, the emblem of Egypt and the inscription, 'Mistress of the World'. But Hatasu's fleet was going on a peaceful errand and required no such panoply of war. Experienced seamen managed it, while soldiers, ambassadors and, some say, even ladies, accompanied it and bore with them a variety of presents to win the friendship and favour of the inhabitants of this strange land. The envoys had a small guard of soldiers, but all included did not number more than 210 men.

The voyagers were met with a friendly welcome and returned with stores of treasures. The inhabitants of Punt lived in little round shaped huts, built on stages and reached by ladders, all under the shade of spreading palms. A picture on the wall of the temple shows the prince of the land Parihu by name, with his wife, Ati or Aty, the latter fat and ungainly (though probably considered a specimen of great beauty by her countrymen), with a donkey to ride upon, followed by two sons and a young daughter, the last giving promise of rivalling her mother in rotundity of outline. Gold, spices, ivory, incense bearing trees, to the number of 31, precious gums, used in the service of the temple and various animals were brought back to Egypt as a result of this most successful journey. The return was celebrated by a high festival in the temple. Hatshepsut or Hatasu appeared in fullest royal attire, adorned in the richest manner, a helmet on her head, a spotted leopard skin covering her shoulders and her limbs 'perfumed like fresh dew'. She offered incense to the god Amen, as his priestess, bearing two bowls full and weighing out gold with her own hand. This was before the sacred boat of Amen Ra, with a ram's head at each end, and carried by high priests, also in leopard skins. The Naka, or incense bearing trees, were borne in tubs, and the weights for weighing the precious metals were gold rings in the shape of recumbent oxen.

Later, as was his iconoclastic wont, Rameses II destroyed some of these pictures and inscriptions and inserted his own name.

Although the name of Tuthmosis II, husband and co-ruler with the queen, is not specially mentioned in connection with this great expedition, he shared in the after festival. He, too, designated by his court name of King Menkhefer-ka-ra, offered incense in the boat of Amen, carried on the shoulders of men. 'Thus,' says Miss Edwards, 'to the sound of trumpets and drums, with waving of green boughs and shouts of triumph, and followed by an ever gathering crowd, the great procession takes its way between avenues of sphinxes, past obelisks and pylons, and up one magnificent flight of steps after another till the topmost terrace of the Great Temple is reached, where the Queen herself welcomed them to the presence of Hathor, the Beautiful, the Lady of the Western Mountain, the Goddess Regent of the Land of Punt.'

At what period is not exactly known, but of course earlier than this, since he is believed to have designed the beautiful temple of Deir el Bahri, the queen called to her assistance the services of the architect Senmut, whose statue is in the Berlin Museum. He, it is implied, usurped the place in Hatasu's affection which rightfully belonged to her husband, but of this it is not possible to speak with any degree of certainty or authority. We only know that he was a man of great ability in his own line, of intelligent mind and skilful hand, and was highly appreciated by her majesty. In an inscription in the Berlin Museum he says his lady ruler made him 'great in both countries' and 'chief of the chiefs' in the whole of Egypt. The buildings which the queen and he erected are said to be among the most tasteful, complete and brilliant in the land. He was of lowly birth, and therefore his position was the more surprising. He appears to have occupied in the queen's counsels something of the place of Disraeli to Queen Victoria, whose Jewish origin made his occupancy of the position he gained remarkable. After Senmut's death Hatasu raised to him a stone memorial as a token of gratitude, with his portrait in black granite and in an attitude of repose. On his shoulder were the short but significant words, 'there was not found in writing his ancestors'. He is also introduced in an inscription, as himself speaking, where he used the male pronoun 'he' in mentioning the queen refers to his own services and ends with styling her 'the lord of the country, the King of Makara'.

Senmut was evidently the chief counsellor and favourite of Hatshepsut, but there was also another highly regarded officer who shared with or succeeded him in the queen's favour and good graces. This was a certain Aahmes, who had also served her father, Tuthmosis I, and whose tomb was discovered by [German Egyptologist Heinrich Karl] Brugsch, and bears this inscription, 'I was during my existence in the favour of the king, and was rewarded by His Holiness, and a divine woman gave me further reward, the defunct great queen Makara (Hashop), because I brought up her daughter, the great queen's daughter, the defunct Nofrerura.' It is of course plain that he survived the queen, but we do not know whether he met with equal favour at the hand of her successor. Possibly the mother's heart, little given to tenderness, may have had an especial softness towards this 'nurse' or tutor of her dead child, her father's trusted servant and perhaps, on that very account, hers also.

Two children were born to the queen, both daughters, Neferura, the heiress, who is spoken of as 'the mistress of both lands', who died in the beginning of the reign of Tuthmosis III, and Hatasu Meri or Merytra, who it is estimated was born about 1512 BCE and became heiress Princess, inheriting all her mother's rights. To establish the throne more firmly therefore, she was married to Tuthmosis III. This king was long supposed to be the youngest son of Tuthmosis I, but the latest authorities, although they do not speak with absolute assurance, incline to believe he was the son of Tuthmosis II, by a concubine, hence he was in one case the uncle, and in the other the half or step-brother of the young princess, but with a less direct title to the throne than she. A certain Renekheb is also spoken of as a tutor of the young queen. This marriage appears to have taken place when they were both children and before the death of Tuthmosis II, which is proved by the cartouches of Tuthmosis

II and Tuthmosis III being found together upon some of the monuments, and at the same time suggests that the juvenile pair, nominally at least, shared in the government.

Tuthmosis II, born about 1533 BCE, appears to have died at about 30, in 1503, and some writers maintain that Hatshepsut usurped the power which rightfully belonged to Tuthmosis III, but Miss Edwards (ever ready to champion her heroine) finds in the above fact strong proof that the queen really protected the interests of her young half-brother or nephew. While Petrie admits that it would be unlikely and perhaps even unnatural that a capable and ambitious woman, still in the prime of life, should immediately hand over the reins of government, placed in her hands by her father, to a young and inexperienced boy and justifies her retention of them, the more that it was she and not he who had the stronger legal claim. Be this as it may, if Tuthmosis III owed gratitude to Hatshepsut for care or protection he showed her little return. Whether from the general unpopularity of mothers-in-law, from her treatment of his brother or uncle, from the feeling that he was suppressed and kept in the background, or from some unknown cause, he evidently hated her. When he came into power he endeavoured to destroy the memorials of her from off the earth and cause her memory even to be forgotten. He injured or erased her name constantly and whenever possible and substituted that of his brother or himself.

Tuthmosis I had continued the building of Thebes and set up his two granite obelisks. Tuthmosis II and Hatshepsut continued building at Karnak, the temple having been in existence, it is said, as far back as the 11th dynasty. So gigantic was the scale on which these architectural works were undertaken that one life seldom saw their completion. Like the coral reef the temples grew and were added to, monarch after monarch of succeeding generations taking a share in the general design.

Tuthmosis I had raised at Karnak two obelisks 21 metres (70 feet) in height, his daughter's far outdid them, for hers were the loftiest then known in Egypt, a flawless block of red granite or rose quartz, rising 32 or 33 metres (108 or 109 feet) into the air. This was erected in the 16th year of her reign and after the death of her husband, which took place some dozen or more years after that of his father. Probably the ceremonial mourning was observed for him, but the heart of Hatshepsut was hard and cold and even if we exonerate her from the implication of being directly concerned in his decease, which stands 'not proven', there seems little doubt that she rejoiced to be comparatively free and hold the reins of power exclusively in her own hands. Nothing seemed missing from her life or her pursuits, which she followed with renewed energy and appeared more constantly than ever in male attire, the short kilt and sandals, the war helmet and even perhaps, as in her reproduction, a beard. Architecture was evidently of great interest to her as to many of her predecessors and obelisks and temples still, after the lapse of centuries, bear witness to her power and skill.

It took 19 months from its first inception to the completion of her great obelisk and even so, when one thinks of its magnificent proportions, the work seems to have proceeded with wonderful celerity. Inscriptions by Senmut record the quarrying. Her brother's name appears at the side. One face was covered with gold, which the queen is believed to have weighed out with her own hand. The beautifully carved centre was inlaid with electrum or silver gilt and related to herself. 'Amen-Khnum Hatasu, the golden Horus, Lord of the two lands hath dedicated to her father, Amen of Thebes, two obelisks of Maket stone (red granite) hewn from the quarries of the South. Their summits were sheathed with pure gold, taken from the chiefs of all nations.' 'His Majesty gave these two gilded obelisks to her father, Amen, that her name should live forever in his temple', and adds towards the conclusion, 'when Ra arises betwixt them as he journeys upward from the heavenly horizon they flood the two Egypts with the glory of their brightness.' [Italian Egyptologist Ippolito] Rosellini says, speaking of the fineness of the work, 'every figure seems rather to have been impressed with a seal than graven with a chisel.' An inscription at the bottom states that it was erected to her father, Tuthmosis I. This obelisk, with its mate, was to occupy a place in the centre court of the palace at Karnak. Dr. Naville, the explorer, discovered the burial chamber of Tuthmosis in 1893 and a great altar erected by the queen.

In an inscription on part of the rock-cut temple of Speos Artemidos, south Beni-hasan, reciting her re-establishment of Egyptian power and worship after destruction by the Hyksos, Hatshepsut says: 'The abode of the mistress of Qes (Kusae on west side) was fallen in ruin, the earth had covered her beautiful sanctuary and children played over her temple – I cleared and rebuilt it anew – I restored that which was in ruins and I completed that which was left unfinished. For there had been Amu in the midst of the Delta and in Hanar and the foreign hordes of their number had destroyed the ancient works. They reigned ignorant of the god Ra.'

The temple of Deir-el-Bahri or 'Dayre-el-Bahari', its present Arabic name, was perhaps the greatest work of Hatshepsut's life and enough of the ruins still remained for the clever French architect, M. Brune, to reconstruct its plan for us. The site was one that would have been chosen by the Greeks for a theatre, but the Egyptian dedicated it to what he deemed a higher object, the worship of the gods. Situated on a green plain, near the tombs of the kings of the 12th dynasty, it was a magnificent natural amphitheatre on the shore of the river and, terrace by terrace, rose from the edge of the water to its steep background of golden-brown rock, in which the inner temple, the 'holy of holies', was excavated. Of its structure Senmut or Sen-Maut was the presiding genius. The name 'Dayre-el-Bahari' means North church, or monastery, and was, of course, applied to it in later times from the ruins of an old monastery which was yet young and modern beside the original erection. An avenue of sphinxes connected the landing for boats with the four terraces. These were supported by earthworks and stone and guarded by hawk-headed figures, in marble, bearing the uraeus. Columns also supported it, some of them polygonal in shape, with the head of the goddess Hathor as a capitol, and were later restored and kept in order till the time of the Ptolemies. 'This temple,' says one writer, 'was a splendid specimen of Egyptian Art history, whether we consider the treatment of the stone or the richness of the coloured decorations,' and it was unique in design and differed from all others. In the inner recesses of the rock-cut chambers was a picture of the queen, representing her as sucking the milk of the sacred cow, the incarnation of the goddess Hathor, thereby intimating her divine origin.

Some 16 or 17 years after the death of Tuthmosis II the cartouche of Tuthmosis III becomes associated with that of

Hatshepsut and then her brilliant career terminates, but the end is wrapped in mystery. Whether she voluntarily laid aside her royal power, which seems unnatural and unlikely, whether she met with foul play or whether she died a natural death, we know not. The remains of many others of her family, more or less illustrious, were found, but hers were not among them. Her place of sepulchre was discovered by Mr. [Archaeologist Alexander Henry] Rhind in 1841 in a cliff side near her temple, but, strange to say, was again lost sight of, and her successor, showing plainly his feeling towards her, has constantly chiselled out her name.

Her cartouche, which may be seen in other works, seems comparatively simple, beside the more elaborate ones of other monarchs. It is a circle with a dot in the centre, a small, seated female figure, wearing the plumes of a goddess and below two right angles joined. The three hieroglyphic signs are explained to mean 'Ma, the sitting figure of the goddess of Truth, Law and Justice; Ka, represented by the hieroglyphic of the uplifted arms and signifying Life, and the sun's disk, representing Ra, the supreme solar god of the universe.'

Many memorials of this great queen, spite of the efforts made to destroy them, remain to us. The ruins of the temple, the great obelisks, one of which is still standing, various statues and statuettes, many sun-dried brick with her cartouche and that of her father, some of which can be seen in our own Metropolitan Museum in New York, a cabinet in wood and ivory, her standard, her signet ring in turquoise and gold, in the possession of an English gentleman, and, most interesting of all perhaps, the remains of her throne chair, now in the British Museum. It is made of a dark wood, not natural to Egypt, and probably from the land of Punt. The legs are decorated with ucilisks in gold, and the carven hoof of some animal. The other parts are ornamented with hieroglyphics in gold and silver and one fragmentary royal oval in which the name of Hatasu appears and thereby identifies the owner of the throne.

Thus ends in comparative mystery, darkness and silence this brilliant life, of which we were long in ignorance.

TUTHMOSIS THE THIRD AND AMENHOTEP THE SECOND

First Expedition of Tuthmosis III into Asia

No sooner had Tuthmosis III burst the leading strings in which his sister had held him for above 20 years, then he showed the mettle of which he was made by at once placing himself at the head of his troops, and marching into Asia. Persuaded that the great god, Ammon, had promised him a long career of victory, he lost no time in setting to work to accomplish his glorious destiny.

Starting from an Egyptian post on the Eastern frontier, called Garu or Zalu, in the month of February, he took his march along the ordinary coast route, and in a short time reached Gaza, the strong Philistine city, which was already a fortress of repute, and regarded as 'the key of Syria'. The day of his arrival was the anniversary of his coronation, and according to his reckoning the first day of his 23rd year. Gaza made no resistance: its chief was friendly to the Egyptians, and gladly opened his gates to the invading army. Having rested at Gaza no more than a single night, Tuthmosis resumed his march, and continuing to skirt the coast, arrived on the 11th day at a fortified town called Jaham, probably Jamnia. Here he was met by his scouts, who brought the intelligence that the enemy was collected at Megiddo, on the edge of the great plain of Esdraelon, the ordinary battlefield of the Palestinian nations. They consisted of 'all the people dwelling between the river of Egypt on the one hand and the land of Naharaïn (Mesopotamia) on the other'. At their head was the king of Kadesh, a great city on the upper Orontes, which afterwards became one of the chief seats of the Hittite power, but was at this time in the possession of the Rutennu (Syrians).

They were strongly posted at the mouth of a narrow pass, behind the ridge of hills which connects Carmel with the Samaritan upland, and Tuthmosis was advised by his captains to avoid a direct attack, and march against them by a circuitous route, which was undefended. But the intrepid warrior scorned this prudent counsel. 'His generals,' he said, 'might take the roundabout road, if they liked; *he* would follow the straight one.' The event justified his determination. Megiddo was reached in a week without loss or difficulty, and a great battle was fought in the fertile plain to the north-west of the fortress, in which the Egyptian king was completely victorious, and his enemies were scattered like chaff before him.

The Syrians must have fled precipitately at the first attack; for they lost in killed no more than 83, and in prisoners no more than 240, or according to another account 340, while the chariots taken were 924, and the captured horses 2,132. Megiddo was near at hand, and the bulk of the fugitives would reach easily the shelter of its walls. Others may have dispersed themselves among the mountains. The Syrian camp was, however, taken, together with vast treasures in silver and gold, lapis lazuli, turquoise and alabaster; and the son of the king of Kadesh fell into Tuthmosis' hands. Megiddo itself, soon afterwards, surrendered, as did the towns of Inunam, Anaugas, and Hurankal or Herinokol. An immense booty in corn and cattle was also carried off. Tuthmosis returned to Egypt in triumph, and held a prolonged festival to Ammon-Ra in Thebes, accompanied by numerous sacrifices and offerings. Among the last we find included three of the cities taken from the Rutennu, which were assigned to the god in order that they might 'supply a yearly contribution to his sacred food'.

His Second and Subsequent Campaigns

It is a familiar saying, that 'increase of appetite doth grow by what it feeds on'. Tuthmosis certainly found his appetite for conquest whetted, not satiated, by his Syrian campaign. If we may trust M. [François] Lenormant [French Assyriologist], he took the field in the very year that followed his victory of Megiddo, and after traversing the whole of Syria, and ravaging the country about Aleppo, proceeded to Carchemish, the great Hittite town on the Upper Euphrates, and there crossed the river into Naharaïn, or Mesopotamia, whence he carried off a number of prisoners.

Two other campaigns, which cannot be traced in detail, belong to the period between his 24th and his 29th year. Thenceforward to his 40th year his military expeditions scarcely knew any cessation. At one time he would embark his troops on board a fleet, and make descents upon the coast of Syria, coming as unexpectedly and ravaging as ruthlessly as the Normans of the Middle Ages. He would cut down the fruit trees, carry off the crops, empty the magazines of grain, lay hands upon all valuables that were readily removable and carry them on board his ships, returning to Egypt with a goodly store of gold and silver, of lapis lazuli and other precious stones, of vases in silver and in bronze, of corn, wine, incense, balsam, honey, iron, lead, emery and male and female slaves. At another, he would march by land, besiege and take the inland towns, demand and obtain the sons of the chiefs as hostages, exact heavy war contributions and bring back with him horses and chariots, flocks and herds, strange animals, trees and plants.

Great Expedition of his Thirty-third Year

Of all his expeditions, that undertaken in his 33rd year was perhaps the most remarkable. Starting from the country of the Rutennu, he on this occasion directed the main force of his attack upon the Mesopotamian region, which he ravaged far and wide, conquering the towns, and 'reducing to a level plain the strong places of the miserable land of Naharaïn', capturing 30 kings or chiefs, and erecting two tablets in the region, to indicate its subjection. It is possible that he even crossed the Tigris into Adiabene or the Zab country, since he relates that on his return he passed through the town of Ni or Nini, which many of the best historians of Egypt identify with Nineveh. Nineveh was not now (about 1500 BCE) the capital of Assyria, which was lower down the Tigris, at Asshur or Kileh Sherghat, but was only a provincial town of some magnitude. Still it was within the dominions of the Assyrian monarch of the time, and any attack upon it would have been an insult and a challenge to the great power of Upper Mesopotamia, which ruled from the alluvium to the mountains. It is certain that the king of

Assyria did not accept the challenge, but preferred to avoid an encounter with the Egyptian troops.

Both at this time and subsequently he sent envoys with rich presents to court the favour of Tuthmosis, who accepted the gifts as 'tribute', and counted 'the chief of Assuru' among his tributaries. Submission was also made to him at the same time by the 'prince of Senkara', a name which still exists in the lower Babylonian marsh region. Among the gifts which this prince sent was 'lapis lazuli of Babylon'. It is an exaggeration to represent the expedition as having resulted in the conquest of the great empires of Assyria and Babylon; but it is quite true to say that it startled and shook those empires, that it filled them with a great fear of what might be coming, and brought Egypt into the position of the principal military power of the time. Assyrian influence especially was checked and curtailed.

There is reason to believe, from the Egyptian remains found at Arban on the Khabour, that Tuthmosis added to the Egyptian empire the entire region between the Euphrates and its great eastern affluent – a broad tract of valuable territory – and occupied it with permanent garrisons. The Assyrian monarch bought off the further hostility of his dangerous neighbour by an annual embassy which conveyed rich gifts to the court of the pharaohs, gifts that were not reciprocated. Among these we find enumerated gold and silver ornaments, lapis lazuli, vases of Assyrian stone (alabaster?), slaves, chariots adorned with gold and silver, silver dishes and silver beaten out into sheets, incense, wine, honey, ivory, cedar and sycamore wood, mulberry trees, vines, and fig trees, buffaloes, bulls and a gold habergeon with a border of lapis lazuli.

Adventure with an Elephant

A curious episode of the expedition is related by Amenemheb, an officer who accompanied it, and was in personal attendance upon the Egyptian monarch. It appears that in the time of Tuthmosis III, the elephant haunted the woods and jungles of the Mesopotamian region, as he now does those of the peninsula of Hindustan. The huge unwieldy beasts were especially abundant in the neighbourhood of Ni or Nini, the country between the middle Tigris and the Zagros range. As Amenemhat I had delighted in the chase of the lion and the crocodile, so Tuthmosis III no sooner found a number of elephants within his reach than he proceeded to hunt and kill them, mainly no doubt for the sport, but partly in order to obtain their tusks. No fewer than 120 are said to have been killed or taken. On one occasion, however, the monarch ran a great risk. He was engaged in the pursuit of a herd, when the 'rogue', or leading elephant, turned and made a rush at the royal sportsman, who would probably have fallen a victim, gored by a tusk or trampled to death under the huge beast's feet, had not Amenemheb hastened to the rescue, and by wounding the creature's trunk drawn its rage upon himself. The brute was then, after a short struggle, overpowered and captured.

Further Expeditions: Amount of Plunder and Tribute

Further expeditions were led by Tuthmosis into Asia in his 34th, 35th, 38th, 39th, 40th, and 42nd years; but in none of them does he seem to have outdone the exploits of the great campaign of the year 33. The brunt of his attacks at this time fell upon the Zahi, or Tahai, of northern Phoenicia, and upon the Naïri of the Mesopotamian region, who continually rebelled, and had to be reconquered. The Rutennu seem for the most part to have paid their tribute without resistance and without much difficulty. This may have been partly owing to the judicious system which Tuthmosis had established among them, whereby each chief was forced to give a son or brother as hostage for his good behaviour, and if the hostage died to send another in his place. It was certainly not because the tribute was light, since it consisted of a number of slaves, silver vases of the weight of 345 kilograms (762 pounds), 19 chariots, 276 head of cattle, 1,622 goats, several hundredweight of iron and lead, a number of suits of armour, and 'all kinds of good plants'. The Rutennu had also to supply the stations along the military road, whereby Tuthmosis kept up the communications between Egypt and Mesopotamia, with bread, wine, dates, incense, honey and figs.

Interest in Natural History

While thus engaged in enlarging the limits of his empire towards the north and the north-east, the careful monarch did not allow the regions brought under Egyptian influence by former rulers to escape him. He took a tribute of gold, spices, male and female slaves, cattle, ivory, ebony and panther skins from the land of Punt, of cattle and slaves from Cush, and of the same products from the Uauat. Altogether he is said to have carried off from the subject countries above 11,000 captives, 1,670 chariots, 3,639 horses, 4,491 of the larger cattle, more than 35,000 goats, silver to the amount of 1,787 kilograms (3,940 pounds), and gold to the amount of 4,106 kilograms (9,054 pounds). He also conveyed to Egypt from the conquered lands enormous quantities of corn and wine, together with incense, balsam, honey, ivory, ebony and other rare woods, lapis lazuli, furniture, statues, vases, dishes, basins, tent poles, bows, habergeons, fruit trees, live birds and monkeys! With a curiosity which was insatiable, he noted all that was strange or unusual in the lands which he visited, and sought to introduce the various novelties into his own proper country. Two unknown kinds of birds, and a variety of the goose, which he found in Mesopotamia, and transported from the valley of the Khabour to that of the Nile, are said to have been 'dearer to the king than anything else'. His artists had instructions to make careful studies of the different objects, and to represent them faithfully on his monuments. We see on these 'waterlilies as high as trees, plants of a growth like cactuses, all sorts of trees and shrubs, leaves, flowers and fruits, including melons and pomegranates; oxen and calves also figure, and among them a wonderful animal with three horns. There are likewise herons, sparrowhawks, geese and doves. All these objects appear gaily intermixed in the pictures, as suited the simple childlike conception of the artist.' An inscription tells the intention of the monarch. 'Here,' it runs, 'are all sorts of plants and all sorts of flowers of the Holy Land, which the king discovered when he went to the land of Ruten to conquer it. Thus says the king – I swear by the sun, and I call to witness my father Ammon, that all is plain truth; there is no trace of deception in that which I relate. What the splendid soil brings forth in the way of productions, I have had portrayed in these pictures, with the intention of offering them to my father Ammon, as a memorial for all times.'

Employment of a Navy; Song of Victory on the Walls of the Temple of Karnak

Besides his army, Tuthmosis also maintained a naval force, and used it largely in his expeditions. According to one writer, he placed a fleet on the Euphrates, and in an action which took place with the Assyrians, defeated and chased the enemy for a distance of between 11 and 13 kilometres (seven and eight miles). He certainly upon some occasions made his attacks on Syria and Phoenicia from the sea; nor is it improbable that his maritime forces reduced Cyprus (which was conquered and held in a much less flourishing period by Amasis) and plundered the coast of Cilicia; but a judicious criticism will scarcely extend the voyages of his fleet, as has been done by another writer, to Crete, and the islands of the Aegean, the seaboards of Greece and Asia Minor, the southern coast of Italy, Algeria and the waters of the Euxine! There is no evidence in the historical inscriptions of Tuthmosis of any such far-reaching expeditions. The supposed evidence for them is in a song of victory, put into the mouth of the god, Ammon, and inscribed on one of the walls of the great temple of Karnak. The song is interesting, but it scarcely bears out the deductions that have been drawn from it, as will appear from the subjoined translation.

(AMMON loquitur.)

I came, and thou smotest the princes of Zahi;
I scattered them under thy feet over all their lands;
I made them regard thy Holiness as the blazing sun;
Thou shinest in sight of them in my form.

I came, and thou smotest them that dwell in Asia;
Thou tookest captive the goat-herds of Ruten;

I made them behold thy Holiness in thy royal adornments,
As thou graspest thy weapons in the war-chariot.

I came, and thou smotest the land of the East;
Thou marchedst against the dwellers in the Holy Land;
I made them behold thy Holiness as the star Canopus,
Which sends forth its heat and disperses the dew.

I came, and thou smotest the land of the West;
Kefa and Asebi (i.e. Phœnicia and Cyprus) held thee in fear;
I made them look upon thy Holiness as a young bull,
Courageous, with sharp horns, which none can approach.

I came, and thou smotest the subjects of their lords;
The land of Mathen trembled for fear of thee;
I made them look upon thy Holiness as upon a crocodile,
Terrible in the waters, not to be encountered.

I came, and thou smotest them that dwelt in the Great Sea;
The inhabitants of the isles were afraid of thy war-cry;
I made them behold thy Holiness as the Avenger,
Who shews himself at the back of his victim.

I came, and thou smotest the land of the Tahennu;
The people of Uten submitted themselves to thy power;
I made them see thy Holiness as a lion, fierce of eye,
Who leaves his den and stalks through the valleys.

I came, and thou smotest the hinder (i.e. northern) lands;
The circuit of the Great Sea is bound in thy grasp;

I made them behold thy Holiness as the hovering hawk.
Which seizes with his glance whatever pleases him.

I came, and thou smotest the lands in front:
Those that sat upon the sand thou carriedst away captive;
I made them behold thy Holiness like the jackal of the South,
Which passes through the lands as a hidden wanderer.

I came, and thou smotest the nomad tribes of Nubia,
Even to the land of Shut, which thou holdest in thy grasp;
I made them behold thy Holiness like thy pair of brothers,
Whose hands I have united to give thee power.

Architectural Works

It is impossible to conclude this sketch of Tuthmosis III without some notice of his buildings. He was the greatest of Egyptian conquerors, but he was also one of the greatest of Egyptian builders and patrons of art. The grand temple of Ammon at Thebes was the especial object of his fostering care; and he began his career of builder and restorer by repairs and restorations, which much improved and beautified that edifice. Before the southern propylæa he re-erected, in the first year of his independent reign, colossal statues of his father, Tuthmosis I, and his grandfather, Amenhotep, which had been thrown down in the troublous time succeeding Tuthmosis the First's death. He then proceeded to rebuild the central sanctuary, the work of Usurtasen I, which had probably begun to decay, and, recognizing its importance as the very *penetrale* of the temple, he resolved to reconstruct it in granite, instead of common stone, that he might render it, practically, imperishable.

With a reverence and a self-restraint that it might be wished restorers possessed more commonly, he preserved all the lines and dimensions of the ancient building, merely reproducing in a better material the work of his great predecessor. Having accomplished this pious task, he gave a vent to his constructive ambition by a grand addition to the temple on its eastern side. Behind the cell, at the distance of about 45 metres (150 feet), he erected a magnificent hall, or pillared chamber, of dimensions previously unknown in Egypt, or elsewhere in the world at the time – an oblong square, 43 metres (143 feet) long by 16 metres (53 feet) wide, or nearly half as large again as the nave of Canterbury Cathedral. The whole of the apartment was roofed in with slabs of solid stone; it was divided in its longest direction into five avenues or vistas by means of rows of pillars and piers, the former being towards the centre, and attaining a height of nine metres (30 feet), with bell capitals, and the latter towards the sides, with a height of six metres (20 feet). This arrangement enabled the building to be lighted by means of a clerestory, in the manner shown by the accompanying woodcut. In connection with this noble hall, on three sides of it, northwards, eastwards, and southwards, Tuthmosis further erected chambers and corridors, partly open, partly supported by pillars, which might form convenient store-chambers for the vestments of the priests and the offerings of the people.

Tuthmosis also added propylæa to the temple on the south, and erected in front of the grand entrance which was (as usual) between the pylons of the propylæa, two or perhaps four great obelisks, one of which exists to the present day, and is the largest and most magnificent of all such monuments now extant. It stands in front of the Church of St. John Lateran at Rome, and has a height of 32 metres (105 feet), exclusive of the base, with a width diminishing from 2.8 metres (nine feet six inches) to 2.6 metres (eight feet seven inches). It is estimated to weigh above 450 tons, and is covered with well-cut hieroglyphics. No other obelisk approaches within 3.5 metres (12 feet) of its elevation, or within fifty tons of its weight. Yet, if we may believe an inscription of Tuthmosis, found on the spot, the pair of obelisks whereof this was one shrank into insignificance in comparison with another pair, also placed by him before his propylæa, the height of which was 50 metres (162 feet,) and their weight consequently from seven hundred to eight hundred tons! As no trace has been found of these monsters, and as it seems almost impossible that they should have been removed, and highly improbable that they could have been broken up without leaving some indication of their existence, perhaps we may conclude that they were designed rather than executed, and that the inscription was set up in anticipation of an achievement contemplated but never effected.

Other erections of the Great Tuthmosis are the enclosure of the famous Temple of the Sun at Heliopolis, the temple of Phthah at Thebes, the small temple at Medinet-Abou, a temple to Kneph adorned with obelisks at Elephantine, and a series of temples and monuments erected at Ombos, Esneh, Abydos, Coptos, Denderah, Eileithyia, Hermonthis, and Memphis in Egypt, and at Amada, Corte, Talmis, Pselcis, Semneh, Koummeh, and Napata in Nubia. Extensive ruins of many of these buildings still remain, particularly at Koummeh, Semneh, Napata, Denderah, and Ombos. Altogether, Tuthmosis III is pronounced to have left behind him more monuments than any other Pharaoh excepting Rameses II, and though occasionally showing himself, as a builder, somewhat capricious and whimsical, still, on the whole, to have worked in a pure style and proved that he was not deficient in good taste.

It has happened, moreover, by a curious train of circumstances, that Tuthmosis III is, of all the pharaohs, the one whose great works are most widely diffused, and display Egyptian skill and taste to the largest populations, and in the most important cities, of the modern world. Rome, as we have seen, possesses his grandest obelisk, which is at the same time the greatest of all extant monoliths.

Tuthmosis Compared with Alexander

Tuthmosis III has been called 'the Alexander of Egyptian history'. The phrase is at once exaggerated and misleading. It is exaggerated as applied to his military ability; for, though beyond a doubt this monarch was by far the greatest of Egyptian conquerors, and possessed considerable military talent, much personal bravery and an energy that has seldom been exceeded, yet, on the other hand, his task was trivial as compared with that of the Macedonian general, and his achievements insignificant. Instead of plunging with a small force into the midst of populous countries, and contending with armies 10 or 20 times as numerous as his own, defeating them and utterly subduing a vast empire, Tuthmosis marched at the head of a numerous disciplined army into thinly peopled regions, governed by petty chiefs jealous one of another, fought scarcely a single great battle, and succeeded in conquering two regions of a moderate size, Syria and Upper Mesopotamia, as far as the

Khabour river. Alexander overran and subdued the entire tract between the Aegean and the Sutlej, the Persian Gulf and the Oxus. He conquered Egypt, and founded a dynasty there which endured for nearly three centuries. Tuthmosis subdued not a tenth part of the space, and the empire which he established did not endure for much more than a century. It is thus absurd to compare Tuthmosis III to Alexander the Great as a conqueror.

Alexander was, besides, much more than a conqueror; he was a first-rate administrator. Had he lived 20 years longer he would probably have built up a universal monarchy, which might have lasted for a millennium. As it was, he so organized the East that it continued for nearly three centuries mainly under Greek rule, in the hands of the monarchs who are known as his 'successors'. Tuthmosis III, on the contrary, organized nothing. He left his conquests in such a condition that they, all of them, revolted at his death. His successor had to reconquer all the countries that had submitted to his father, and to re-establish over them the Egyptian sovereignty.

Description of His Person

In person the great Egyptian monarch was not remarkable. He had a long, well-shaped, and somewhat delicate nose, which was almost in line with his forehead, an eye prominent and larger than that of most Egyptians, a shortish upper lip, a resolute mouth with rather over-full lips, and a rounded, slightly retreating chin. The expression of his portrait statues is grave and serious, but lacks strength and determination. Indeed, there is something about the whole countenance that is a little womanish, though his character certainly presents no appearance of effeminacy. He died after a reign of 54 years, according to his own reckoning, having practically exercised the sovereign power for about 32 of the 54. His age at his death must have been about 60.

Short Reign of Amenhotep II

Tuthmosis III was succeeded by his son, Amenhotep, whom historians commonly term Amenophis the Second. This king was a warrior like his father, and succeeded in reducing, without much difficulty, the various nations that had thrown off the authority of Egypt on receiving the news of his father's death. He even carried his arms, according to some, as far as Nineveh, which he claims to have besieged and taken; he does not, however, mention the Assyrians as his opponents. His contests were with the Naïri, the Rutennu and the Shasu (Arabs) in Asia, with the Tahennu (Libyans) and Nubians in Africa. On all sides victory crowned his arms; but he stained the fair fame that his victories would have otherwise secured him by barbarous practices, and cruel and unnecessary bloodshed.

He tells us that at Takhisa in northern Syria he killed seven kings with his own hand, and he represents himself in the act of destroying them with his war club, not in the heat of battle, but after they have been taken prisoners. He further adds that, after killing them, he suspended their bodies from the prow of the vessel in which he returned to Egypt, and brought them, as trophies of victory, to Thebes, where he hung six of the seven outside the walls of the city, as the Philistines hung the bodies of Saul and Jonathan on the wall of Beth-shan; while he had the seventh conveyed to Napata in Nubia, and there similarly exposed, to terrify his enemies in that quarter. It has been said of the Russians – not perhaps without some justice – 'Grattez le Russe et vous trouverez le Tartare'; with far greater reason may we say of the ancient Egyptians, that, notwithstanding the veneer of civilization which they for the most part present to our observation, there was in their nature, even at the best of times, an underlying ingrained barbarism which could not be concealed, but was continually showing itself.

Amenophis II appears to have had a short reign; his seventh year is the last noted upon his monuments. As a builder he was unenterprising. One temple at Amada, one hall at Thebes, and his tomb at Abd-el-Qurnah, form almost the whole of his known constructions. None of them is remarkable. Egypt under his sway had a brief rest before she braced herself to fresh efforts, military and architectural.

AMENHOTEP III AND HIS GREAT WORKS – THE VOCAL MEMNON

The 'Twin Colossi' of Thebes: Their Impressiveness

The fame of Amenhotep the Third, the grandson of the great Tuthmosis, rests especially upon his Twin Colossi, the grandest, if not actually the largest, that the world has ever beheld. Imagine sitting figures, formed of a single solid block of sandstone, which have sat for above 3,000 years, mouldering gradually away under the influence of time and weather changes, yet which are still more than 18 metres (60 feet) high, and must originally, when they wore the tall crown of an Egyptian king, have reached very nearly the height of 21 metres (70 feet). We think a statue vast, colossal, of magnificent dimensions, if it be as much as ten or twenty feet high – as Chantrey's statue of Pitt, or Phidias's chryselephantine statue of Jupiter. What, then, must these be, which are of a size so vastly greater? Let us hear how they impress an eye-witness of world-wide experience. 'There they sit,' says Harriet Martineau, 'together, yet apart, in the midst of the plain, serene and vigilant, still keeping their untired watch over the lapse of ages and the eclipse of Europe. I can never believe that anything else so majestic as this pair has been conceived of by the imagination of art. Nothing certainly, even in nature, ever affected me so unspeakably; no thunderstorms in my childhood, nor any aspect of Niagara, or the great lakes of America, or the Alps, or the Desert, in my later years.... The pair, sitting alone amid the expanse of verdure, with islands of ruins behind them, grew more striking to us every day. To-day, for the first time, we looked up to them from their base. The impression of sublime tranquillity which they convey when seen from distant points, is confirmed by a nearer approach. There they sit, keeping watch – hands on knees, gazing straight forward; seeming, though so much of the face is gone, to be looking over to the monumental piles on the other side of the river, which became gorgeous temples, after these throne-seats were placed here – the most immovable thrones that have ever been established on this earth!'

The Account Given of Them by Their Sculptor

The design of erecting two such colossi must be attributed to the monarch himself, and we must estimate, from the magnificence of the design, the grandeur of his thoughts and the wonderful depth of his artistic imagination; but the skill to execute, the genius to express in stone such dignity, majesty, and repose as the statues possess, belongs to the first-rate sculptor, who turned the rough blocks of stone, hewn by the masons in a distant quarry, into the glorious statues that have looked down upon the plain for so many ages. The sculptors of Egyptian works are, in general, unknown; but, by good fortune, in this particular case, the name of the artist has remained on record, and he has himself given us an account of the feelings with which he saw them set up in the places where they still remain. The sculptor, who bore the same name as his royal master, i.e. Amenhotep or Amen-hept, declares in the exultation of his heart: 'I immortalized the name of the king, and no one has done the like of me in my works. I executed two portrait-statues of the king, astonishing for their breadth and height; their completed form dwarfed the temple tower – forty cubits was their measure; they were cut in the splendid sandstone mountain on either side, the eastern and the western. I caused to be built eight ships, whereon the statues were carried up the river; they were emplaced in their sublime temple; they will last as long as heaven. A joyful event was it when they were landed at Thebes and raised up in their place.'

The Eastern Colossus; Why It Is Called 'The Vocal Memnon'

A peculiar and curious interest attaches to one – the more eastern – of the two statues. It was known to the Romans of the early empire as 'The Vocal Memnon', and formed one of the chief attractions which drew travellers to Egypt, from the fact, which is quite indisputable, that at that time, for two centuries or perhaps more, it emitted in the early morning a musical sound, which was regarded as a sort of standing miracle. The fact is mentioned by Strabo, Pliny the elder, Pausanias, Tacitus, Juvenal, Lucian, Philostratus, and others, and is recorded by a number of ear-witnesses on the lower part of the colossus itself in inscriptions which may be seen at the present day. Amenhotep, identified by the idle fancy of some Greek or Roman scholar with the Memnon of Homer, son of Tithonus and Eos (Dawn), who led an army of Ethiopians to the assistance of Priam of Troy against the Greeks, was regarded as a god, and to hear the sound was not only to witness a miracle, but to receive an assurance of the god's favourable regard. For the statue did not emit a sound – the god did not speak – every day. Sometimes travellers had to depart disappointed altogether, sometimes they had to make a second, a third, or a fourth visit before hearing the desired voice. But still it was a frequent phenomenon; and a common soldier has recorded the fact on the base of the statue, that he heard it no fewer than thirteen times. The origin of the sound, the time when it began to be heard, and the circumstances under which it ceased, are all more or less doubtful. Some of those exceedingly clever persons who find priest-craft everywhere, think that the musical sound was the effect of human contrivance, and explain the whole matter to their entire satisfaction by 'the jugglery of the priests'. The priests either found a naturally vocal piece of rock, and intentionally made the statue out of it; or they cunningly introduced a pipe into the interior of the figure, by which they could make musical notes issue from the mouth at their pleasure. It is against this view that in the palmy days of the Egyptian hierarchy, the vocal character of the statue was entirely unknown; we have no evidence of the sound having been heard earlier than the time of Strabo (25–10 BCE), when Egypt was in the possession of the Romans, and the priests had little influence. Moreover, the theory is disproved by the fact that, during the two centuries of the continuance of the marvel, there were occasions when Memnon was obstinately silent, though the priests must have been most anxious that he should speak, while there were others when he spoke freely, though they must have been perfectly indifferent. The wife of a prefect of Egypt made two visits to the spot to no purpose; and the Empress Sabina, wife of the Emperor Hadrian, was, on her first visit, also disappointed, so that 'her venerable features were inflamed with anger.' On the other hand, as already mentioned, a common Roman soldier heard the sound thirteen times.

Earliest Testimony to Its Being 'Vocal'

With respect to the time when, and the circumstances under which, the phenomenon first showed itself, all that can be said is, that the earliest literary witness to the fact is Strabo (about 25 BCE); that the earliest of the inscriptions on the base that can be dated belongs to the reign of Nero, and that it is at least questionable whether the sound ever issued from the stone before 27 BCE. In that year there was an earthquake which wrought great havoc at Thebes; and it is an acute suggestion, that it was this earthquake which at once shattered the upper part of the colossus, and so affected the remainder of the block of stone that it became vocal then for the first time. For centuries the figure remained a *torso*, and it was while a *torso* that it emitted the musical tone—

'Dimidio magicæ resonabant Memnone chordæ.'

After a long interval of years, probably about 174 CE, that restoration of the monument took place which is to be seen to the present day. Five blocks of stone, rudely shaped into a form like that of the unharmed colossus, were emplaced upon the *torso*, which was thus reconstructed. The intention was to do Memnon honour; but the effect was to strike him dumb. The peculiar condition of the stone, which the earthquake had superinduced, and which made it vocal, being changed by the new arrangement, the sound ceased, and has been heard no more.

Rational Account of the Phenomenon

It is a fact well known to scientific persons at the present day, that musical sounds are often given forth both by natural rocks and by quarried masses of stone, in consequence of a sudden change of temperature. Baron Humboldt, writing on the banks of the Oronooko, says: 'The granite rock on which we lay is one of those where travellers have heard from time to time, towards sunrise, subterraneous sounds, resembling those of the organ. The missionaries call these stones *loxas de musica*. "It is witchcraft," said our young Indian pilot.... But the existence of a phenomenon that seems to depend on a certain state of the atmosphere cannot be denied. The shelves of rock are full of very narrow and deep crevices. They are heated during the day to about 50°. I often found their temperature during the night at 39°. It may easily be conceived that the difference of temperature between the subterraneous and the external air would attain its maximum about sunrise.' Analogous phenomena occur among the sandstone rocks of El Nakous, in Arabia Petræa, near Mount Maladetta in the Pyrenees, and (perhaps) in the desert between Palestine and Egypt. 'On the fifth day of my journey,' says the accomplished author of *Eothen*, 'the sun growing fiercer and fiercer, ... as I drooped my head under his fire, and closed my eyes against the glare that surrounded me, I slowly fell asleep – for how many minutes or moments I cannot tell – but after a while I was gently awakened by a peal of church bells – my native bells – the innocent bells of Marlen that never before sent forth their music beyond the Blagdon hills! My first idea naturally was that I still remained fast under the power of a dream. I roused myself, and drew aside the silk that covered my eyes, and plunged my bare face into the light. Then at least I was well enough awakened, *but still those old Marlen bells rang on*, not ringing for joy, but properly, prosily, steadily, merrily ringing "for church". *After a while the sound died away slowly*; it happened that neither I nor any of my party had a watch to measure the exact time of its lasting; but it seemed to me that about ten minutes had passed before the bells ceased.' The gifted writer proceeds to give a metaphysical explanation of the phenomena; but it may be questioned whether he did not hear actual musical sounds, emitted by the rocks that lay beneath the sands over which he was moving.

And similar sounds have been heard when the stones that sent them forth were quarried blocks, no longer in a state of nature, but shaped by human tools, and employed in architecture. Three members of the French Expedition, MM. Jomard, Jollois, and Devilliers, were together in the granite cell which forms the centre of the palace-temple of Karnak, when, according to their own account, they 'heard a sound, resembling that of a chord [instrument string] breaking, issue from the blocks at sunrise.' Exactly the same comparison is employed by Pausanias to describe the sound that issued from 'the vocal Memnon'.

On the whole, we may conclude that the musical qualities of his remarkable colossus were unknown alike to the artist who sculptured the monument and to the king whom it represented. To them, in its purpose and object, it belonged, not to Music, but wholly to the sister art of Architecture. 'The Pair' sat at one extremity of an avenue leading to one of the great palace-temples reared by Amenhotep III – a palace-temple which is now a mere heap of sandstone, 'a little roughness in the plain.' The design of the king was, that this grand edifice should be approached by a *dromos* or paved way, 225 metres (1,100 feet) long, which should be flanked on either side by nine similar statues, placed at regular intervals along the road, and all representing himself. The egotism of the monarch may perhaps be excused on account of the grandeur of his idea, which we nowhere else find repeated, avenues of sphinxes being common in Egypt, and avenues of sitting human *life-size* figures not unknown to Greece, but the history of art containing no other instance of an avenue of colossi.

Amenhotep's Temple at Luxor

Another of Amenhotep's palace-temples has been less unkindly treated by fortune than the one just mentioned. The temple of Luxor, or El-Uksur, on the eastern bank of the river, a little over two kilometres (about a mile and a half) to the south of the great temple of Karnak, is a magnificent edifice to this day; and though some portions of it, and some of its most remarkable features, must be assigned to Rameses II, yet still it is, in the main, a construction of Amenhotep's, and must be regarded as being, even if it stood alone, sufficient proof of his eminence as a builder. The length of the entire building is about 243 metres (800 feet), the breadth varying from about 30 to 60 metres (100 to 200 feet).

Its general arrangement comprised, first, a great court, at a different angle from the rest, being turned so as to face Karnak. In front of this stood two colossal statues of the founder, together with two obelisks, one of which has been removed to France, and now adorns the centre of the Place de la Concorde at Paris. Behind this was a great pillared hall, of which only the two central ranges of columns are now standing. Still further back were smaller halls and numerous apartments, evidently meant for the king's residence, rather than for a temple or place exclusively devoted to worship. The building is remarkable for its marked affectation of irregularity. 'Not only is there a considerable angle in the direction of the axis of the building, but the angles of the courtyards are hardly ever right angles; the pillars are variously spaced, and pains seem to have been gratuitously taken to make it as irregular as possible in nearly every respect.'

His Other Buildings

Besides this grand edifice, Amenhotep built two temples at Karnak to Ammon and Maut, embellished the old temple of Ammon there with a new propylon, raised temples to Kneph, or Khnum, at Elephantine and built a shrine to contain his own image at Soleb in Nubia, another shrine at Napata, and a third at Sedinga. He left traces of himself at Semneh, in the island of Konosso, on the rocks between Philae and Assouan, at El-Kaab, at Toora near Memphis, at Silsilis, and at Sarabit-el-Khadim in the Sinaitic peninsula. He was, as M. Lenormant remarks, 'un prince essentiellement batisseur'. The scale and number of his works are such as to indicate unremitting attention to sculpture and building during the entire duration of his long reign of 36 years.

His Wars and Expeditions

On the other hand, as a general he gained little distinction. He maintained, indeed, the dominion over Syria and Western Mesopotamia, which had been established by Tuthmosis III, and his cartouche has been found at Arban on the Khabour; but there is no appearance of his having made any additional conquests in this quarter. The subjected peoples brought their tribute regularly, and the neighbouring nations, whether Hittites, Assyrians or Babylonians, gave him no trouble. The dominion of Egypt over Western Asia had become 'an accomplished fact', and was generally recognized by the old native kingdoms. It did not extend, however, beyond Taurus and Niphates towards the north, or beyond the Khabour eastward or southward, but remained fixed within the limits which it had attained under the Third Tuthmosis.

The only quarter in which Amenhotep warred was towards Ethiopia. He conducted in person several expeditions up the valley of the Nile, against the Black tribes of the Soudan. But these attacks were not so much wars as raids, or razzias. They were not made with the object of advancing the Egyptian frontier, or even of extending Egyptian influence, but partly for the glorification of the monarch, who thus obtained at a cheap rate the credit of military successes, and partly – probably mainly – for the material gain which resulted from them through the capture of highly valuable slaves. The Black races have always been especially sought for this purpose, and were in great demand in the Egyptian slave market: ladies of rank were pleased to have for their attendants Black boys, whom they dressed in a fanciful manner; and the court probably indulged in a similar taste. Amenhotep's aim was certainly rather to capture than to kill. In one of his most successful raids the slain were only 312, while the captives consisted of 205 men, 250 women and 285 children, or a total of 740; and the proportion in the others was similar. The trade of slave hunting was so lucrative that even a great king could not resist the temptation of having a share in its profits.

His Lion Hunts; His Physiognomy and Character

When Amenhotep was not engaged in hunting men, his favourite recreation was to indulge in the chase of the lion. On one of his scarabaei he states that between his first and his 10th year he slew with his own hand 110 of these ferocious beasts. Later on in his reign he presented to the priests who had the charge of the ancient temple of Karnak a number of live lions, which he had probably caught in traps. The lion was an emblem both of Horus and of Turn, and may, when tamed, have been assigned a part in religious processions. It is uncertain what was Amenhotep's hunting ground; but the large number of his victims makes it probable that the scene of his exploits was Mesopotamia rather than any tract bordering on Egypt: since lions have always been scarce animals in North-Eastern Africa, but abounded in Mesopotamia even much later than the time of Amenhotep, and are 'not uncommon' there even at the present day. We may suppose that he had a hunting pavilion at Arban, where one of his scarabs has been found, and from that centre beat the reed beds and jungles of the Khabour.

In person, Amenhotep III was not remarkable. His features were good, except that his nose was somewhat too much rounded at the end; his expression was pensive, but resolute; his forehead high, his upper lip short, his chin a little too prominent. He left behind him a character for affectionateness, kindliness and generosity. Some historians have reproached him with being too much under female influence; and certainly in the earlier portion of his reign he deferred greatly to his mother, Mutemua, and in the latter portion to his wife, Tii or Taia; but there is no evidence that any evil result followed, or that these princesses did not influence him for good. It is too much taken for granted by many writers that female influence is corrupting. No doubt it is so in some cases; but it should not be forgotten that there are women whom to have known is 'a liberal education'. Mutemua and Tii may have been of the number.

DEVELOPMENT OF THE CULT OF ATEN UNDER AMENHETEP IV

Amenhetep III was succeeded by his son by his beloved wife Ti, who came to the throne under the name of Amenhetep [also spelled Amenhotep] IV. He reigned about 17 years, and died probably before he was 30. The accuracy of the latter part of this statement depends upon the evidence derived from the mummy of a young man which was found in the Tomb of Queen Ti, and is generally believed to be that of Amenhetep IV. It is thought that this mummy was taken from a royal tomb at Tall al-'Amarnah in mistake for that of Ti, and transported to Thebes, where it was buried as her mummy. Dr. [Grafton] Elliot Smith [professor of anatomy, Egyptologist and anthropologist] examined the skeleton, and decided that it was that of a man 25 or 26 years of age, 'without excluding the possibility that he may have been several years older'. His evidence is very important, for he adds, 'The cranium, however, exhibits in an unmistakable manner the distortion characteristic of a condition of hydrocephalus.' So then if the skeleton be that of Amenhetep IV, the king suffered from water on the brain; and if he was 26 years old when he died he must have begun to reign at the age of nine or 10. But there is the possibility that he did not begin to reign until he was a few years older.

Even had his father lived, he was not the kind of man to teach his son to emulate the deeds of warrior pharaohs like Tuthmosis III, and there was no great official to instruct him in the arts of war, for the long peaceful reign of Amenhetep III made the Egyptians forget that the ease and luxury which they then enjoyed had been purchased by the arduous raids and wars of their forefathers. To all intents and purposes, Ti ruled Egypt for several years after her husband's death, and the boy-king did for a time at least what his mother told him. His wife, Nefertiti, who was his father's daughter probably by a Mesopotamian woman, was no doubt chosen for him by his mother, and it is quite clear from the wall paintings at Tall al-'Amarnah that he was very much under their influence. His nurse's husband, Ai, was a priest of Aten, and during his early years he absorbed from this group of persons the fundamentals of the cult of Aten and much knowledge of the religious beliefs of the Mitannian ladies at the Egyptian Court. These sank into his mind and fructified, with the result that he began to abominate not only Amen, the great god of Thebes, but all the old gods and goddesses of Egypt, with the exception of the solar gods of Heliopolis. In many respects these gods resembled the Aryan gods worshipped by his grandmother's people, especially Varuna, to whom, as to Ra, human sacrifices were sometimes offered, and to them his sympathy inclined. But besides this he saw, as no doubt many others saw, that the priests of Amen were usurping royal prerogatives, and by their wealth and astuteness were becoming the dominant power in the land. Even at that time the revenues of Amen could hardly be told, and the power of his priests pervaded the kingdom from Napata in the South to Syria in the North.

During the first five or six years of his reign Amenhetep IV, probably as the result of the skilful guidance of his mother, made little or no change in the government of the country. But his actions in the sixth and following years of his reign prove that whilst he was still a mere boy, he was studying religious problems with zeal, and with more than the usual amount of boyish understanding. He must have been precocious and clever, with a mind that worked swiftly; and he possessed a determined will and very definite religious convictions and a fearless nature. It is also clear that he did not lightly brook opposition, and that he believed sincerely in the truth and honesty of his motives and actions. But with all these gifts he lacked a practical knowledge of men and things. He never realized the true nature of the duties which as king he owed to his country and people, and he never understood the realities of life. He never learnt the kingcraft of the pharaohs, and he failed to see that only a warrior could hold what warriors had won for him.

Instead of associating himself with men of action, he sat at the feet of Ai the priest, and occupied his mind with religious speculations; and so, helped by his adoring mother and kinswomen, he gradually became the courageous fanatic that the tombs and monuments of Egypt show him to have been. His physical constitution and the circumstances of his surroundings made him what he was. In recent years he has been described by such names as 'great idealist', 'great reformer', the 'world's first revolutionist', the 'first *individual* in human history', etc. But, in view of the known facts of history, and Dr. Elliot Smith's remarks quoted above on the distortion of the skull of Amenhetep IV, we are fully justified in wondering with Dr. Hall if the king 'was not really half insane'. None but a man half insane would have been so blind to facts as to attempt to overthrow Amen and his worship, round which the whole of the social life of the country centred. He suffered from religious madness at least, and spiritual arrogance and self-sufficiency made him oblivious to everything except his own feelings and emotions.

Once having made up his mind that Amen and all the other 'gods' of Egypt must be swept away, Amenhetep IV determined to undertake this work without delay. After years of thought he had come to the conclusion that only the solar gods, Tem, Ra and Horus of the Two Horizons were worthy of veneration, and that some form of their worship must take the place of that of Amen. The form of the Sun-god which he chose for worship was ATEN, i.e., the solar Disk, which was the abode of Tem and later of Ra of Heliopolis. But to him the Disk was not only the abode of the Sun-god, it was the god himself, who, by means of the heat and light which emanated from his own body, gave life to everything on the earth. To Aten, Amenhetep ascribed the attributes of the old gods, Tem, Ra, Horus, Ptah and even of Amen, and he proclaimed that Aten was 'One' and 'Alone'. But this had also been proclaimed by all the priesthoods of the old gods, Tem, Khepera, Khnem, Ra and, later, of Amen. The worshippers of every great god in Egypt had from time immemorial declared that their god was 'One'. 'Oneness' was an attribute, it would seem, of everything that was worshipped in Egypt, just as it is in some parts of India. It is inconceivable that Amenhetep IV knew of the existence of other suns besides the sun he saw, and it was obvious that Aten, the solar disk, was one alone, and without counterpart or equal. Some light is thrown upon Amenhetep's views as to the nature of his god by the title which he gave him. This title is written within two cartouches and reads:

'The Living Horus of the two horizons, exalted in the Eastern Horizon in his name of Shu-who-is-in-the-Disk.'

It is followed by the words, 'ever-living, eternal, great living Disk, he who is in the Set Festival, lord of the Circle (i.e., everything which the Disk shines on in every direction), lord of the Disk, lord of heaven, lord of the earth'. Amenhetep IV worshipped Horus of the two horizons as the 'Shu who was in the disk'. If we are to regard 'Shu' as an ordinary noun, we must translate it by 'heat', or 'heat and light', for the word has these meanings. In this case Amenhetep worshipped the solar heat, or the heat and light which were inherent in the Disk. Now, we know from the Pyramid Texts that Tem or Tem-Ra created a god and a goddess from the emanations or substance of his own body, and that they were called 'Shu' and 'Tefnut', the former being the heat radiated from the body of the god, and the latter the moisture. Shu and Tefnut created Geb (the earth) and Nut (the sky), and they in turn produced Osiris, the god of the river Nile, Set, the god of natural decay and death, and their shadowy counterparts, Isis and Nephthys. But, if we regard 'Shu' as a proper name in the title of Amenhetep's god, we get the same result, and can only assume that the king deified the heat of the sun and worshipped it as the one, eternal, creative, fructifying and life-sustaining force. The old Heliopolitan tradition made Tem or Tem-Ra, or Khepera, the creator of Aten the Disk, but this view Amenhetep IV rejected, and he asserted that the Disk was self-created and self-subsistent.

The common symbol of the solar gods was a disk encircled by a serpent, but when Amenhetep adopted the disk as the symbol of his god, he abolished the serpent and treated the disk in a new and original fashion. From the disk, the circumference of which is sometimes hung round with symbols of 'life' (☥), he made a series of rays to descend, and at the end of each ray was a hand, as if the ray was an arm, bestowing 'life' on the earth. This symbol never became popular in the country, and the nation as a whole preferred to believe that the Sun-god travelled across the sky in two boats, the Sektet and the Atet. The form of the old Heliopolitan cult of the Sun-god that was evolved by Amenhetep could never have appealed to the Egyptians, for it was too philosophical in character and was probably based upon esoteric doctrines that were of foreign origin. Her and Suti, the two great overseers of the temples of Amen at Thebes, were content to follow the example of their king Amenhetep III, and bow the knee to Aten and, like other officials, to sing a hymn in his praise. But they knew the tolerant character of their master's religious views, and that outwardly at least he was a loyal follower of Amen, whose blood, according to the dogma of his priests, flowed in the king's veins.

To Amenhetep III a god more or less made no difference, and he considered it quite natural that every priesthood should extol and magnify the power of its god. He was content to be a counterpart of Amen, and to receive the official worship due to him as such. But with his son it was different. The heat of Aten gave him life and maintained it in him, and whilst that was in him Aten was in him. The life of Aten was his life, and his life was Aten's life, and therefore he was Aten; his spiritual arrogance made him believe that he was an incarnation of Aten, i.e., that he was God – not a mere 'god' or one of the 'gods' of Egypt – and that his acts were divine. He felt therefore that he had no need to go to the temple of Amen to receive the daily supply of the 'fluid of life', which not only maintained the physical powers of kings, but gave them wisdom and understanding to rule their country. Still less would he allow the high priest of Amen to act as his vicar. Finally he determined that Amen and the gods must be done away and all the dogmas and doctrines of their priesthoods abolished, and that Aten must be proclaimed the One, self-created, self-subsisting, self-existing god, whose son and deputy he was.

Without, apparently, considering the probable effect of his decision when translated into action, he began to build the temple of Gem-Aten in Per-Aten, at Thebes. In it was a chamber or shrine, in which the *ben*, or *benben*, i.e., the 'Sun-stone', was placed, and in doing this he followed the example of the priests of Heliopolis. The site he selected for this temple was a piece of ground about halfway between the Temple of Karnak and the Temple of Luxor. He decided that this temple should be the centre of the worship of Aten, which should henceforward be the one religion of his country. The effect of the king's action on the priests of Amen and the people of Thebes can be easily imagined when we remember that with the downfall of Amen their means of livelihood disappeared. But Amenhetep was the king, the blood of the Sun-god was in his veins, and pharaoh was the master and owner of all Egypt, and of every person and thing in it. Priests and people were alike unable to resist his will, and, though they cursed Aten and his fanatical devotee, they could not prevent the confiscation of the revenues of Amen and the abolition of his services. Not content with this, Amenhetep caused the name of Amen to be obliterated on the monuments, and in some cases even his father's name, and the word for 'gods' was frequently cut out. Not only was there to be no Amen, but there were to be no gods; Aten was the only god that was to be worshipped.

The result of the promulgation of this decree can be easily imagined. Thebes became filled with the murmurings of all classes of the followers of Amen, and when the temple of Aten was finished, and the worship of the new god was inaugurated, these murmurings were changed to threats and curses, and disputes between the Amenites and Atenites filled the city. What exactly happened is not known and never will be known, but the result of the confusion and uproar was that Amenhetep

IV found residence in Thebes impossible, and he determined to leave it, and to remove the court elsewhere. Whether he was driven to take this step through fear for the personal safety of himself and his family, or whether he wished still further to insult and injure Amen and his priesthood, cannot be said, but the reason that induced him to abandon his capital city and to destroy its importance as such must have been very strong and urgent.

Having decided to leave Thebes he sought for a site for his new capital, which he intended to make a City of God, and found it in the north, at a place which is about 257 kilometres (160 miles) to the south of Cairo and 80 kilometres (50 miles) to the north of Asyut. At this point the hills on the east bank of the Nile enclose a sort of plain which is covered with fine yellow sand. The soil was virgin, and had never been defiled with temples or other buildings connected with the gods of Egypt whom Amenhetep IV hated, and the plain itself was eminently suitable for the site of a town, for its surface was unbroken by hills or reefs of limestone or sandstone. This plain is nearly five kilometres (three miles) from the Nile in its widest part and is about eight kilometres (five miles) in length. The plain on the other side of the river, which extended from the Nile to the western hills, was very much larger than that on the east bank, and was also included by the king in the area of his new capital. He set up large stelae on the borders of it to mark the limits of the territory of Aten, and had inscriptions cut upon them stating this fact.

We have already seen that Amenhetep IV had, whenever possible, caused the name of Amen to be chiselled out from stelae, statues and other monuments, and even from his father's cartouches, whilst at the same time the name of Amen formed part of his name as the son of Ra. It was easy to remedy this inconsistency, and he did so by changing his name from Amenhetep, which means 'Amen is content', to AAKHUNATEN, a name which by analogy should mean something like 'Aten is content'. This meaning has already been suggested by more than one Egyptologist, but there is still a good deal to be said for keeping the old translation, 'Spirit of Aten'. I transcribe the new name of Amenhetep IV, Aakhunaten, not with any wish to add another to the many transliterations that have been proposed for it, but because it represents with considerable accuracy the hieroglyphs. How the name was pronounced we do not know and never shall know, but there is no good ground for thinking that 'Ikhnaton' or 'Ikh-en-aton' represents the correct pronunciation. In passing we may note that *Aten* has nothing to do with the Semitic *'adhon*, 'lord'.

At this time Amenhetep IV adopted two titles in connection with his new name, i.e., 'Ankh-em-Maat' and 'Aa-em-aha-f', the former meaning, 'Living in Truth' and the latter 'great in his life period'. What is meant exactly by 'living in truth' is not clear. *Maat* means what is straight, true, real, law, both physical and moral, the truth, reality, etc. He can hardly have meant 'living in or by the law', for he was a law to himself, but he may have meant that in Atenism he had found the truth or the 'real' thing, and that all else in religion was a phantom, a sham. Aten lived in *maat*, or in truth and reality, and the king, having the essence of Aten in him, did the same. The exact meaning which Amenhetep IV attached to the other title, 'great in his life-period', is also not clear. He, as was every pharaoh who preceded him, was a 'son of Ra', but he did not claim, as they did, to 'live like Ra for ever', and only asserted that his life-period was great. Amenhetep IV called his new capital Aakhutaten, i.e., 'the Horizon of Aten', and he and his followers regarded it as the one place in which Aten was to be found. It was to them the visible symbol of the splendour and benevolence and love of the god, the sight of it rejoiced the hearts of all beholders, and its loveliness, they declared, was beyond compare. It was to them what Babylon was to the Babylonians, Jerusalem to the Hebrews, and Makkah to the Arabs; to live there and to behold the king, who was Aten's own son, bathed in the many-handed, life-giving rays of Aten, was to enjoy a foretaste of heaven, though none of the writers of the hymns to Aten deign to tell us what the heaven to which they refer so glibly was like. Having taken up his abode in this city, Amenhetep set to work to organize the cult of Aten, and to promulgate his doctrine, which, like all writers of moral and religious aphorisms, he called his 'Teaching', *Sbait*.

Having appointed himself High Priest, he, curiously enough, adopted the old title of the High Priest of Heliopolis and called himself 'Ur-maa', i.e., the 'Great Seer'. But he did not at the same time institute the old semi-magical rites and ceremonies which the holders of the title in Heliopolis performed. He did not hold the office very long, but transferred it to Merira, one of his loyal followers.

When still a mere boy, probably before he ascended the throne and rejected his name of Amenhetep, he seems to have dreamed of building temples to Aten, and so when he took up his residence in his new city he at once set to work to build a sanctuary for that god. Among his devoted followers was one

Bek, an architect and master builder, who claims to have been a pupil of the king, and who was undoubtedly a man of great skill and taste. Him the king sent to Sun, the Syene of the Greek writers, to obtain stone for the temple of Aten, and there is reason to think that, when the building was finished, its walls were most beautifully decorated with sculptures and pictures painted in bright colours. A second temple to Aten was built for the Queen-mother Ti, and a third for the princess Baktenaten, one of her daughters; and we should expect that one or more temples were built in the western half of the city across the Nile. With the revenues filched from Amen Aakhunaten built several temples to Aten in the course of his reign. Thus he founded Per-gem-Aten in Nubia at a place in the Third Cataract; Gem-pa-Aten em. Per-Aten at Thebes; Aakhutaten in Southern Anu (Hermonthis); the House of Aten in Memphis; and Res-Ra-em-Anu. It will be noticed that no mention is made of Aten in the name of this last temple of Aten. He also built a temple to Aten in Syria, which is mentioned on one of the Tall al-'Amarnah tablets in the British Museum under the form Hi-na-tu-na.

As the buildings increased in Aakhutaten and the cult of Aten developed, the king's love for his new city grew, and he devoted all his time to the worship of his god. Surrounded by his wife and family and their friends, and his obedient officials, who seem to have been handsomely rewarded for their devotion, the king had neither wish nor thought for the welfare of his kingdom, which he allowed to manage itself. His religion and his domestic happiness filled his life, and the inclinations and wishes of the ladies of his court had more weight with him than the counsels and advice of his ablest officials. We know nothing of the forms and ceremonies of the Aten worship, but hymns and songs and choruses must have filled the temple daily. And the stele of Tutankhamen proves that a considerable number of dancing men and acrobats were maintained by the king in connection with the service of Aten. Not only was the king no warrior, he was not even a lover of the chase. As he had no son to train in manly sports and to teach the arts of government and war, for his offspring consisted of seven daughters, his officers must have wondered how long the state in which they were then living would last. The life in the City of Aten was no doubt pleasant enough for the court and the official classes, for the king was generous to the officers of his government in the city, and, like the pharaohs of old, he gave them when they died tombs in the hills in which to be buried. The names of many of these officers are well known, e.g., Merira I, Merira II, Pa-nehsi (the Negro), Hui, Aahmes, Penthu, Mahu, Api, Rames, Suti, Nefer-kheperu-her-sekheper, Parennefer, Tutu, Ai, Mai, Ani, etc.

The tombs of these men are different from all others of the same class in Egypt. The walls are decorated with pictures representing (1) the worship of Aten by the king and his mother; (2) the bestowal of gifts on officials by the king; (3) the houses, gardens and estates of the nobles; (4) domestic life, etc. The hieroglyphic texts on the walls of the tombs contain the names of those buried in them, the names of the offices which they held under the king, and fulsome adulation of the king, and of his goodness, generosity and knowledge. Then there are prayers for funerary offerings, and also Hymns to Aten. The long Hymn in the tomb of Ai is not by the king, as was commonly supposed; it is the best of all the texts of the kind in these tombs, and many extracts from it are found in the tombs of his fellow officials. A shorter Hymn occurs in some of the tombs, and of this it is probable that Aakhunaten was the author. We look in vain for the figures of the old gods of Egypt, Ra, Horus, Ptah, Osiris, Isis, Anubis, and the cycles of the gods of the dead and of the Tuat (Underworld), and not a single ancient text, whether hymn, prayer, spell, incantation, litany, from the Book of the Dead in any of its Recensions is to be found there. To the Atenites the tomb was a mere hiding place for the dead body, not a model of the Tuat, as their ancestors thought. Their royal leader rejected all the old funerary Liturgies like the 'Book of Opening the Mouth', and the 'Liturgy of Funerary Offerings', and he treated with silent contempt such works as the 'Book of the Two Ways', the 'Book of the Dweller in the Tuat', and the 'Book of Gates'. Thus it would appear that he rejected *en bloc* all funerary rites and ceremonies, and disapproved of all services of commemoration of the dead, which were so dear to the hearts of all Egyptians.

The absence of figures of Osiris in the tombs of his officials and all mention of this god in the inscriptions found in them suggests that he disbelieved in the Last Judgment, and in the dogma of rewards for the righteous and punishments for evil doers. If this were so, the Field of Reeds, the Field of the Grasshoppers, the Field of Offerings in the Elysian Fields, and the Block of Slaughter with the headsman Shesmu, the five pits of the Tuat, and the burning of the wicked were all ridiculous fictions to him. Perhaps they were, but they were ineradicably fixed in the minds of his subjects, and he gave them nothing to put in the place of these fictions and the cult of Aten did not satisfy them.

Another question arises: did the Atenites mummify their dead? It is clear from the existence of the tombs in the hills about Aakhunaten that important officials were buried; but what became of the bodies of the working-class folk and the poor? Were they thrown to the jackals 'in the bush'? All this suggests that the Atenites adored and enjoyed the heat and light which their god poured upon them, and that they sang and danced and praised his beneficence, and lived wholly in the present. And they worshipped the triad of life, beauty and colour. They abolished the conventionality and rigidity in Egyptian painting and sculptures and introduced new colours into their designs and crafts, and, freed from the control of the priesthoods, artists and workmen produced extraordinarily beautiful results. The love of art went hand in hand with their religion and was an integral part of it. We may trace its influence in the funerary objects, even of those who believed in Osiris and were buried with the ancient rites and ceremonies especially in figures, vases, etc., made of pottery. Perhaps the brightly coloured vignettes, which are found in the great rolls of the Book of the Dead that were produced at this period, were painted by artists who copied the work of Atenite masters.

Now whilst Aakhunaten was organizing and developing the cult of Aten, and he and his Court and followers were passing their days and years in worshipping their god and in beautifying their houses, what was happening to the rest of Egypt? Tutankhamen tells us that the revenues of the gods were diverted to the service of Aten, that the figures of the gods had disappeared from their thrones, that the temples were deserted, and that the Egyptians generally were living in a state of social chaos. For the first 12 years or so of Aakhunaten's reign, the tribute of the Nubians was paid, for the Viceroy of Nubia had at hand means for making the tribes bring gold, wood, slaves, etc., to him. In the north of Egypt General Heremheb, the commander-in-chief, managed to maintain his lord's authority, but there is no doubt, as events showed when he became king of Egypt, that he was not a wholly sincere worshipper of Aten, and that his sympathies lay with the priesthoods of Ptah of Memphis and Ra of Heliopolis. The Memphites and the Heliopolitans must have resented bitterly the building of temples to Aten in their cities, and there can be little doubt that that astute soldier soon came to an understanding with them. Moreover, he knew better than his king what was happening in Syria, and how the Khabiru were threatening Phoenicia from the south, and how the Hittites were consolidating their position in Northern Syria, and increasing their power in all directions. He, and everyone in Egypt who was watching the course of events, must have been convinced that no power which the king could employ could stop the spread of the revolt in Western Asia, and that the rule of the Egyptians there was practically at an end.

When the king as Amenhetep IV ascended the throne, all his father's friends in Babylonia, Assyria, Mitanni, the lands of the Kheta and Cyprus hastened to congratulate him, and all were anxious to gain and keep the friendship of the new king of Egypt. Burraburiyash, king of Karduniash, hoped that the new king and he would always exchange presents, and that the old friendship between his country and Egypt would be maintained. Ashuruballit sent him gifts and asked for 20 talents of gold in return. Tushratta, king of Mitanni, addressed him as 'my son-in-law', sent greetings to Queen Ti, and spoke with pride of the old friendship between Mitanni and Egypt. He also wrote to Queen Ti, and again refers to the old friendship. But Aakhunaten did not respond in the manner they expected, and letters sent by them to him later show that the gifts which he sent were mean and poor. Clearly he lacked the open-handedness and generosity of his father Amenhetep III. As years went on, the governors of the towns and cities that were tributaries of Egypt wrote to the king protesting their devotion, fidelity and loyalty, many of them referring to favours received and asking for new ones. Very soon these protestations of loyalty were coupled with requests for Egyptian soldiers to be sent to protect the king's possessions. Thus, one Shuwardata writes: To the king, my lord, my gods and my Sun. Thus saith Shuwardata, the slave: Seven times and seven times did I fall down at the feet of the king my lord, both upon my belly and upon my back. Let the king, my lord, know that I am alone, and let the king, my lord, send troops in great multitudes, let the king, my lord, know this.

The people of Tunip, who were vassals of Tuthmosis III, wrote and told the king that Aziru had plundered an Egyptian caravan, and that if help were not sent Tunip would fall as Ni had already done. Rib-Adda of Byblos writes: We have no food to eat and my fields yield no harvest because I cannot sow corn. All my villages are in the hands of the Khabiru. I am shut up like a bird in a cage, and there is none to deliver me. I have written to the king, but no one heeds. Why wilt thou not attend to the affairs of thy country? That 'dog', Abd-Ashratum, and the Khabiri have taken Shigata and Ambi and Simyra. Send soldiers and an able officer. I beseech the king not to neglect this matter. Why is there no answer to my letters? Send chariots and I will try to hold out, else in two months' time Abd-Ashratum will be master of the whole country. Gebal (Byblos) will fall, and all the country as far as Egypt will be in the hands of the Khabiri. We have no grain; send grain. I have sent my possessions to Tyre, and also my sister's daughters for safety. I have sent my own son to thee, hearken to him. Do as thou wilt with me, but do not forsake thy city Gebal. In former times when Egypt neglected our city we paid no tribute; do not thou neglect it. I have sold my sons and daughters for food and have nothing left. Thou sayest, 'Defend thyself', but how can I do it? When I sent my son to thee he was kept three months waiting for an audience. Though my kinsmen urge me to join the rebels, I will not do it.

Abi-Milki of Tyre writes: To the king, my lord, my gods, my Sun. Thus saith Abi-Milki, thy slave. Seven times and seven times do I fall down at the feet of the king my lord. I am the dust under the sandals of the king my lord. My lord is the sun that riseth over the earth day by day, according to the bidding of the Sun, his gracious Father. It is he in whose moist breath I live, and at whose setting I make my moan. He maketh all the lands to dwell in peace by the might of his hand; he thundereth in the heavens like the Storm-god, so that the whole earth trembleth at his thunder. Behold, now, I said to the Sun, the Father of the king my Lord, When shall I see the face of the king my Lord? And now behold also I am guarding Tyre, the great city, for the king my lord until the king's mighty hand shall come forth unto me to give me water to drink and wood to warm myself withal. Moreover, Zimrida, the king of Sidon, sendeth word day by day unto the traitor Aziru, the son of

Abd-Ashratum, concerning all that he hath heard from Egypt. Now behold, I have written unto my lord, for it is well that he should know this.

In a letter from Lapaya the writer says: If the king were to write to me for my wife I would not refuse to send her, and if he were to order me to stab myself with a bronzed dagger I would certainly do so. Among the writers of the Letters is a lady who reports the raiding of Ajalon and Sarha by the Khabiri. All the letters tell the same story of successful revolt on the part of the subjects of Egypt and the capture and plundering and burning of towns and villages by the Khabiri, and the robbery of caravans on all the trade routes. And whilst all this was going on the king of Egypt remained unmoved and only occupied himself with the cult of his god! The general testimony of the Tall al-'Amarnah Letters proves that he took no trouble to maintain the friendly relations that had existed between the kings of Babylonia and Mitanni and his father. He seems to have been glad enough to receive embassies and gifts from Mesopotamia, and to welcome flattering letters full of expressions of loyalty and devotion to himself, but the gifts which he sent back did not satisfy his correspondents. He sent little or no gold to be used in decorating temples in Mesopotamia and for making figures of gods, and some of the letters seem to afford instances of double-dealing on the part of the king of Egypt. At all events, he waged no wars in Mesopotamia, and when one city after another failed to send tribute he made no attempt to force them to do so. It is uncertain how much he really knew of what was happening in Western Asia, but when Tushratta and others sent him dispatches demanding compensation for attacks made upon their caravans, when passing through his territory, he must have realized that the power of Egypt in that country had greatly weakened. As the years went on he must have known that the Egyptians hated his god and loathed his rule, and such knowledge must have, more or less, affected the health of a man of his physique and character.

During the earlier years of his reign, painters and sculptors gave him the conventional form of an Egyptian king, but later he is represented in an entirely different manner. He had naturally a long nose and chin and thick, protruding lips, and he was somewhat round-shouldered, and had a long slim body, and he must have had some deformity of knees and thighs. On the bas-reliefs and in the paintings all these physical characteristics are exaggerated, and the figures of the king are undignified caricatures. But these must have been made with the king's knowledge and approval, and must be faithful representations of him as he appeared to those who made them. In other words, they are examples of the realism in art (which he so strongly inculcated in the sculptors and artists who claimed to be his pupils) applied to himself. History is silent as to the last years of his reign, but the facts now known suggest that, overwhelmed by troubles at home and abroad, and knowing that he had no son to succeed him, and that he had failed to make the cult of Aten the national religion, his proud and ardent spirit collapsed, and with it his health, and that he became a man of sorrow. Feeling his end to be near, he appointed as co-regent Sakara tcheser-kheperu, who had married his eldest daughter Merit-Aten, and died probably soon afterwards. He was buried in a rock-hewn tomb, which he had prepared in the hills five miles away on the eastern bank of the Nile instead of in the western hills, where all the kings of the 18th dynasty were buried. Even in the matter of the position of his tomb he would not follow the custom of the country. This tomb was found in 1887–88 by native diggers, who cut out the cartouches of the king and sold them to travellers.

The facts known about the life and reign of Aakhunaten seem to me to prove that from first to last he was a religious fanatic, intolerant, arrogant and obstinate, but earnest and sincere in his seeking after God and in his attempts to make Aten the national god of Egypt. Modern writers describe him as a 'reformer', but he reformed nothing. He tried to force the worship of 'Horus of the Two Horizons in his name of Shu (i.e., Heat) who is in the Aten' upon his people and failed. When he found that his subjects refused to accept his personal views about an old, perhaps the oldest, solar god, whose cult had been dead for centuries, he abandoned the capital of his great and warlike ancestors in disgust, and like a spoilt child, which no doubt he was, he withdrew to a new city of his own making.

Like all such religious megalomaniacs, so long as he could satisfy his own peculiar aspirations and gratify his wishes, no matter at what cost, he was content. Usually the harm which such men do is limited in character and extent, but he, being a king, was able to inflict untold misery on his country during the 17 years of his reign. He spent the revenues of his country on the cult of his god, and in satisfying his craving for beauty in shape and form, and for ecstatic religious emotion; Though lavish in the rewards in good gold and silver to all those who ministered to this craving, he was mean and niggardly when it came to spending money for the benefit of his country. The Tall al-'Amarnah Letters make this fact quite clear. The peoples of Western Asia might think and say that the King of Egypt had 'turned Fakir', but there was little asceticism in his life. His boast of 'living in reality', or 'living in truth', which suggests that he lived a perfectly natural and simple life, seeing things as they really were, on the face of it seems to be ludicrous.

TUTANKHAMEN

Tut-ankh-Amen was the son-in-law, as everyone knows, of that most written-about, and probably most overrated, of all the Egyptian pharaohs, the heretic king Akh-en-Aten. Of his parentage we know nothing. He may have been of the blood royal and had some indirect claim to the throne on his own account. He may on the other hand have been a mere commoner. The point is immaterial, for, by his marriage to a king's daughter, he at once, by Egyptian law of succession, became a potential heir to the throne.

A hazardous and uncomfortable position it must have been to fill at this particular stage of his country's history. Abroad, the Empire founded in the 15th century BCE by Tuthmosis III, and held, with difficulty it is true, but still held, by succeeding monarchs, had crumpled up like a pricked balloon. At home dissatisfaction was rife. The priests of the ancient faith, who had seen their gods flouted and their very livelihood compromised, were straining at the leash, only waiting the most convenient moment to slip it altogether: the soldier class, condemned to a mortified inaction, were seething with discontent, and apt for any form of excitement: the foreign harem element, women who had been introduced into the court and into the families of soldiers in such large numbers since the wars of conquest, were now, at a time of weakness, a sure and certain focus of intrigue: the manufacturers and merchants, as foreign trade declined and home credit was diverted to a local and extremely circumscribed area, were rapidly becoming sullen and discontented: the common populace, intolerant of change, grieving, many of them, at the loss of their old familiar gods, and ready enough to attribute any loss, deprivation or misfortune, to the jealous intervention of these offended deities, were changing slowly from bewilderment to active resentment at the new heaven and new earth that had been decreed for them. And through it all Akh-en-Aten, Gallio of Gallios, dreamt his life away at Tell el Amarna.

The question of a successor was a vital one for the whole country, and we may be sure that intrigue was rampant. Of male heirs there was none, and interest centres on a group of little girls, the eldest of whom could not have been more than 15 at the time of her father's death. Young as she was, this eldest princess, Mert-Aten by name, had already been married some little while, for in the last year or two of Akh-en-Aten's reign we find her husband associated with him as co-regent, a vain attempt to avert the crisis which even the arch-dreamer Akh-en-Aten must have felt to be inevitable. Her taste of queenship was but a short one, for Smenkh-ka-Re, her husband, died within a short while of Akh-en-Aten. He may even, as evidence in this tomb seems to show, have predeceased him, and it is quite possible that he met his death at the hands of a rival faction. In any case he disappears, and his wife with him, and the throne was open to the next claimant.

The second daughter, Makt-Aten, died unmarried in Akh-en-Aten's lifetime. The third, Ankh-es-en-pa-Aten, was married to Tut-ankh-Aten as he then was, the Tut-ankh-Amen with whom we are now so familiar. Just when this marriage took place is not certain. It may have been in Akh-en-Aten's lifetime, or it may have been contracted hastily immediately after his death, to legalize his claim to the throne. In any event they were but children. Ankh-es-en-pa-Aten was born in the eighth year of her father's reign, and therefore cannot have been more than 10; and we have reason to believe, from internal evidence in the tomb, that Tut-ankh-Amen himself was little more than a boy.

Clearly in the first years of this reign of children there must have been a power behind the throne, and we can be tolerably certain who this power was. In all countries, but more particularly in those of the Orient, it is a wise rule, in cases of doubtful or weak succession, to pay particular attention to the movements of the most powerful Court official. In the Tell el Amarna Court this was a certain Ay, Chief Priest, Court Chamberlain and practically Court everything else. He himself was a close personal friend of Akh-en-Aten's, and his wife Tyi was nurse to the royal wife Nefertiti, so we may be quite sure there was nothing that went on in the palace that they did not know. Now, looking ahead a little, we find that it was this same Ay who secured the throne himself after Tut-ankh-Amen's death. We also know, from the occurrence of his cartouche in the sepulchral chamber of the newly found tomb, that he made himself responsible for the burial ceremonies of Tut-ankh-Amen, even if he himself did not actually construct the tomb.

It is quite unprecedented in The Valley to find the name of a succeeding king upon the walls of his predecessor's sepulchral monument. The fact that it was so in this case seems to imply a special relationship between the two, and we shall probably be safe in assuming that it was Ay who was largely responsible for establishing the boy king upon the throne. Quite possibly he had designs upon it himself already, but, not feeling secure enough for the moment, preferred to bide his time and utilize the opportunities he would undoubtedly have, as minister to a young and inexperienced sovereign, to consolidate his position. It is interesting to speculate, and when we remember that Ay in his turn was supplanted by another of the leading officials of Akh-en-Aten's reign, the General Hor-em-heb, and that neither of them had any real claim to the throne, we can be reasonably sure that in this little byway of history, from 1375 to 1350 BCE, there was a well set stage for dramatic happenings.

However, as self-respecting historians, let us put aside the tempting 'might have beens' and 'probablys' and come back to the cold hard facts of history. What do we really know about this Tut-ankh-Amen with whom we have become so surprisingly familiar? Remarkably little, when you come right down to it. In the present state of our knowledge, we might say with truth that the one outstanding feature of his life was the fact that he died and was buried. Of the man himself – if indeed he ever arrived at the dignity of manhood – and of his personal character we know nothing. Of the events of his short reign we can glean a little, a very little, from the monuments. We know, for instance, that at some time during his reign he abandoned the heretic capital of his father-in-law, and removed the court back to Thebes.

That he began as an Aten worshipper, and reverted to the old religion, is evident from his name Tut-ankh-Aten, changed to Tut-ankh-Amen, and from the fact that he made some slight additions and restorations to the temples of the old gods at Thebes. There is also a stela in the Cairo Museum, which originally stood in one of the Karnak temples, in which he refers to these temple restorations in somewhat grandiloquent language. 'I found,' he says, 'the temples fallen into ruin, with their holy places overthrown, and their courts overgrown with weeds. I reconstructed their sanctuaries, I re-endowed the temples, and made them gifts of all precious things. I cast statues of the gods in gold and electrum, decorated with lapis lazuli and all fine stones.' We do not know at what particular period in his reign this change of religion took place, nor whether it was due to personal feeling or was dictated to him for political reasons. We know from the tomb of one of his officials that certain tribes in Syria and in the Sudan were subject to him and brought him tribute, and on many of the objects in his own tomb we see him trampling with great gusto on prisoners of war, and shooting them by hundreds from his chariot, but we must by no means take for granted that he ever in actual fact took the field himself. Egyptian monarchs were singularly tolerant of such polite fictions.

That pretty well exhausts the facts of his life as we know them from the monuments. From his tomb, so far, there is singularly little to add. We are getting to know to the last detail what he had, but of what he was and what he did we are still sadly to seek. There is nothing yet to give us the exact length of his reign. Six years we knew before as a minimum: much more than that it cannot have been. We can only hope that the inner chambers will be more communicative. His body, if, as we hope and expect, it still lies beneath the shrines within the sepulchre, will at least tell us his age at death, and may possibly give us some clue to the circumstances.

Just a word as to his wife, Ankh-es-en-pa-Aten as she was known originally, and Ankh-es-en-Amen after the reversion to Thebes. As the one through whom the king inherited, she was a person of considerable importance, and he makes due acknowledgment of the fact by the frequency with which her name and person appear upon the tomb furniture. A graceful figure she was, too, unless her portraits do her more than justice, and her friendly relations with her husband are insisted on in true Tell el Amarna style. There are two particularly charming representations of her. In one, on the back of the throne, she anoints her husband with perfume: in the other, she accompanies him on a shooting expedition, and is represented crouching at his feet, handing him an arrow with one hand, and with the other pointing out to him a particularly fat duck which she fears may escape his notice. Charming pictures these, and pathetic, too, when we remember that at 17 or 18 years of age the wife was left a widow. Well, perhaps. On the other hand, if we know our Orient, perhaps not, for to this story there is a sequel, provided for us by a number of tablets, found some years ago in the ruins of Boghozkeui, and only recently deciphered. An interesting little tale of intrigue it outlines, and in a few words we get a clearer picture of Queen Ankh-es-en-Amen than Tut-ankh-Amen was able to achieve for himself in his entire equipment of funeral furniture.

She was, it seems, a lady of some force of character. The idea of retiring into the background in favour of a new queen did not appeal to her, and immediately upon the death of her husband she began to scheme. She had, we may presume, at least two months' grace, the time that must elapse between Tut-ankh-Amen's death and burial, for until the last king was buried it was hardly likely that the new one would take over the reins. Now, in the past two or three reigns there had been constant intermarriages between the royal houses of Egypt and Asia. One of Ankh-es-en-Amen's sisters had been sent in marriage to a foreign court, and many Egyptologists think that her own mother was an Asiatic princess. It was not surprising, then, that in this crisis she should look abroad for help, and we find her writing a letter to the King of the Hittites in the following terms: 'My husband is dead and I am told that you have grown-up sons. Send me one of them, and I will make him my husband, and he shall be king over Egypt.'

It was a shrewd move on her part, for there was no real heir to the throne in Egypt, and the swift dispatch of a Hittite prince, with a reasonable force to back him up, would probably have brought off a very successful coup. Promptitude, however, was the one essential, and here the queen was reckoning without the Hittite king. Hurry in any matter was well outside his calculations. It would never do to be rushed into a scheme of this sort without due deliberation, and how did he know that the letter was not a trap? So he summoned his counsellors and the matter was talked over at length. Eventually it was decided to send a messenger to Egypt to investigate the truth of the story. 'Where,' he writes in his reply – and you can see him patting himself on the back for his shrewdness – 'is the son of the late king, and what has become of him?'

Now, it took some 14 days for a messenger to go from one country to the other, so the poor queen's feelings can be imagined, when, after a month's waiting, she received, in answer to her request, not a prince and a husband, but a dilatory futile letter. In despair she writes again: 'Why should I deceive you? I have no son, and my husband is dead. Send me a son of yours and I will make him king.' The Hittite king now decides to accede to her request and to send a son, but it is evidently too late. The time had gone by. The document breaks off here, and it is left to our imagination to fill in the rest of the story.

Did the Hittite prince ever start for Egypt, and how far did he get? Did Ay, the new king, get wind of Ankh-es-en-Amen's schemings and take effectual steps to bring them to naught? We shall never know. In any case, the queen disappears from the scene and we hear of her no more. It is a fascinating little tale. Had the plot succeeded there would never have been a Rameses the Great.

RAMESES THE GREAT

1303–1213 BCE

The central figure of Egyptian history has always been, probably always will be, Rameses II. He holds this place partly by right, partly by accident. He was born to greatness; he achieved greatness; and he had borrowed greatness thrust upon him. It was his singular destiny not only to be made a posthumous usurper of glory, but to be forgotten by his own name and remembered in a variety of aliases. As Sesoosis, as Osymandias, as Sesostris, he became credited in course of time with all the deeds of all the heroes of the new Empire, beginning with Tuthmosis III, who preceded him by 300 years, and ending with Sheshonk, the captor of Jerusalem, who lived four centuries after him. Modern science, however, has repaired this injustice; and, while disclosing the long-lost names of a brilliant succession of sovereigns, has enabled us to ascribe to each the honours which are his due. We know now that some of these were greater conquerors than Rameses II. We suspect that some were better rulers. Yet the popular hero keeps his ground. What he has lost by interpretation on the one hand, he has gained by interpretation on the other; and the beau sabreur of the Third Sallier Papyrus remains to this day the representative pharaoh of a line of monarchs whose history covers a space of 50 centuries, and whose frontiers reached at one time from Mesopotamia to the ends of the Soudan.

The interest that one takes in Rameses II begins at Memphis, and goes on increasing all the way up the river. It is a purely living, a purely personal interest; such as one feels in Athens for Pericles, or in Florence for Lorenzo the Magnificent. Other pharaohs but languidly affect the imagination. Tuthmosis and Amenhotep are to us as Darius or Artaxerxes – shadows that come and go in the distance. But with the second Rameses we are on terms of respectful intimacy. We seem to know the man – to feel his presence – to hear his name in the air. His features are as familiar to us as those of Henry VIII or Louis XIV. His cartouches meet us at every turn. Even to those who do not read the hieroglyphic character, those well-known signs convey, by sheer force of association, the name and style of Rameses, beloved of Amen. [...]

Youth of Rameses the Great

Rameses II was the son of Seti I, the second pharaoh of the 19th Dynasty, and of a certain Princess Tuaa, described on the monuments as 'royal wife, royal mother and heiress and sharer of the throne'. She is supposed to have been of the ancient royal line of the preceding dynasty, and so to have had, perhaps, a better right than her husband to the double crown of Egypt. Through her, at all events, Rameses II seems to have been in some sense born a king, equal in rank, if not in power, with his father; his rights, moreover, were fully recognized by Seti, who accorded him royal and divine honours from the hour of his birth, or, in the language of the Egyptian historians, while he was 'yet in the egg'. The great dedicatory inscription of the Temple of Osiris at Abydos relates how his father took the royal child in his arms, when he was yet little more than an infant, showed him to the people as their king, and caused him to be invested by the great officers of the palace with the double crown of the two lands. The same inscription states that he was a general from his birth, and that as a nursling he 'commanded the bodyguard and the brigade of chariot-fighters'; but these titles must of course have been purely honorary.

At 12 years of age, he was formally associated with his father upon the throne, and by the gradual retirement of Seti I from the cares of active government, the co-royalty of Rameses became, in the course of the next 10 or 15 years, an undivided responsibility. He was probably about 30 when his father died; and it is from this time that the years of his reign are dated. In other words, Rameses II, in his official records, counts only from the period of his sole reign, and the year of the death of Seti is the 'year one' of the monumental inscriptions of his son and successor. In the second, fourth and fifth years of his monarchy, he personally conducted campaigns in Syria, more than one of the victories then achieved being commemorated on the rock-cut tablets of Nahr-el-Kelb near Beirut; and that he was by this time recognized as a mighty warrior is shown by the stela of Dakkeh, which dates from the 'third year', and celebrates him as terrible in battle – 'the bull powerful against Ethiopia, the griffin furious against the negroes, whose grip has put the mountaineers to flight'. The events of the campaign of his 'fifth year' (undertaken in order to reduce to obedience the revolted tribes of Syria and Mesopotamia) are immortalized in the poem of Pentaur. It was on this occasion that he fought his famous single-handed fight, against overwhelming odds, in the sight of both armies under the walls of Kadesh. Three years later, he carried fire and sword into the land of Canaan, and in his 11th year, according to inscriptions yet extant upon the ruined pylons of the Ramesseum at Thebes, he took, among other strong places on sea and shore, the fortresses of Asealon and Jerusalem.

Treaty with the Kheta

The next important record transports us to the 21st year of his reign. Ten years have now gone by since the fall of Jerusalem, during which time a fluctuating frontier warfare has probably been carried on, to the exhaustion of both armies. Khetasira, Prince of Kheta, sues for peace. An elaborate treaty is thereupon framed, whereby the said prince and 'Rameses, Chief of Rulers, who fixed his frontiers where he pleases', pledge themselves to a strict offensive and defensive alliance, and to the maintenance of goodwill and brotherhood forever. This treaty, we are told, was engraved for the Khetan prince 'upon a tablet of silver adorned with the likeness of the figure of Sutekh, the Great Ruler of Heaven'; while for Rameses Mer-Amen it was graven on a wall adjoining the Great Hall at Karnak, where it remains to this day.

According to the last clause of this curious document, the contracting parties enter also into an agreement to deliver up to each other the political fugitives of both countries; providing at the same time for the personal safety of the offenders. 'Whosoever shall be so delivered up,' says the treaty, 'himself, his wives, his children, let him not be smitten to death; moreover, let him not suffer in his eyes, in his mouth, in his feet; moreover, let not any crime be set up against him.' This is the earliest instance of an extradition treaty upon record; and it is chiefly remarkable as an illustration of the clemency with which international law was at that time administered.

Finally, the convention between the sovereigns is placed under the joint protection of the gods of both countries: 'Sutekh of Kheta, Amen of Egypr, and all the thousand gods, the gods male and female, the gods of the hills, of the rivers, of the great sea, of the winds and the clouds, of the land of Kheta and of the land of Egypt.'

His Wives

The peace now concluded would seem to have remained unbroken throughout the rest of the long reign of Rameses II. We hear, at all events, of no more Avars; and we find the king married presently to a Khetan princess, who in deference to the gods of her adopted country takes the official name of Ma-at-iri-neferu-Ra, or 'Contemplating the Beauties of Ra'. The names of two other queens – Nefer-t-ari and Ast-nefert – are also found upon the monuments.

These three were probably the only legitimate wives of Rameses II, though he must also have been the lord of an extensive harem. His family, at all events, as recorded upon the walls of the Temple at Wady Sabooah, amounted to no less than 170 children, of whom 111 were princes. This may have been a small family for a great king 3,000 years ago. It was but the other day, comparatively speaking, that Lepsius saw and talked with old Hasan, Kashef of Derr – the same petty ruler who gave so much trouble to [Giovanni] Belzoni, [Johann Ludwig] Burckhardt and other early travellers – and he, like a patriarch of old, had in his day been the husband of 64 wives, and the father of something like 200 children.

His Great Works

For 46 years after the making of the Khetan treaty, Rameses the Great lived at peace with his neighbours and tributaries. The evening of his life was long and splendid. It became his passion and his pride to found new cities, to raise dikes, to dig canals, to build fortresses, to multiple statues, obelisks and inscriptions, and to erect the most gorgeous and costly temples in which man ever worshipped. To the monuments founded by his predecessors he made additions so magnificent that they dwarfed the designs they were intended to complete. He caused artesian wells to be pierced in the stony bed of the desert. He carried on the canal begun by his father, and opened a waterway between the Mediterranean and the Red Sea. No enterprise was too difficult, no project too vast, for his ambition. 'As a child,' says the stela of Dakkeh, 'he superintended the public works, and his hands laid their foundations.' As a man, he became the supreme Builder. Of his gigantic structures, only certain colossal fragments have survived the ravages of time; yet those fragments are the wonder of the world.

The Captivity

To estimate the cost at which these things were done is now impossible. Every temple, every palace, represented a hecatomb of human lives. Slaves from Ethiopia, captives taken in war, Syrian immigrants settled in the Delta, were alike pressed into the service of the state. We know how the Hebrews suffered, and to what an extremity of despair they were reduced by the tasks imposed upon them. Yet even the Hebrews were less cruelly used than some who were kidnapped beyond the frontiers. Torn from their homes without hope of return, driven in herds to the mines, the quarries and the brickfields, these hapless victims were so dealt with that not even the chances of desertion were open to them. The Blacks from the south were systematically drafted to the north; the Asiatic captives were transported to Ethiopia. Those who laboured underground were goaded on without rest or respite, till they fell down in the mines and died.

Pithom and Rameses

That Rameses II was the pharaoh of the captivity, and that Meneptah, his son and successor, was the pharaoh of the Exodus, are now among the accepted presumptions of Egyptological science. The Bible and the monuments confirm each other upon these points, while both are again corroborated by the results of recent geographical and philological research. The 'treasure-cities Pithom and Raamses' which the Israelites built for pharaoh with bricks of their own making, are the Pa-Tum and Pa-Rameses of the inscriptions, and both have recently been identified by M. Naville in the course of his excavations conducted in 1883 and 1886 for the Egypt Exploration Fund.

The discovery of Pithom, the ancient Biblical 'treasure city' of the first chapter of Exodus, has probably attracted more public attention, and been more widely discussed by European savants, than any archaeological event since the discovery of Nineveh. It was in February 1883 that M. Naville opened the well-known mound of Tel-el-Maskhutah, on the south bank of the new sweet-water canal in the Wady Tumilat, and there discovered the foundations and other remains of a fortified city of the kind known in Egyptian as a Bekhen, or store-fort. This Bekhen, which was surrounded by a wall nine metres (30 feet) in thickness, proved to be about 12 acres in extent. In one corner of the enclosure were found the ruins of a temple built by Rameses II. The rest of the area consisted of a labyrinth of subterraneous rectangular cellars, or store chambers, constructed of sun-dried bricks of large size, and divided by walls varying from 2½ to 3 metres (8 to 10 feet) in thickness.

In the ruins of the temple were discovered several statues more or less broken, a colossal hawk inscribed with the royal ovals of Rameses II, and other works of art dating from the reigns of Osorkon II, Nectanebo and Ptolemy Philadelphus. The hieroglyphic legends engraved upon the statues established the true value of the discovery by giving both the name of the city and the name of the district in which the city was situate; the first being Pa-Tum (Pithom), the 'Abode of Tum', and the second being Thuku-t (Succoth); so identifying 'Ta-Tum, in the district of Thuku-t', with Pithom, the treasure city built by the forced labour of the Hebrews, and Succoth, the region in which they made their first halt on going forth from the land of bondage. Even the bricks with which the great wall and the walls of the store-chambers are built bear eloquent testimony to the toil of the suffering colonists, and confirm in its minutest details the record of their oppression, some being duly kneaded with straw; others, when the straw was no longer forthcoming, being mixed with the leafage of a reed common to the marshlands of the Delta; and the remainder, when even this substitute ran short, being literally 'bricks without straw', moulded of mere clay crudely dried in the sun.

The researches of M. Naville further showed that the Temple to Tum, founded by Rameses II, was restored, or rebuilt, by Osorkon II of the 22nd dynasty; while at a still higher level were discovered the remains of a Roman fortress. That Pithom was still an important place in the time of the Ptolemies is proved by a large and historically important tablet found by M. Naville in one of the store chambers, where it had been thrown in with other sculptures and rubbish of various kinds. This table records repairs done to the canal, an expedition to Ethiopia, and the foundation of the city of Arsinoe. Not less important from a geographical point of view was the finding of a Roman milestone which identifies Pithom with Hero (Heroopolis), where, according to the Septuagint, Joseph went forth to meet Jacob. This milestone gives nine Roman miles as the distance from Heroopolis to Clysma. A very curious manuscript lately discovered by Signore Gamurrini in the library of Arezzo, shows that even so late as the fourth century of the Christian era, this ancient walled enclosure – the camp, or 'Ero Castra', of the

Roman period, the 'Pithom' of the Bible – was still known to pious pilgrims as 'the Pithom built by the Children of Israel'; that the adjoining town, external to the camp, at that time established within the old Pithom boundaries, was known as 'Heroopolis'; and that the town of Rameses was distant from Pithom about 20 Roman miles.

As regards Pa-Rameses, the other 'treasure city' of Exodus, it is conjecturally, but not positively, identified by M. Naville with the mound of Saft-el-Henneh, the scene of his explorations in 1886. That Saft-el-Henneh was identical with 'Kes', or Goshen, the capital town of the 'Land of Goshen', has been unequivocally demonstrated by the discoverer; and that it was also known, in the time of Rameses II as 'Pa-Rameses' is shown to be highly probable. There are remains of a temple built of black basalt, with pillars, fragments of statues, and the like, all inscribed with the cartouches of Rameses II; and the distance from Pithom is just 20 Roman miles.

It was from Pa-Rameses that Rameses II set out with his army to attack the confederate princes of Asia Minor then lying in ambush near Kadesh; and it was hither that he returned in triumph after the great victory. A contemporary letter written by one Panbesa, a scribe, narrates in glowing terms the beauty and abundance of the royal city, and tells how the damsels stood at their doors in holiday apparel, with nosegays in their hands and sweet oil upon their locks, 'on the day of the arrival of the War-God of the world'. This letter is in the British Museum.

Kauiser and Keniamon

Other letters written during the reign of Rameses II have by some been supposed to make direct mention of the Israelites.

'I have obeyed the orders of my master,' writes the scribe Kauiser to his superior Bak-en-Ptah, 'being bidden to serve out the rations to the soldiers, and also to the Aperiu [Hebrews?] who quarry stone for the palace of King Kameses Mer-Amen.' A similar document written by a scribe named Keniamon, and couched in almost the same words, shows these Aperiu on another occasion to have been quarrying for a building on the southern side of Memphis; in which case Turra would be the scene of their labours.

These invaluable letters, written on papyrus in the hieratic character, are in good preservation. They were found in the ruins of Memphis, and now form part of the treasures of the Museum of Leyden. They bring home to us with startling nearness the events and actors of the Bible narrative. We see the toilers at their task, and the overseers reporting them to the directors of public works. They extract from the quarry those huge blocks which are our wonder to this day. Harnessed to rude sledges, they drag them to the riverside and embark them for transport to the opposite bank.

Some are so large and so heavy that it takes a month to get them down from the mountain to the landing-place. Other labourers are elsewhere making bricks, digging canals, helping to build the great wall which reached from Pelusium to Heliopolis, and strengthening the defences not only of Pithom and Rameses, but of all the cities and forts between the Red Sea and the Mediterranean. Their lot is hard; but not harder than the lot of other workmen. They are well fed. They intermarry. They increase and multiply. The season of their great oppression is not yet come. They make bricks, it is true, and those who are so employed must supply a certain number daily; but the straw is not yet withheld, and the task, though perhaps excessive, is not impossible. For we are here in the reign of Rameses II, and the time when Meneptah shall succeed him is yet far distant. It is not till the king dies that the children of Israel sigh, 'by reason of the bondage'. [...]

An unusually long reign, the last 46 years of which would seem to have been spent in peace and outward prosperity, enabled Rameses II to indulge his ruling passion without interruption. To draw up anything like an exhaustive catalogue of his known architectural works would be equivalent to writing an itinerary of Egypt and Ethiopia under the 19th dynasty. His designs were as vast as his means appear to have been unlimited. From the Delta to Gebel Barkal, he filled the land with monuments dedicated to his own glory and the worship of the gods. Upon Thebes, Abydos and Tanis, he lavished structures of surpassing magnificence. In Nubia, at the places now known as Gerf Hossayn, Wady Sabooah, Derr and Abou Simbel, he was the author of temples and the founder of cities. These cities, which would probably be better described as provincial towns, have disappeared; and but for the mention of them in various inscriptions we should not even know that they had existed. Who shall say how many more have vanished, leaving neither trace nor record? A dozen cities of Rameses may yet lie buried under some of those nameless mounds which follow each other in such quick succession along the banks of the Nile in Middle and Lower Egypt. Only yesterday, as it were, the remains of what would seem to have been a magnificent structure decorated in a style absolutely unique, were accidentally discovered under the mounds of Tel-el-Yahoodeh, about 12 miles to the north-east of Cairo.

There are probably 50 such mounds, none of which have been opened, in the Delta alone; and it is no exaggeration to say that there must be some hundreds between the Mediterranean and the First Cataract.

An inscription found of late years at Abydos shows that Rameses II reigned over his great kingdom for the space of 67 years. 'It is thou,' says Rameses IV, addressing himself to Osiris, 'it is thou who wilt rejoice me with such length of reign as Rameses II, the great God, in his 67 years. It is thou who wilt give me the long duration of this great reign.'

If only we knew at what age Rameses II succeeded to the throne, we should, by help of this inscription, know also the age at which he died. No such record has, however, transpired, but a careful comparison of the length of time occupied by the various events of his reign, and above all the evidence of age afforded by the mummy of this great pharaoh, discovered in 1886, show that he must have been very nearly, if not quite, a centenarian.

'Thou madest designs while yet in the age of infancy,' says the stela of Dakkeh. 'Thou wert a boy wearing the sidelock, and no monument was erected, and no order was given without thee. Thou wert a youth aged 10 years, and all the public works were in thy hands, laying their foundations.' These lines, translated literally, cannot, however, be said to prove much. They certainly contain nothing to show that this youth of 10 was, at the time alluded to, sole king and ruler of Egypt. That he was titular king, in the hereditary sense, from his birth and during the lifetime of his father, is now quite certain. That he should, as a boy, have designed public buildings and superintended their construction is extremely probable. The office was one which might well have been discharged by a crown-prince who delighted in architecture, and made it his peculiar study. It was, in fact, a very noble office – an office which from the earliest days of the ancient Empire had constantly been confided to princes of the royal blood; but it carried with it no evidence of sovereignty. The presumption, therefore, would be that the stela of Dakkeh (dating as it does from the third year of the sole reign of Rameses II) alludes to a time long since past, when the king as a boy held office under his father.

The same inscription, as we have already seen, makes reference to the victorious campaign in the South. Rameses is addressed as 'the bull powerful against Ethiopia; the griffin furious against the negroes'; and that the events hereby alluded to must have taken place during the first three years of his sole reign is proved by the date of the tablet. The great dedicatory inscription of Abydos shows, in fact, that Rameses II was prosecuting a campaign in Ethiopia at the time when he received intelligence of the death of his father, and that he came down the Nile, northwards, in order, probably, to be crowned at Thebes.

Now the famous sculptures of the commemorative chapel at Bayt-el-Welly relate expressly to the events of this expedition; and as they are executed in that refined and delicate style which especially characterises the bas-relief work of Gournah, of Abydos, of all those buildings which were either erected by Seti I, or begun by Seti and finished during the early years of Rameses II, I venture to think we may regard them as contemporary, or very nearly contemporary, with the scenes they represent. In any case, it is reasonable to conclude that the artists employed on the work would know something about the events and persons delineated, and that they would be guilty of no glaring inaccuracies.

All doubt as to whether the dates refer to the associated reigns of Seti and Rameses, or to the sole reign of the latter, vanish, however, when in these same sculptures we find the conqueror accompanied by his son, Prince Amenherkhopeshef, who is of an age not only to bear his part in the field, but afterwards to conduct an important ceremony of state on the occasion of the submission and tribute-offering of the Ethiopian commander. Such is the unmistakable evidence of the bas-reliefs at Bayt-el-Welly, as those who cannot go to Bayt-el-Welly may see and judge for themselves by means of the admirable casts of these great tableaux which line the walls of the Second Egyptian Room at the British Museum. To explain away Prince Amenherkhopeshef would be difficult. We are accustomed to a certain amount of courtly exaggeration on the part of these who record with pen or pencil the great deeds of the pharaohs. We expect to see the king always young, always beautiful, always victorious. It seems only right and natural that he should be never less than six metres (20 feet), and sometimes more than 18 metres (60 feet) in height. But that any flatterer should go so far as to credit a lad of 13 with a son at least as old as himself is surely quite incredible.

The Birth of Moses

Lastly, there is the evidence of the Bible.

Joseph being dead and the Israelites established in Egypt, there comes to the throne a pharaoh who takes alarm at the increase of this alien race, and who seeks to check their too rapid multiplication. He not only oppresses the foreigners, but ordains that every male infant born to them in their bondage shall be cast into the river. This pharaoh is now universally believed to be Rameses II. Then comes the old, sweet, familiar Bible story that we know so well. Moses is born, cast adrift in the ark of bulrushes, and rescued by the king's daughter. He becomes to her 'as a son'. Although no dates are given, it is clear that the new pharaoh has not been long upon the throne when these events happen. It is equally clear that he is no mere youth. He is old in the uses of statecraft; and he is the father of a princess of whom it is difficult to suppose that she was herself an infant.

On the whole, then, we can but conclude that Rameses II, though born a king, was not merely grown to manhood, but wedded, and the father of children already past the period of infancy, before he succeeded to the sole exercise of sovereign power. This is, at all events, the view taken by Professor [Gaston] Maspero [French Egyptologist], who expressly says, in the latest edition of his *Histoire Ancienne*, 'that Rameses II, when he received news of the death of his father, was then in the prime of life, and surrounded by a large family, some of whom were of an age to fight under his own command'.

Brugsch places the birth of Moses in the sixth year of the reign of Rameses II. This may very well be. The four-score years that elapsed between that time and the time of the Exodus correspond with sufficient exactness to the chronological data furnished by the monuments. Moses would thus see out the 61 remaining years of the king's long life, and release the Israelites from bondage towards the close of the reign of Menepthah, who sat for about 20 years on the throne of his fathers. The correspondence of dates this time leaves nothing to be desired.

The Sesostris of Diodorus Siculus went blind, and died by his own hand; which act, says the historian, as it conformed to the glory of his life, was greatly admired by his people. We are here evidently in the region of pure fable. Suicide was by no means an Egyptian, but a classical virtue. Just as the Greeks hated age, the Egyptians reverenced it; and it may be doubted whether a people who seem always to have passionately desired length of days, would have seen anything to admire in a wilful shortening of that most precious gift of the gods. With the one exception of Cleopatra – the death of Nitocris the rosy-cheeked being also of Greek, and therefore questionable, origin – no Egyptian sovereign is known to have committed suicide; and even Cleopatra, who was half Greek by birth, must have been influenced to the act by Greek and Roman example. Dismissing, then, altogether this legend of his blindness and self-slaughter, it must be admitted that of the death of Rameses II we know nothing certain [see opposite].

Character of Rameses the Great

Such are, very briefly, the leading facts of the history of this famous pharaoh. Exhaustively treated, they would expand into a volume. Even then, however, one would ask, and ask in vain, what manner of man he was. Every attempt to evolve his personal character from these scanty data, is in fact a mere exercise of fancy. That he was personally valiant may be gathered, with due reservation, from the poem of Pentaur; and that he was not unmerciful is shown in the extradition clause of the Khetan treaty. His pride was evidently boundless. Every temple which he erected was a monument to his own glory; every colossus was a trophy; every inscription a paean of self-praise. At Abou Simbel, at Derr, at Gerf Hossayn, he seated his own image in the sanctuary among the images of the gods. There are even instances in which he is depicted under the twofold aspect of royalty and divinity – Rameses the Pharaoh burning incense before Rameses the Deity.

For the rest, it is safe to conclude that he was neither better nor worse than the general run of Oriental despots – that he was ruthless in war, prodigal in peace, rapacious of booty and unsparing in the exercise of almost boundless power. Such pride and such despotism were, however, in strict accordance with immemorial precedent, and with the temper of the age in which he lived. The Egyptians would seem, beyond all doubt, to have believed that their king was always, in some sense, divine. They wrote hymns and offered up prayers to him, and regarded him as the living representative of Deity. His princes and ministers habitually addressed him in the language of worship. Even his wives, who ought to have known better, are represented in the performance of acts of religious adoration before him. What wonder, then, if the man so deified believed himself a god?

THE DEATH OF RAMSES II

c. 1285 BCE

Ramses II enjoyed a long reign. The monuments expressly testify to a reign of 67 years' duration, of which, apparently, more than half should be reckoned to his rule conjointly with his father. The jubilee celebration of his 30th year as (sole?)

pharaoh gave occasion for great festivities throughout the country, of which the inscriptions in Silsilis, El-Kab, Biggeh, Sehel and even on several scarabs, make frequent mention. The prince and high priest of Memphis, Khamuas, journeyed through the chief cities of the country in this connection, that he might have the great and joyful festival in honour of his father prepared in a worthy fashion by the different governors. The anniversary of the festival was calculated according to a fixed cycle, and apparently fell when the lunar and solar years coincided at short intervals of three or four years. It was observed as a solemn feast.

Great in the field, active in works of peace, Ramses appears to have also tasted heaven's richest blessings in his family life. The outer surface of the front of the temple of Abydos reveals to us the portraits and the names, now only partially preserved, of 119 children (59 sons and 60 daughters), which besides the lawful consorts known to us, the favourite wife Isinefer, mother of Khamaus, the queens Nefert-ari, Meri-mut, and the daughter of the king of Kheta, implies a large number of inferior wives.

It is scarcely probable that the great Ramses departed this life leaving his earthly kingdom in a peaceful condition. Already in his old age a numerous progeny of sons and grandsons were disputing over their father's inheritance. The seed of periods of storm and unrest was laid. According to historical tradition these bearings were confirmed in the most striking manner by subsequent events.

The body of Pharaoh was consigned to its death chamber in the rocky valley of Biban-el-Moluk. In spite of the large number of his children, Seti's grateful son had left no offspring behind him who would have prepared a tomb for his father worthy of his deeds and of his name; a tomb which might, if only in some degree, have approached the dignity of Seti's noble funeral vaults. The tomb of Ramses is an insignificant, rather tasteless erection, seldom visited by travellers to the Nile Valley, who probably scarcely suspect that the great Sesostris of Greek story has found his last resting place in this modest place. This pharaoh might have repeated of himself at his death, as formerly in his struggle against the Kheta he said, 'I stood alone; none other was with me'.

THE PERIOD OF DECAY

19th–25th Dynasties: *c.* 1285–655 BCE

After the summit, the inevitable decline. The first of world powers under the Ramessides, Egypt again becomes degenerate, and, after some 500 years of reanimation, passes into the power of the priests, who in turn are supplanted by invading hosts, this time from Ethiopia. Then the Assyrian conquerors, taking their turn at world domination, invade Egypt along the route which Tuthmosis III and Ramses had followed of old in invading Assyria. Dismembered Egypt falls an easy prey to Esarhaddon. It revolts under Asshurbanapal again and again, and is as often reconquered. But a mixed population of Ethiopians and Assyrians again gives a certain measure of new vitality to the old body, and, the destruction of the Assyrian empire having rid the Egyptians of one of their enemies, they were presently able, under Psamthek I

(Psammetichus), to overthrow the Ethiopian 'usurpers', and establish once more a 'native' dynasty.

For about three-quarters of a century Egypt retained autonomy, and even struggled back to a shadow of its old-time power, illustrating once again the vitality that resides in an old stock. Then the final *coup* was given by Cambyses the Persian; and the last contest was over. Taken by themselves, these long-drawn-out struggles of a dying nation – extending over half a thousand years – are full of interest; but in the comparative scale they are unimportant. We have seen the great nation at its floodtide of power, and we need not dwell at very great length upon the time of its ebbing fortunes; for other nations, off to the east, have now taken the place of Egypt as the world-centres, and are beckoning attention.

MENEPTAH

c. 1285–1250 BCE

The disappearance of the old hero, Ramses II, did not produce many changes in the condition of affairs in Egypt. Meneptah from this time forth possessed as pharaoh the power which he had previously wielded as regent. He was now no longer young. Born somewhere about the beginning of the reign of Ramses II, he was now 60, possibly 70, years old; thus an old man succeeded another old man at a moment when Egypt must have needed more than ever an active and vigorous ruler. The danger to the country did not on this occasion rise from the side of Asia, for the relations of the pharaoh with his Kharu [Phoenician] subjects continued friendly, and, during a famine which desolated Syria, he sent wheat to his Hittite allies.

The nations, however, to the north and east, in Libya and in the Mediterranean islands, had for some time past been in a restless condition, which boded little good to the empires of the Old World. The Tamahu, some of them tributaries from the 12th, and others from the first years of the 18th dynasty, had always been troublesome, but never really dangerous neighbours. From time to time it was necessary to send light troops against them, who, sailing along the coast or following the caravan routes, would enter their territory, force them from their retreats, destroy their palm groves, carry off their cattle and place garrisons in the principal oases – even in Siwa itself. For more than a century, however, it would seem that more active and numerically stronger populations had entered upon the stage. A current of invasion, having its origin in the region of the Atlas, or possibly even in Europe, was setting toward the Nile, forcing before it the scattered tribes of the Sudan.

Who were these invaders? Were they connected with the race which had planted its dolmens over the plains of the Maghreb? Whatever the answer to this question may be, we know that a certain number of Berber tribes – the Libu and Mashauasha – who had occupied a middle position between Egypt and the people behind them, and who had only irregular communications with the Nile Valley, were now pushed to the front and forced to descend upon it.

The Libu might very well have gained the mastery over the other inhabitants of the desert at this period, who had become enfeebled by the frequent defeats which they had sustained at the hands of the Egyptians. At the moment when Meneptah ascended the throne, their king, Marajui, son of Did, ruled over immense territory.

A great kingdom had risen capable of disturbing Egyptian control. The danger was serious. The Hittites, separated from the Nile by the broad breadth of Phoenicia, could not directly threaten any of the Egyptian cities: but the Libyans, lords of the desert, were in contact with the Delta, and could in a few days fall upon any point in the valley they chose. Meneptah, therefore, hastened to resist the assault of the Westerners, as his father had formerly done that of the Easterners; and, strange as it may seem, he found among the troops of his new enemies some of the adversaries with whom the Egyptians had fought under the walls of Kadesh 60 years before. The Shardana, Lycians and others, having left the coasts of the Delta and the Phoenician seaports, owing to the vigilant watch kept by the Egyptians over their waters, had betaken themselves to the Libyan littoral, where they met with a favourable reception. Whether they had settled in some places, and formed there those colonies of which a Greek tradition of a more recent age speaks, we cannot say. They certainly followed the occupation of mercenary soldiers, and many of them hired out their services to the native princes, while others were enrolled among the troops of the king of Kheta or of the Pharaoh himself. Marajui brought with him Achaeans [Aqauasha], Shardana, Turisha, Shakalisha and Lycians in considerable numbers when he resolved to begin the strife.

This was not one of those conventional little wars which aimed at nothing further than the imposition of the payment of a tribute upon the conquered, or the conquest of one of their provinces. Marajui had nothing less in view than the transport of his whole people into the Nile Valley, to settle permanently there as the Hyksos had done before him. He set out on his march toward the end of the fourth year of the pharaoh's reign, or the beginning of his fifth, surrounded by the elite of his troops, 'the first choice from among all the soldiers and all the heroes in each land'. The announcement of their approach spread terror among the Egyptians. The peace which they enjoyed for 50 years had cooled their warlike ardour, and the machinery of their military organization had become somewhat rusty. The standing army had almost melted away; the regiments of archers and charioteers were no longer effective, and the neglected fortresses were not strong enough to protect the frontier.

As a consequence, the oases of Farafrah and of the Natron lakes fell into the hands of the enemy at the first attack, and the western provinces of the Delta became the possession of the invader before any steps could be taken for their defence. Memphis, which realized the imminent danger, broke out into open murmurs against the negligent rulers who had given no heed to the country's ramparts, and had allowed the garrisons of its fortresses to dwindle away. Fortunately, Syria remained quiet. The Kheta, in return for the aid afforded them by Meneptah during the famine, observed a friendly attitude, and the pharaoh was thus enabled to withdraw the troops from his Asiatic provinces. He could with perfect security take the necessary measures for insuring 'Heliopolis, the city of Tmu', against surprise, 'for arming Memphis, the citadel of Ptah-Tanen, and for restoring all things which were in disorder; he fortified Pa-Bailos (Bilbeis), in the neighbourhood of the

Shakana canal, on a branch of that of Heliopolis'; and he rapidly concentrated his forces behind these quickly organized lines. Marajui, however, continued to advance; in the early months of the summer he had crossed the Canopic branch of the Nile, and was now about to encamp not far from the town of Pa-Arshop (Proposis).

The pharaoh did not stir from his position. Marajui had, in the meantime, arranged his attack for the first of Epiphi, at the rising of the sun: it did not take place however until the third. 'The archers of his Majesty made havoc of the barbarians for six hours; they were cut off by the edge of the sword.'

When Marajui saw the carnage, 'his heart failed him; he betook himself to flight as fast as his feet could bear him to save his life, so successfully that his bow and arrows remained behind him in his precipitation, as well as everything else he had upon him'. His treasure, his arms, his wife, together with the cattle which he had brought with him for his use, became the prey of the conqueror; 'he tore out the feathers from his headdress, and took flight with such of those wretched Libyans as escaped the massacre, but the officers who had the care of his Majesty's team of horses followed in their steps' and put most of them to the sword. Marajui succeeded, however, in escaping in the darkness, and regained his own country without water or provisions, and almost without escort. The conquering troops returned to the camp laden with booty, and driving before them asses carrying, as bloody tokens of victory, quantities of hands and phalli cut from the dead bodies of the slain. The bodies of six generals and of 6,359 Libyan soldiers were found upon the field of battle, together with 222 Shakalisha, 724 Turisha and some hundreds of Shardana and Aqauasha [Achaeans];

several thousands of prisoners passed in procession before the pharaoh, and were distributed among such of his soldiers as had distinguished themselves.

Meneptah lived for some time after this memorable year, and the number of monuments which belong to this period shows that he reigned in peace. We can see that he carried out works in the same places as his father before him – at Tanis as well as Thebes, in Nubia as well as in the Delta. He worked the sandstone quarries for his building materials, and continued the custom of celebrating the feasts of the Inundation, at Silsilis. One at least of the steles which he set up on the occasion of these feasts is really a chapel, with its architraves and columns, and still excites the admiration of the traveller on account both of its form and of its picturesque appearance. The last years of his life were troubled by the intrigues of princes who aspired to the throne, and by the ambition of the ministers to whom he was obliged to delegate his authority. One of the latter, a man of Semite origin, named Ben-Azana, of Zor-bisana, who had assumed the appellation of his first patron Ramses-uparna-Ra, appears to have acted for him as regent. [Chronological reasons demand that we place the Exodus of the Hebrews from Egypt in the reign of this pharaoh.]

c. 1250–1235 BCE

Meneptah was succeeded, apparently, by one of his sons, called Seti, after his great-grandfather. Seti II had doubtless reached middle age at the time of his accession, but his portraits represent him, nevertheless, with the face and figure of a young man. The expression in these is gentle, refined, haughty and somewhat melancholy. It is the type of Seti I and Ramses II, but enfeebled and, as it were, saddened. An inscription of his second year attributes to him victories in Asia, but others of the same period indicate the existence of disturbances similar to those which had troubled the last years of his father. Seti died, it would seem, without having time to finish his tomb. We do not know whether he left any legitimate children, but two sovereigns succeeded him who were not directly connected with him, but were probably the grandsons of the Amenmes and the Siptah, whom we meet with among the children of Ramses.

The first of these was also called Amenmes, and he held sway for several years over the whole of Egypt, and over its foreign possessions. The second, who was named Siptah-Meneptah, ascended 'the throne of his father', thanks to the devotion of his minister, Bi, but in a greater degree to his marriage with a certain princess called Ta-user. He maintained himself in this position for at least six years, during which he made an expedition into Ethiopia, and received in audience at Thebes messengers from all foreign nations. He kept up so zealously the appearance of universal dominion that to judge from his inscriptions he must have been the equal of the most powerful of his predecessors at Thebes. Egypt, nevertheless, was proceeding at a quick pace toward its downfall. No sooner had this monarch disappeared than it began to break up.

As in the case of the Egyptians of the Greek period, we can see only through a fog what took place after the deaths of Meneptah and Seti II. We know only for certain that the chiefs of the nomes were in perpetual strife with each other, and that a foreign power was dominant in the country as in the time of Apophis. The days of the kingdom would have been numbered if a deliverer had not promptly made his appearance. The direct line of Ramses II was extinct, but his innumerable sons by innumerable concubines had left a posterity out of which some at least might have the requisite ability and zeal, if not to save the empire, at least to lengthen its duration, and once more give to Thebes days of glorious prosperity.

Egypt had set out some five centuries before this for the conquest of the world, and fortune had at first smiled upon her enterprise. Tuthmosis I, Tuthmosis III, and the several pharaohs bearing the name of Amenhotep, had marched with their armies from the upper waters of the Nile to the banks of the Euphrates, and no power had been able to withstand them. New nations, however, soon rose up to oppose her, and the Hittites in Asia and the Libyans of the Sudan together curbed her ambition. Neither the triumphs of Ramses II nor the victory of Meneptah had been able to restore her prestige, or the lands of which her rivals had robbed her beyond her ancient frontier. Now her own territory itself was threatened, and her own well-being was in question; she was compelled to consider, not how to rule other tribes, great or small, but how to keep her own possessions intact and independent; in short, her very existence was at stake.

FROM SETNEKHT TO RAMSES VIII AND MERI-AMEN MERI-TMU

c. 1230–1220 BCE

In the midst of the unsettled state of affairs a new dynasty arose under the leadership of Setnekht, a descendant of

Ramses II and governor of Thebes, who with some difficulty succeeded in quelling the rebels and subjugating the Syrian Arisu. 'He was like the gods Kheper and Sutekh in his energy, repairing the state of disorder of the whole country, killing the barbarians who were in the Delta, and purifying the great realm of Egypt. He was regent of the two countries on the throne of Tmu (the chief god of Heliopolis) devoting himself so well to the reorganization of what had been upset, that each one found a brother in every one of those from whom they had been so long separated; and re-establishing the temples and sacrifices so well that the traditional homage was rendered to the divine cycles.'

His son, Ramses III, who had been his co-regent, was the last of the great sovereigns of Egypt. His ambition during the 32 years of his reign was to follow in the steps of his namesake, Ramses the Great, in re-establishing the integrity of the empire abroad, and the prosperity of the country at home. But in spite of his father's successful warfare, the Syrian provinces were lost, and the frontiers encroached upon. On the east, the Bedouins attacked the fortified ports of the Delta, and the mining colonies of Sinai; on the west, the nations of Libya had invaded the Nile. Led by their chiefs Did (probably the son of Marajui, the contemporary of Meneptah), Mashaknu, Zamar, and Zautmar, the Tuhennu, the Tamahu, the Kahaka and their neighbours, left the sandy plains of the desert and conquered the Mareotic nome or district of the Saïd, at the mouth of the Nile, as far as the great arm of the river, in short all the western part of the Delta from the town of Karbria on the west to the outskirts of Memphis on the south.

c. 1220–1195 BCE

After repulsing the Bedouins, Ramses III turned his arms against the Libyans in the year five [of his reign] and completely conquered them. 'They were as terrified as goats attacked by a bull, that tramples with his foot, strikes with his horns, and makes the mountains tremble in his rush upon those that approach him.' The raids of the barbarians had exasperated the Egyptians, they gave no quarter; the Libyans fled in disorder, and some of their tribes, lingering in the Delta, were taken off and incorporated in the auxiliary army.

Scarcely was this trouble over when Ramses attacked Syria. Whilst Egypt was being ruined with civil wars, her old enemy, the Kheta, made her lose the rest of her empire. The nations of Asia Minor, continually pushed forward by the arrival of new races, had left their homes and penetrated into the distant regions of Syria and Egypt, attracted by reports of the riches of those countries; the Danau, the Tyrians, the Shakalisha, the Teucrians, who had succeeded the Dardani in the hegemony of the Trojan nations, and the Lycians and the Philistines joined the confederation. Those on the ships attacked the coasts, and the others crossed Syria and laid siege to the fortresses of the isthmus. With forces increased by the people they subjugated on the way, they penetrated Cilicia, forced the Kati and Kheta [Hittites] to follow them, picked up the contingent of Carchemish, Arathu, and Kadesh, and after staying some time in the environs of this town in the country of the Amorites, pushed straight on to Egypt.

But prompt as this action had been, Ramses was quite prepared to meet it. After having armed the mouth of the Nile and the places of the Delta, he started to oppose the enemy.

The encounter of the two armies and the two fleets took place in the year eight between Raphia and Pelusium under the walls of the castle, called the Tower of Ramses III.

'The mouth of the river was like a mighty wall of ships and vessels of every kind, filled from prow to poop with brave armed men. The infantry soldiers, the picked men of the army of Egypt, were there like roaring lions on the mountains; the charioteers, chosen from the swiftest of heroes, were led by every kind of experienced officers; the horses trembled in every limb and longed to trample nations under foot.

'As for me,' says Ramses, 'I was like Mentu, the warlike. I rose before them and they saw the work of my hands. I, the King Ramses, I have acted like a hero, who knows his valour and who stretches his arm over his people in the day of the struggle. Those who have violated frontiers will no longer cultivate the land, the time for their souls to pass into eternity is fixed. Those who were upon the shore were prostrated on the banks of the water, massacred as in a charnel house. I destroyed their vessels, and their goods were swallowed up by the waters.'

Prompt as this victory was, it did not conclude the wars of Ramses III. The Libyans, the old allies of the maritime races, would gladly have joined against Egypt in the year eight; and if they did not do so, it was doubtless because they had not had time to repair their losses. As soon as they were ready, they reappeared upon the scene, and in the year 11 the chief Kapur and his son Mashashal led the Mashauasha [Maxyes], the Sabita, the Kaikasha and other less important tribes, aided by the people of Tyre and Lycia, to the invasion of the Delta.

'For the second time their hearts told them that they would pass their lives in the nomes of Egypt, and that they would till the valleys and plains like their own land.'

But the attempt did not meet with success. 'Death came upon them in Egypt for they had run with their own feet to the furnace, which consumes corruption, to the fire of the bravery of the king which descends like Baal from the heights of the skies! All his members are imbued with victorious strength. With his right hand he seizes multitudes; his left extends like arrows over those before him to destroy them; his sword-blade is as sharp as that of his father, Mentu. Kapur, who had come to demand homage, blinded by fear, cast his arms from him and his troops did likewise: he raised a supplicating cry to Heaven and his son supported his arms. But lo, there stood by him the god, who knew his most secret thoughts.

'His Majesty fell upon their heads like a mountain of granite, he crushed them and watered the earth with their blood, their army and their soldiers were massacred they were taken, they were struck, their arms were tied, and like birds, imprisoned in the hold of a ship, they were in the power of His Majesty. The king was like Mentu, his victorious feet trampled on the heads of the enemy; the chiefs who opposed him were struck and held by the wrists.'

So the Libyans were careful henceforth not to disturb the peace of Egypt.

The victories of these 12 years healed the wounds of the preceding period. A voyage of the fleet along the coasts made the ancient Syrian provinces return to their allegiance and the allied nations of the Kheta [Hittites], of Carchemish and of the Kati, seeing the subjugation of the maritime people, soon followed suit. A second maritime expedition was directed against Arabia.

'I equipped vessels and galleys, armed with numerous sailors and workmen. The captains of the maritime auxiliary forces were there with overseers and managers to provision the ships with the countless products of Egypt. There were tens of thousands of every kind passing through the great sea of Kati. They arrived at the country of the Punt without any misadventure, and prepared to load the galleys and vessels with the products of Tonutir, with all the mysterious wonders of the country, and with considerable quantities of the perfumes of Punt. Their sons, the chiefs of the Tonutir came themselves to Egypt bringing tribute; they came safe and sound to the country of Coptos and landed in the country with their riches. They brought them in caravans of asses and men, and embarked them on the river at the port of Coptos.'

Other expeditions to the peninsula of Sinai restored the mining districts to the possession of pharaoh. So the Egyptian empire was reconstituted as it was in the preceding century in the time of Ramses II. The Shardana, Tyrians, Lycians and Trojans no longer landed *en masse* on the coasts of Africa.

The tide of Asiatic emigration now turned from the valley of the Nile, which had been its direction for the last one hundred and fifty years, towards the west, and inundated Italy, at the same time that the Phoenician colonists arrived there. The Tyrians took the land at the north of the mouth of the Tiber, the Shardana occupied the large island, which later was called Sardinia, and soon nothing remained of them in Egypt but the recollection of their raids and the legendary recital of their migrations from the shores of the Archipelago to the coasts of the western Mediterranean.

The Philistines were the only people of the confederation allowed to settle in Syria, and they took root along the southern coast between Joppa and the river of Egypt, in the districts hitherto peopled by the Canaanites, and there they primarily lived under the yoke of pharaoh. On the other frontier of the Delta, a Libyan tribe, called Mashauasha, likewise obtained a concession of territory, and the Mashauasha soldiers raised in Libya, from that portion of the tribe encamped on the bank of the Nile, formed a picked corps, the Ma, the leaders of which played a great part in the internal history of Egypt.

Herodotus relates that on the return of Sesostris (the name given by that historian to Ramses II) he was nearly killed by treachery. His brother, to whom he had intrusted the government during his absence, invited him and his children to a great feast; then he surrounded the house with wood and gave orders for it to be set alight. The king, learning this, immediately consulted with his wife, who was with him, and she advised him to take two of their six children and lay them on the burning wood, so that they could use their bodies as a bridge by which to pass over. Sesostris did this, and thus burned two of his children, and the others were saved with the parents.

The monuments have proved that the Sesostris of this legend of Herodotus is not Ramses II but his namesake, Ramses III. One of the brothers of the king mentioned in official documents under the pseudonym of Pen-ta-ur conspired against him with a large number of courtiers and ladies of the harem, with the object of killing pharaoh and putting his brother in his place. The plot was discovered, the conspirators cited before the tribunals and condemned, some to death and others to perpetual imprisonment.

The last years of the reign of Ramses III were passed in peace. He built at Thebes, in memory of his wars, the great palace of Medinet Habu; he enlarged Karnak and restored Luxor. The details of these pious works in the Delta have been preserved in a manuscript at the library of Heliopolis, the great Harris papyrus.

One sees by this document that Egypt not only regained her foreign empire, but her commercial and industrial activity. The prosperous days of Tuthmosis III and Ramses II seemed to have returned.

Nevertheless, the decadence was at hand. Egypt, exhausted by four centuries of perpetual warfare, became more and more incapable of serious effort. The population decimated by recruiting, inefficiently replaced by the incessant introduction of foreign elements, had lost the patience and enthusiasm of early times. The upper classes, accustomed to comfort and riches, now only cared for the civil professions, and thought lightly of what was military.

c. 1195–945 BCE

This was especially seen to be the case in the course of the 20th Dynasty. In the year 32, Ramses, tired of government, called his son Ramses IV to share it. He died two years later, and Ramses IV, after a reign of not more than three or four years, was followed by a distant relation who was Ramses V. Then came the four sons of Ramses III: Ramses VI, Ramses VII, Ramses VIII and Meri-Amen Meri-Tmu, who succeeded each other rapidly on the throne. These Ramses made some expeditions here and there, but never great wars. They passed their days in peace abroad, and peace at home, and if it be true that people are happy who have no history, Egypt was very happy under their rule.

No more constant struggles, no more distant marches to the mountains of Cilicia and to the plains of the Upper Nile. Syria continued to pay tribute for some time; for if Egypt, exhausted by victory, had scarcely the strength to enforce obedience, Syria was exhausted with defeat, and had no more strength to revolt. But there was this difference between the two countries, the one bordered on old age and never revived, while the other soon rallied from its reverses. The kingdom of Egypt died of exhaustion in full prosperity.

A WEAKENING STATE

Following Ramses II, the strength and power of Egypt appeared to weaken. Even before the end of the New Kingdom (nineteenth and twentieth dynasties), the state was characterised by short and unremarkable reigns.

This was then followed by the Third Intermediate Period, characterised in turn by invasions from the Libyans (twenty-second–twenty-third dynasties), the Nubians (twenty-fifth dynasty) and the Saites (twenty-sixth dynasty,) as well as by dynasties ruling concurrently from different parts of Egypt.

The Late Period was equally confusing, with dynasties 27 and 31 representing Persian invasions and again short reigns. These left the landscape ripe for Alexander the Great to enter and take over in 332 BCE, ending the thirty-first dynasty and the reign of Darius III.

We finish the chapter with Leigh North's (1906) description of the reign of Cleopatra VII and the downfall of Egypt under Roman occupation. This occupation brought to an end a period of unrest and instability, and what is often thought of as ancient Egyptian history.

EGYPT UNDER THE DOMINION OF MERCENARIES

The first sign of weakness in an empire seems to be scented. Egypt, decaying within, attracted speedy attention from the ambitious, who turned greedy eyes towards her hoarded wealth.

After the death of Ramses III, Egypt had ceased to exercise any influence upon Syria. A time of increasing inaction and stagnation had set in for Egypt, which at last led to Her-Hor, the Theban high priest, being placed upon the throne. How long Her-Hor ruled over Egypt, we know not, but we see that his son Piankhi and his grandson Painet'em I did not have royal power but only succeeded their father as high priests, and, as such, had uncontrolled power in Thebes and its environs.

c. 1000 BCE

Another ruling house of foreign (Libyan) origin arose at this time in Tanis. King Se-Amen (according to Manetho, Smendes) was its chief. His name is seen on the walls of a temple at Tanis, and upon an obelisk of Heliopolis. He also reigned over Thebes. In the 16th year of his reign he had the mummies of Ramses I, Seti I and Ramses II examined and put in another tomb. He evidently overthrew the dominion of the Theban high priests and forced them to recognize his power.

Thereupon Painet'em I added the title of provost (of Thebes) and commander-in-chief of the South and North, to his dignity of high priest, evidently taking, with the Tanitic kings, a position similar to that of Her-Hor with Ramses XII. Se-Amen's son, Pasebkhanu, seems to have gone a step farther; he overcame the party of the Theban priests, and gave the office of chief priest to one of his sons, who, like the grandson of Her-Hor, had, or took, the name of Painet'em II. A few short reigns, among which were those of the Amenemapt, also recognized in Thebes, seem to have followed that of Pasebkhanu I; and then Painet'em ascended the throne.

As 'high priest of Amen' at Thebes, and commander-in-chief, he invested his sons Masaherta and Men-kheper-Ra and then Painet'em (III), the son of the latter, with power; and Hor-Pasebkhanu II seems to have succeeded him in Tanis. The rule of the Tanites seems to have lasted about 120 years (from about 1060 to 943 BCE).

The kingdom, or at all events the part of the country governed by the priests of Amen, was certainly not well organized, for we have several accounts of embezzlements of the properties of the temple of Amen by the stewards and scribes, of the robbing of graves, etc. The constant necessity of removing the mummies of the early kings in the west part of Thebes from their magnificent tombs into secret caves, shows the weakness of the government.

Moreover, the great state trials were conducted on a very simple system. The question Guilty or Not Guilty was put to the statue of Amen, which gave its verdict by the mouth of an oracle.

One sees how perfectly realized is the idea of God's rule in practice. Doubtless the theory was at this time evolved in Thebes, later in Ethiopia, that the king was not only obliged to consult the oracle in all his acts, but also that he was appointed and could be deposed by the oracle.

The title of commander-in-chief borne by the Theban priests, seems to distinguish them as commanders of the soldiers taken from the Egyptian peasants in contradistinction to the mercenaries which, since Seti I, composed the chief part of the army. This force was partially furnished by those domiciled in the country, and partially by fresh supplies from Libya.

There was thus formed in the country an exclusive set similar to the Mamelukes, which held the fate of the country in its hand, and which bequeathed the martial profession from father to son.

These mercenaries were classed together under the name of Ma, derived from the contraction of the Libyan name Mashauasha. We soon see from the surnames of the warriors that the Libyans attained ascendance over them; and although the repeated attacks of the Libyans on Egypt were successfully repulsed, they were now in fact rulers of the country.

It is noteworthy that the corps of the Shardana, so often mentioned in more ancient times, is no more spoken of; it must have been absorbed in the mass of the other soldiers. But the name of Mashau has been retained, and in Coptic *matoei* is still a common name for soldier. One can easily understand that they had frequent opportunities of gaining wealth and land; and the kings granted them exemption from the land tax. At their head stood the 'dukes of the Ma', the grand duke of the Ma having the chief command. But many of such generalissimo may have had equal rank.

c. 945–800 BCE

Buiu-uaua, a Libyan, came to Egypt about Her-Hor's time. His family attained great importance; his fifth descendant, Naromath [Nimrod] was made 'grand duke of the Ma and Generalissimo' sometime under King Painet'em. After his death his son Shashanq succeeded him as commander of the army. An inscription at Abydos shows in what honour he was held, how the king looked after his father's grave, questioned the oracle at Thebes on his behalf, and prayed God for the victory of the general. It is conceivable that Shashanq ended by trying to gain the crown for himself, 943 (?) BCE.

By peaceable or violent means, he was the successor of Hor-Pasebkhanu II, the last Tanite, whose daughter Ka-Ra-maat he married to his son Uasarken, to give support to his dynasty. According to the ruling custom of the Tanites he made Auputh, another of his sons, high priest of Amen and commander-in-chief of all the military forces. By the inscriptions he seems to have been co-regent with his father.

Under the subsequent rulers it remained a custom for one of the king's sons to be endowed with the highest priestly power in Thebes, and also the priesthood of Ptah at Memphis was given to a branch of the royal family, and the other princes were priests as well as generals.

Moreover, Shashanq seems to have brought forward the descendants of the Ramses, for we find a Ramses prince occupying a high military post under him.

The history of the Hebrews shows that the pharaohs of the 21st dynasty were not in a condition to take part in Asiatic affairs. It was early in Solomon's reign that the king of the period, probably Pasebkhanu II, entered into relations with the Israelitish state, took Gaza for Solomon and gave it to his daughter as a dowry, and also gave refuge to political fugitives like Jeroboam and Hadad of Edom to leave a loophole for intervention.

The separation of Judah from Israel and the subsequent long civil war offered an opportunity to renew the expeditions into Syria. So Shashanq repaired to Syria in the fifth year of the reign of Rehoboam. The scanty remains of the annals of the Hebrew kings only report that he carried off the treasures of the temple and palace at Jerusalem; that is, the golden shields which Solomon had hung up there. The long list of the conquered places upon a wall of the temple of Karnak shows that Israelitish strongholds were likewise conquered and plundered.

The pharaoh hardly met with any great resistance anywhere. The inscription of his victory contains, according to the fashion of the time, only religious phrases instead of an account of the war. The expedition was nothing more than a predatory raid for booty; it had no political consequences, and it is quite a mistake to think it was undertaken in the interest of Jeroboam against the king of Judah.

The increase of the Egyptian power, consequent on the accession to the throne of the new dynasty, was of short duration. The successors of Shashanq I – Uasarken I, Takeleth I, Uasarken II, Shashanq II, Takeleth II – are only mentioned by name on the monuments. In Thebes they enlarged the entrance hall of the temple of Amen, begun by Shashanq I. We find further traces of them at Bubastis, the cradle of the dynasty, at Memphis, and elsewhere.

c. 800–735 BCE

The state gradually fell into complete decay under them. The chief generals of the Ma, perhaps partially belonging to the branch lines of the house, founded their own princedoms and shook off the Bubastites. Shashanq III, the successor of Takeleth II, is the last whose name we find in Thebes, where a long and very mutilated inscription of the 29th year of his reign speaks of gifts which he brought to Amen. Then it seems as if the southern portion of the country was taken by the Ethiopians.

Shashanq III reigned 52 years altogether. Then came his son Pamai, who reigned at least two years, and his grandson Shashanq IV, who reigned at least 37 years, until about 735 BCE. We only know of these kings by their being mentioned on several of the monuments to the honour of the Apis bulls which died in their reigns. So their supremacy must at least have been recognized for a time in Memphis. But their dominion must have been limited to the province of Busiris. King Piankhi of Ethiopia mentions in his great inscription a grand duke of the Ma, Shashanq of Busiris, and his successor Pamai, who, presumably, were identical with Shashanq III and Pamai. At the time of this conqueror, about 775 BCE, we find near them a king Nimrod of Hermopolis, a ruler Peftotbast of Heracleopolis Magna, who bore the king's ring, a king Auputh of the Delta cities Tentremu and Ta-an, and a king Uasarken (III) of Bubastis. The latter probably belongs to the Manethan 23rd dynasty which came from Tanis, and, according to Africanus, ascended the throne about 823 BCE. Manetho mentions Petasebast as its founder, and he was succeeded by Uasarken, who is presumably the aforementioned Uasarken III. Manetho evidently did not regard the last rulers of the 22nd dynasty as legitimate, so, although they are mentioned, they are not included in the chronology.

By the side of these 'kings' there are, moreover, numerous princes (*Ur*) of the Ma, designated in other cases as lords (*rpa*) or nomarchs (*ha*). Independent rulers in the few provinces of the Delta, in Athribis, Mendes, Sebennytus, Sais, etc., and the provost of Letopolis bore the title of high priest.

These leading men came mostly from the leaders of the mercenaries, and their possessions and power constantly tottered. It is very possible that the single states formed a slack political confederation, and it is probable that the descendants of the old ruling house were recognized as the chief feudal lords, while those rulers who usurped the title of king laid claim to complete independence.

THE ETHIOPIAN CONQUEST

c. 1000–775 BCE

At the time when a great conquering kingdom was forming itself on the upper Tigris and began to lay hold on all sides around it, the power of the pharaohs in the Nile Valley completely went down. The kingdom of Tuthmosis III had been divided into a succession of small independent principalities and was ruled by dynasties which had arisen from the leaders of the mercenaries. On the other hand, in the upper valley of the Nile, in the lands first joined to Egypt in the time of Usertsen III and afterwards for five centuries by Tuthmosis I, there arose the powerful kingdom of Cush (Greek Ethiopia, now Nubia). Its capital was Napata in the Gebel Barhal, 'the sacred mountain', at the foot of which Amenhotep III had already founded a great sanctuary to the Theban Amen. By its long connection with Egypt, Egyptian culture was completely naturalized in Ethiopia. Egyptian was the official language, the writing was in hieroglyphics, the styling of the kings was after that of the pharaohs. Above all, the Egyptian, and especially the Theban, religion of Amen gained complete dominion in Cush. In the name of Amen the kings went to battle; they were fully dependent on his instructions and oracles; they carefully observed the laws on outer cleanliness and on the food forbidden by religion.

What had remained theory in Egypt, became practice in Ethiopia; a long inscription describes to us how the god himself immediately elects the king through his oracle, and strikingly confirms the accounts of the Greeks. Whence it followed that the priests could command the king in the name of the god to put an end to his life, a prerogative which Ergamenes abolished in the third century BCE. By these circumstances it can be seen why the Egyptian priests described Ethiopia to the Greeks as the Promised Land. From these circumstances it can also be supposed that the rise of the kingdom of Napata was connected with the usurpation of the priests of the Theban Amen at the time of the 21st dynasty, an assumption which is confirmed by many of the kings having borne the name of Piankhi, prominent in the family of Her-Hor. After that time there was no question of the rule of the pharaohs over Cush; so perhaps relatives of the priests of Amen may have founded the Ethiopian town *circa* 1000 BCE.

When the power of the 22nd dynasty became lamed, the kings of Napata could extend their dominion to Upper Egypt. Probably about the end of the reign of Shashanq III, 800 BCE, Thebes may have fallen into their hands; in the first half of the eighth century the valley of the Nile to the vicinity of Hermopolis was under the rule of the Ethiopian king Piankhi. In his time the Prince Tefnekht of Sais succeeded in subjecting the west part of the Delta in Lower Egypt, in winning Memphis, and in making all the numerous princes, kings and small lords of the middle and east Delta, 'all princes of Lower Egypt who wear the feather' (the sign of the warrior casts of the Ma), acknowledge his supremacy. He did not adopt the title of king, probably because he wished to violate as little as possible the relations of rank which existed amongst the mercenary princes. From Memphis he went south, subjected Crocodilopolis, Oxyrhynchus and others, besieged Heracleopolis, the royal residence of Peftotbast, and compelled King Nimrod of Hermopolis to submit. Then Piankhi stepped forward, called to help by the adversaries of Tefnekht. His army conquered a hostile fleet on the Nile, drove Tefnekht back at Heracleopolis, besieged Nimrod in Hermopolis, and seized a number of small places. Then the king himself appeared at the seat of war; he compelled Nimrod to capitulate, and received rich presents from him. After the fall of Hermopolis, all the small places subjected themselves, only Memphis had to be taken by storm, after a plan of Tefnekht to relieve it had failed. Then Piankhi advanced to the Delta; small princes hastened together before him to swear allegiance and bring him rich gifts. Thus Tefnekht was no longer strong enough to assert his position; Piankhi may also have had misgivings as to waging a dangerous war in the west Delta. He contented himself with Tefnekht's taking the oath of allegiance in the presence of the ambassador of the Ethiopian king and sending him presents after being promised safety.

c. 775–704 BCE

The campaigns of Piankhi, which fell in the year 21 of his reign (*c.* 775 BCE), do not seem to have resulted in a lasting subjection of Egypt. If the vassal king Uasarken (III) of Bubastis was the second ruler of the 23rd Dynasty, the Ethiopians must by that time have been expelled from Upper Egypt; for we meet with the third ruler of this house, Psamus, in two small inscriptions in the temple of Karnak. In the monuments Manetho lets him be succeeded by an unauthenticated king, Zet. Then follows the 24th Dynasty, which, according to him, only consists of the Saïte Bakenranf (probably 733–729 BCE), who, according to the reliable Greek reports, was a son of Tnephachthus, that is to say, of Tefnekht, Piankhi's adversary. In tradition he is praised as a wise prince and great legislator; from the monuments we only know that in his sixth year, an Apis was placed in the same sepulchral chamber with one that died under Shashanq IV; according to this he probably succeeded the last title-bearing king of the 22nd Dynasty, but must already have reigned for some time previously in Sais.

In Ethiopia, Piankhi (it is not known whether after one or more interregnums) was followed by Kashta, who was married to Shepenapet, a daughter of King Uasarken, probably Uasarken III of Bubastis. His son Shabak repeated the expedition to Egypt, conquered Bakenranf – according to Manetho he burnt him alive – and compelled the local dynasties to acknowledge his supremacy (728 BCE). He took the title of a king of Egypt, but as real rulers of the land he established his sister Ameniritis and her husband, Piankhi (II?). We often meet with Shabak and his sister in the temples of Thebes, likewise in Hammamat and elsewhere; an exquisite alabaster statue of the queen has been found in Karnak. Greek tradition asserts that the Ethiopian king reigned very mildly over Egypt, executions never took place, criminals were made to build canals and dams. But a fixed and uniform dominion was never practised by the Ethiopians over Egypt. As in the time of Piankhi, the local dynasties remained in possession of their dominions, and amongst them in all probability also the successors of Tefnekht and Bakenranf in Sais, the ancestors of the 26th dynasty.

Although in the year 725 BCE and in 720 (Annals of Sargon), Shabak is called 'King of Egypt', yet in 715 BCE Sargon speaks of the tribute of 'Pharaoh, King of Egypt'; in 711 he mentions the same together with the King of Melukhkha (i.e. Cush), and in Sennacherib's time the 'Kings of Egypt' appear together with 'the troops of the King of Melukhkha'.

Numerous battles for the possession of the Lower Nile occupied the reigns of Shabak and his successors; it made it impossible for them to take part in the affairs of Asia, no matter how much they desired so to do.

c. 704–672 BCE

Shabak of Cush and Egypt was succeeded in the year 716 (?) by Shabatakh who, according to Manetho, was his son, and of whom only scattered monuments have been preserved in Karnak and Memphis. But in the year 704 he was succeeded by a younger, more vigorous prince, Tirhaqa. The latter appears not to have belonged to the royal family, but to have acquired the throne by marriage with the wife of Shabak and to have seized the government in the name of the latter's son, Tanut-Amen; in Karnak the two conjointly raised a temple to Osiris Ptah, and are here both called kings in exactly the same terms.

Tirhaqa was 20 years old when he obtained the double crown. The numerous princes of the Egyptian cities acknowledged his supremacy, and he was able to turn his attention to renewing Shabak's interference in Syria. A number of Syrian princes were ready to join the liberator from the Assyrian yoke, especially Elulaeus of Tyre, Hezekiah of Judah, who, in the year 714, had succeeded Ahaz, and Zidqa of Askalon. King Padi of Ekron remained faithful to the Assyrians, but his magnates revolted against him and delivered him up to Hezekiah. It might have been hoped that Sennacherib would be detained for a long time in Babylonia. We learn that Merodach-baladan had opened negotiations with Hezekiah, so that a great coalition against Assyria seems to have been planned.

Yet this time also the Assyrians were able to forestall their adversaries. Before their preparations were completed, in the beginning of 701, Sennacherib appeared in Syria and turned first against Elulaeus. Sidon, Sarepta, Akko and the other towns subject to him submitted, and he himself fled to Cyprus. From Phoenicia, Sennacherib marched to Philistia, having received in every way the homage of those vassals who had remained loyal. Zidqa of Askalon was captured, his towns reduced, and a new king set up. Then, the Great King further informs us, he marched against Ekron, when the army of the King of Cush (Assyrian, Melukhkha) and the princes of Egypt came to its assistance. At Altaku he defeated this force, took that city and Timnath, reduced Ekron where he punished the instigator of the rebellion, and restored King Padi, who had been taken as a prisoner to Jerusalem.

Trusting in Pharaoh and in Jehovah, Hezekiah persisted in resisting. Meantime the army of Tirhaqa, King of Cush, marched up. Sennacherib advanced against him and again demanded the surrender of Jerusalem. But Hezekiah, trusting in Jehovah's word as announced to him by the prophet Isaiah, once more refused. In the night the Mal'ak-Yahveh (the angel of the Lord) smites the Assyrian army, so that 185,000 men die, and Sennacherib had to return to Nineveh.

c. 672–663 BCE

The Egyptians gave Herodotus a similar account: after the Ethiopian Sabaco [Shabak], a former priest of Ptah, Sethos, who had been at enmity with the warrior caste, ruled over Egypt. Now when Sennacherib, 'King of the Arabians and Assyrians', made an expedition against Egypt, the warriors refused to fight, and Sethos was in great distress. But the gods sent fieldmice against the hostile army which was encamped at Pelusium, and the mice gnawed the bows and all the leather trappings of the enemy, so that on the following day they could easily be defeated by the Egyptian artisans and merchants that had been impressed into service.

We can never be completely clear as to what did happen, especially so long as the position of the places mentioned is not positively ascertained. This much is established, that although Sennacherib may have exaggerated the importance of the victory at Altaku, he did not suffer defeat at the hands of the Egyptians. For in that case Tirhaqa would have followed up his victory – while, as a matter of fact, he did not again interfere in Syria for the space of 30 years – and the Egyptians would have spoken of a victory and not of a miracle. It is much more likely that it was some natural visitation, presumably a pestilence, which compelled Sennacherib to give up the invasion of Egypt and raise the siege of Jerusalem. There was, however, no further hope of aid from Egypt, so Hezekiah made his peace with the Great King and sent to his capital the heavy contribution which could, only with great difficulty, be raised by the little city.

In spite of the half compulsory retreat, the supremacy over Syria was secured; during the next decades none of the petty states ventured to dream of a revolt from the Assyrian. It was not till towards the end of his reign, after 672 BCE, that Esarhaddon undertook a great campaign. Again had rebellion broken out in Syria in reliance on Ethiopian support: King Baal of Tyre had renounced his allegiance. Esarhaddon determined to find some means of putting an end to the ever-recurring danger. Tyre was blockaded anew, but the main army marched straight on Egypt. The prince of the desert Arabs furnished camels, and the toilsome march from Raphia to Pelusium was successfully accomplished. We do not know whether Tirhaqa was in a position to offer resistance; at all events Memphis was taken, and the Assyrian army penetrated as far as Thebes. Tirhaqa had to retreat to Ethiopia, and the numerous provincial princes of Egypt submitted, and were confirmed in possession as tributary vassals. No less than 20 of them are mentioned as being summoned to Thebes from the Delta and the towns of Upper Egypt. The most powerful amongst them was Neku, the lord of Sais and Memphis (according to Manetho 671–664 BCE), whose forefathers, Stephinates and Nechepsos, had already risen in power in Sais, and were probably the direct successors of Tefnekht and Bocchoris (Bakenranf).

At the bidding of the Assyrian king, Neku had to change the name of Sais into Karbilmatati, 'garden of the lord of the countries'; in the same way his son Psamthek received the Assyrian name of Nabu-shezib-anni. From this time Esarhaddon styles himself 'King of the Kings of Misir (Lower Egypt), Patoris (Upper Egypt), and Cush'. On the 12th of Airu (April), 668 BCE, Esarhaddon laid down the government. He set his illegitimate son Shamash-shum-ukin over the Babylonian provinces as vice-king, while Asshurbanapal inherited the crown of the Assyrian empire. The change of rulers encouraged Tirhaqa to attempt to win back Egypt. Mentu-em-ha, the governor of Thebes, hailed him as a deliverer. Memphis was also won, and in Thebes restoration works were even taken in hand. But the success was not a lasting one; an army despatched by Asshurbanapal beat the Ethiopian troops, and Tirhaqa had to fly to Thebes but did not manage to hold it (about 667 BCE). It is true that several Egyptian princes, Neku, Pakruru of Pisept and Sharludari of Tanis (Pelusium), now attempted to overthrow the rule of the foreigner and bring back Tirhaqa: but the Assyrian generals anticipated them; Neku and Sharludari were taken and the rebel towns severely punished. In Neku, Asshurbanapal hoped to be able to win a firm support for his rule, and presumably on information of warlike preparations in Ethiopia, he released him from his captivity with rich presents and reinstated him in his principality.

663–655 BCE

In the year 664 Tirhaqa died; he was succeeded by his stepson Tanut-Amen, who was already advanced in years. A dream which promised him the double crown, induced him, so he states in an inscription, to lead his army from Napata against Egypt in the very beginning of his reign. At Thebes he encountered no resistance; before Memphis the enemy's troops were beaten and the town taken. In one of these engagements Neku, the most powerful of the Assyrian vassals, probably met his death:

Herodotus relates that he was slain by the Ethiopian king, and according to Manetho he died 663 BCE. On the other hand, the attempt to conquer the towns of the Delta was unsuccessful: but some of the vassals, including Pakruru of Pisept, presented themselves at the court at Memphis. Tanut-Amen's inscription tells only of the long theological discourses which the king held before them, and how, after having been well entertained, each returned to his own town. Silence is preserved as to the sequel; from Asshurbanapal's annals we learn that the feeble prince, who was completely under the dominion of theological fancies, evacuated the country before the Assyrian army, without striking a blow, and returned to his own land. This terminated the Ethiopian rule for all time (about 662 BCE): Thebes fell again into the hands of the Assyrians and rich booty was carried to Nineveh. The memory of the retreat of the Ethiopians was preserved down to a late period; the priests told Herodotus that Shabak, the representative of the Ethiopian rule, had voluntarily evacuated Egypt after a reign of 50 years, in consequence of a dream. It is true that they omitted to mention that as a result of this the country fell into the hands of the Assyrians.

THE CLOSING SCENES

Dynasties 26–31: 655–332 BCE

A great nation in its time of decline does not sink into utter insignificance without making spasmodic efforts at recuperation. Such efforts were made by Egypt in the 26th Dynasty, when there sat upon the throne of Egypt several monarchs who recalled something of the days of yore. Notable among these were Psamthek I (Psammetichus) and Aahmes II, under whose beneficent rule Egypt was voluntarily opened up to commerce with the outside world. These rulers built no lasting monuments comparable to the pyramids or the Labyrinth, and attempted no conquests like those of Thutmosis and Ramses. But their reigns were marked by a period of national prosperity such as had not been known in Egypt for several centuries; and they were also notable because at this time the first recorded observations that have come down to us were made by foreigners regarding Egyptian history and the Egyptian people. We shall, therefore, consider some details of this dynasty before passing on to a brief consideration of the reign of the Persians in Egypt and an even briefer analysis of the remaining dynasties. In this sweeping view more than 300 years are covered. During this period the centres of world-historic influence are shifted from Assyria to Babylonia; from Babylonia to Persia; and thence to Greece; but never again does Egypt occupy her old position. Her reminiscent glory only serves to make her the more coveted as a conqueror's prize. But first there is the bright spot of Psamthek's reign.

PSAMTHEK

655–612 BCE

It was no longer the time of Tuthmosis and Ramses. It was the turn of Egypt to be enslaved, now by the 'vile race of the Cushites', now by the 'vile race of the Kheta'. The Egyptian monuments, which register only victories, would not have sufficed to make known to us the history of this troubled epoch; it is only since the Assyrian inscriptions have been deciphered that we have been able to learn of the double conquest of Egypt by Kings Esarhaddon and Asshurbanapal.

The princes of the Delta received investiture from these Asiatic conquerors, for whom they had perhaps less aversion than for the Ethiopian kings. Twice, however, was Egypt reconquered by Tirhaqa and by his successor, Tanut-Amen. But all these successive invasions had broken the bond which attached the nomes to the national unity; all that remained was an Egypt parcelled out like feudal Europe after the invasion of the Northmen.

The princes of the South continued to recognize the authority of the Ethiopian dynasty; those of the Delta, to the number of 12, formed a sort of federation which the Greek authors call the Dodecarchy. But at the end of 15 years, the prince of Sais, Psamthek, became an object of suspicion to his colleagues. Herodotus tells us the occasion.

'At the very commencement of their reign, an oracle had foretold to them that he amongst them who should make libations in the temple of Hephaistos (Ptah) with a brazen cup, would have the empire of all Egypt. Sometime later, as they were on the point of making libations, after having offered sacrifices in the temple, the high priest presented them with cups of gold; but he made a mistake in the number, and instead of twelve cups, he only brought eleven for the twelve kings. Then Psammetichus [Psamthek], who happened to be in the first rank, took his helmet, which was of bronze, and used it for the libations. The other kings, reflecting on his action and on the oracle, and recognising that he had not acted from premeditated design, thought that it would be unjust to put him to death; but they despoiled him of the greater part of his power, and relegated him to the marshes, forbidding him to leave them or to keep up any correspondence with the rest of Egypt.

'Smarting under this outrage, and resolved to avenge himself on the authors of his exile, he sent to Buto to consult the oracle of Leto, the most veracious of the Egyptian oracles. Answer was returned that he would be avenged by men of bronze, coming from the sea. At first he could not persuade himself that men of bronze could come to his aid; but a short time after, some Ionian and Carian pirates, being obliged to put into Egypt, came on shore clothed in bronze armour. An Egyptian ran to carry the news to Psammetichus, and as this Egyptian had never seen men armed in such a manner, he told them that men of bronze, coming from the sea, were pillaging the countryside. The king, perceiving that the oracle was accomplished, made alliance with the Ionians and Carians, and engaged them by large promises to take his part. With these auxiliary troops and the Egyptians who had remained faithful to him, he dethroned the eleven kings.'

Upper Egypt submitted without resistance, and the names of the Ethiopian kings were struck off the Theban monuments. They seem, however, to have retained some partisans, for Psamthek espoused a wife of their race, the means employed by each dynasty to legitimatize its usurpation. He recompensed his auxiliaries by giving them territories near the Pelusiac mouth of the Nile, and made them his guard of honour. This was not an innovation; for a long time the kings of Egypt had been wont to take foreigners into their pay, and there is no doubt that there were in the native army many soldiers of Libyan or Ethiopian race; but they were annoyed at the favour shown the newcomers, and emigrated into Ethiopia to the number of 200,000 men. Psamthek tried to detain them by appealing to their patriotism, but they struck their lances on their shields and answered that so long as they had arms they would find their own country wherever they chose to establish themselves.

This wholesale desertion was a benefit to Egypt, which it thus relieved from military rule. Conquests lead to inevitable reprisals. Armies, like all privileged classes, end by becoming corrupted, and then, useless in the face of the enemy, they become a heavy burden and an instrument of civil war. Psamthek had no reason to regret these soldiers, who had been unable to repel foreign invasion.

The labours of peace repaired the recent disasters; the temples were rebuilt; the arts shone with a new brilliancy; the whole activity of the nation was turned towards commerce and industry. Psamthek inaugurated a new policy by opening the country to foreigners.

'He received those who visited Egypt with hospitality,' says Diodorus; 'he was the first of the Egyptian kings to open markets to other nations, and to give great security to navigators.'

The Greeks, who had helped to conquer the throne, were particularly favoured. Encouraged by the example of the Ionian and Carian adventurers whose services he had paid so well, some Milesian colonists anchored 30 ships at the entrance of the Bolbitinic mouth of the Nile, and there founded a fortified trading establishment. To facilitate commercial relations for the future, Psamthek confided some Egyptian children to the Greeks established in Egypt, that they might learn Greek, and thus arose those interpreters who formed a distinct class in the towns of the Delta. It even appears, according to Diodorus, that Psamthek had his own children taught Greek. The intercourse of the Greeks with the Egyptians became from that time so constant that from the reign of Psammetichus, says Herodotus, we know with certainty all that passed in that country.

The accession of Psamthek and the 26th dynasty is fixed at the year 655 before the Christian era, and it is only from this period that we have certain dates for the history of Egypt. The complete chronology of the 26th dynasty has been recovered in the monuments of the tomb of Apis, discovered by Mariette Bey, in the excavation of the Serapeum of Memphis, and now in the Louvre. This chronology differs somewhat sensibly from that which it had been possible to draw up from Manetho's lists, so that we are, says [French Egyptologist Emmanuel] De Rougé, obliged to distrust figures preserved in those lists, which a few years ago were regarded as an infallible criterion. An attempt has been made to restore to them the credit they had lost as an instrument of chronology, by attaching to them an undisputed synchronism. According to the calculation of M. Biot, a rising of the star Sothis (Sirius), indicated at Thebes under Ramses III, towards the commencement of the 20th dynasty, would fall at the beginning of the 13th century BCE.

Psamthek had his reign dated from the death of Tirhaqa (664 BCE), without taking the Dodecarchy into account, and this is doubtless the reason why Herodotus gives him 54 years' reign, although in reality he reigned only 44. He had built the southern pylon of the temple of Ptah at Memphis, and a peristyle court where the Apis bull was fed. The walls were covered with bas-reliefs, and colossi, 12 ells high, took the place of columns; these were probably caryatides like those which are seen at Thebes and Abu Simbel. These structures have disappeared, like all the other buildings of Memphis. The only monuments of the reign of Psamthek which still exist are the 12 columns, 21 metres (about 69 feet) high, whose ruins are seen in the first court of the temple of Karnak, where they formed a double rank. One only of these columns is still upright. It is not known whether they were raised to form the centre avenue of a hypostyle hall like that of Seti, or whether they were intended to bear symbolic images which served the Egyptians as military ensigns, such as the ram, the ibis, the sparrowhawk, the jackal, etc.

Psamthek and his successors, though not residing at Thebes, restored its monuments and repaired the disasters of the Assyrian invasion. In the Louvre and the British Museum there are numerous sculptures of the Saitic epoch, which is one of the grand epochs of Egyptian art.

In the reign of Psamthek, the Scythians, driving the Cimmerians before them, had invaded Asia and were threatening Egypt. Psamthek preferred to buy their retreat by a money payment, rather than expose the country to the danger of invasion, and the barbarians retraced their steps northward. But in order to protect Egypt on the north-east, it was necessary to have a foothold in Palestine, and Psamthek therefore laid siege to the town of Ashdod.

612–594 BCE

This siege, says Herodotus, lasted 29 years, but perhaps, as M. Maspero thinks, Herodotus' interpreters meant to say that the taking of Ashdod took place in the 29th year of Psamthek's reign. His son, Neku II, who succeeded him in 612 BCE, desiring to profit by the changes which had supervened in Asia, and to re-establish the dominion of Egypt, gave battle to the Jews and Syrians near Megiddo. Josiah, king of Judah, was killed, his son Jehoahaz, whom the Jews had proclaimed king, was dethroned by Neku, who put in his place Eliakim, another son of Josiah, and remained master of all Syria. But he soon found a redoubtable adversary in front of him, for the kingdom of Babylon had succeeded to that of Nineveh. Beaten by Nebuchadnezzar at Carchemish on the banks of the Euphrates, Neku lost all his conquests and returned precipitately to Egypt.

His name remains connected with an enterprise more important than his military expeditions. Two kings of the 19th dynasty, Seti I and Ramses II, had had a canal of communication dug between the eastern branch of the Nile and the Red Sea. But whether it was that this canal had not been finished, or that it was blocked up by the sands, Neku desired to restore it. The canal began a little above Bubastis. According to Herodotus, 120,000 workmen perished in digging it, and Neku had it discontinued in consequence of an oracle, which warned him that he was labouring for the barbarians; an oracle which was accomplished, for the canal was finished by the Persians. In our own day, when it was desired to open direct communication between the Red Sea and the Mediterranean, the operations were begun with the restoration of Neku's canal, to supply fresh water for the workmen who were digging the maritime canal.

After abandoning his project, Neku conceived another which might have had still more important consequences. He sent some Phoenician sailors to make a voyage of circumnavigation round Africa.

'The Phoenicians,' says Herodotus, 'having embarked on the Erythraean Sea, sailed into the Southern Sea. As the autumn was come they landed on that part of Libya at which they found themselves, and sowed corn. They then awaited the time of the harvest, and having gathered it again took to the sea. Having voyaged thus for two years, in the third year they doubled the pillars of Heracles and, returning to Egypt, related what I do not believe, but which others may perhaps credit; that whilst sailing round Libya they had the sun on their right.'

THE GOOD KING SABACH [SHABAK] AND PSAMMETICHUS

728–612 BCE

Psamthek was well known to classic writers under the name Psammetichus. The old historian Diodorus picturesquely tells of his accession. We prefer to quote the old translation of G. Booth, 1700: 'After a long time, one Sabach an Ethiopian came to the Throne, going beyond all his Predecessors in his Worship of the Gods, and kindness to his Subjects. Any Man may judge and have a clear Evidence of his gentle Disposition in this, that when the Laws pronounced the severest Judgment (I mean Sentence of Death) he chang'd the Punishment, and made an Edict that the Condemn'd Persons should be kept to work in the Towns in Chains, by whose Labour he rais'd many Mounts, and made many Commodious Canals; conceiving by this means he should not only moderate the severity of the Punishment, but instead of that which was unprofitable, advance the publick Good, by the Service and Labours of the Condemn'd.

'A Man may likewise judge of his extraordinary Piety from his Dream, and his Abdication of the Government; for the Tutelar God of Thebes, seem'd to speak to him in his Sleep, and told him that he could not long reign happily and prosperously in Egypt, except he cut all the Priests in Pieces, when he pass'd through the midst of them with his Guards and Servants; which Advice being often repeated, he at length sent for the Priests from all parts, and told them that if he staid in Egypt any longer, he found that he should displease God, who never at any time before by Dreams or Visions commanded any such thing. And that he would rather be gone and lose his Life, being pure and innocent, than displease God, or enjoy the Crown of Egypt, by staining his Life with the horrid Murder of the Innocent.

'And so at length giving up the Kingdom into the Hands of the People, he return'd into Ethiopia. Upon this there was an Anarchy for the space of Two Years; but the People falling into Tumults and intestine Broyls and Slaughters one of another, 12 of the chief Nobility of the Kingdom joyn'd in a Solemn Oath, and then calling a Senate at Memphis, and making some Laws for the better directing and cementing of them in mutual peace and fidelity, they took upon them the Regal Power and Authority.

'After they had govern'd the Kingdom very amicably for the space of Fifteen Years (according to the Agreement which they had mutually sworn to observe), they apply'd themselves to the building of a Sepulcher, where they might all lye together; that as in their Lifetime they had been equal in their Power and Authority, and had always carried it with love and respect one towards another; so after Death (being all bury'd together in one Place) they might continue the Glory of their Names in one and the same Monument.

'To this end they made it their business to excel all their Predecessors in the greatness of their Works: For near the Lake of Myris in Lybia, they built a Four-square Monument of Polish'd Marble, every square a Furlong in length, for curious Carvings and other pieces of Art, not to be equall'd by any that should come after them. When you are enter'd within the Wall, there's presented a stately Fabrick, supported round with Pillars, Forty on every side: The Roof was of one entire Stone, whereon was curiously carv'd Racks and Mangers for Horses, and other excellent pieces of Workmanship, and painted and adorn'd with divers sorts of Pictures and Images; where likewise were portray'd the Resemblances of the Kings, the Temples, and the Sacrifices in most beautiful Colours. And such was the Cost and Stateliness of this Sepulcher, begun by these Kings, that (if they had not been dethron'd before it was perfected) none ever after could have exceeded them in the state and magnificence of their Works. But after they had reign'd over Egypt Fifteen Years, all of them but one lost their Sovereignty in the manner following.

655–612 BCE

'Psammeticus Saïtes [Psamthek I], one of the Kings, whose Province was upon the Sea Coasts, traffickt with all sorts of Merchants, and especially with the Phenicians and Grecians; by this means enriching his Province, by vending his own Commodities, and the importation of those that came from Greece, he not only grew very wealthy, but gain'd an interest in the Nations and Princes abroad; upon which account he was envy'd by the rest of the Kings, who for that reason made War upon him. Some antient Historians tell a Story, That these Princes were told by the Oracle, That which of them should first pour Wine out of a brazen Viol to the God ador'd at Memphis, should be sole Lord of all Egypt. Whereupon Psammeticus when the Priest brought out of the Temple Twelve Golden Viols, pluckt off his Helmet, and pour'd out a Wine Offering from thence; which when his Collegues took notice of, they forbore putting him to death, but depos'd him, and banish'd him into the Fenns, bordering upon the Sea Coasts.

'Whether therefore it were this, or Envy as is said before, that gave Birth to this Dissention and Difference amongst them, it's certain Psammeticus hir'd Souldiers out of Arabia, Caria and Ionia, and in a Field-Fight near the City Moniemphis, he got the day. Some of the Kings of the other side were slain, and the rest fled into Africa, and were not able further to contend for the Kingdom.

'Psammeticus having now gain'd possession of the whole, built a Portico to the East Gate of the Temple at Memphis, in honour of that God, and encompass'd the Temple with a Wall, supporting it with Colosses of 12 Cubits high in the room of Pillars. He bestow'd likewise upon his Mercenary Soldiers many large Rewards over and above their Pay promis'd them.'

To return to later and less credulous historians, it will be well to note a more authoritative account of this period.

THE RESTORATION IN EGYPT

655–612 BCE

When Asshurbanapal again subjected the petty princes of Egypt, he had favoured none so much as Neku I of Sais. The latter had fallen in battle against Tanut-Amen;

his son Psamthek had sought refuge with the Assyrians and had been brought back to his dominions by them. As soon as circumstances allowed, he threw off the Assyrian yoke, as his father had done before him. At the same time, he took up the task begun by Tefnekht, his predecessor and courageous ancestor, of suppressing the petty princes and uniting Egypt. King Gyges of Lydia sent him auxiliaries; they were the Carian and Ionian troops, which, according to Herodotus, landed in Egypt one day and were employed by Psamthek against his rivals. Soon the first mercenaries were followed by others; they formed the backbone of the king's army.

What took place in the individual fights is not known; that is, we have no knowledge of the battles with the Assyrians. But about the year 655 BCE the object was obtained, Egypt freed and united. So as to establish his rule safely, the king married Shepenapet, daughter of Queen Ameniritis.

The chief opponents of the new ruler were doubtless the mercenaries organized as a warrior caste, the Ma, who had shared the land under the Ethiopian and Assyrian supremacy. Herodotus relates that 240,000 warriors 'who stood to the left of the king' had wandered to Ethiopia, under Psamthek, since for three years they were not relieved in the garrisons; the king, who hastened after them, could not persuade them to return. Although the recital is legendary with regard to the immense number, the fact fits in clearly with the history of the times that a considerable number of the warrior caste, who would not submit to the new circumstances, should have left the land, been taken up by the king of Napata and colonized the valley of the Upper Nile.

It has already been mentioned that Psamthek, so as to protect himself against the renewed invasion of the Assyrians, also turned to Asia. As Aahmes I, after the expulsion of the Hyksos, invested Sherohan in Palestine, so for 29 years Psamthek took the field against Ashdod, until he conquered the town. His power does not seem to have extended farther south than the First Cataract. His grandson, Psamthek II, first took the field against Ethiopia. To his time probably belong the inscriptions which Greek, Carian and Phoenician soldiers have inscribed on the colossi of the temples of Abu Simbel in their mother tongues. Southern Nubia did not remain long conquered. The three strong border fortresses of Elephantine in the south, Daphne in the east and Marea in the west essentially determine the limits of Egyptian power.

The new state, in which, after some 200 years of anarchy, the kingdom of the Pharaohs was again established, was only partly national. The dynasty was, as the name teaches, not of Egyptian origin, but in all probability Libyan. The troops which the princes of Sais could raise were doubtless for the greater part Libyans, and the particular characteristic was due to the mercenaries who had come across the sea. In future days the Ionians and Carians who were colonised in the 'camps' between Bubastis and Pelusium, on that most dangerous east border of the land, were the chief support of the throne; under Uah-ab-Ra [Apries] their number increased to 30,000 men.

612–596 BCE

Thus from the beginning the kings of the restoration, like the Ptolemies, held a much freer position, which raised them far above their predecessors. They, manifestly with intention, held

Sais as residence, although Memphis was honoured as the oldest capital, and structures were built on the ruins of ancient Thebes. With full knowledge they carried on a considerable commerce. Psamthek's son, Neku II (612–596 BCE), began to build a canal from the Nile to the Red Sea; he sent out a Phoenician fleet to circumnavigate Africa, which returned to the Mediterranean three years after its departure from Suez. A fleet was maintained on the Arabian as well as in the Mediterranean Sea.

With the Greeks, who in earlier times came to Egypt only as pirates or were driven there by storms, but now sought to draw all the coasts of the Mediterranean into their commerce, active negotiations were taken up. From trading with them arose the numerous caste of the interpreters. Neku II sends oblations to Brandichae; to his son, Psamthek II, there came an embassy from Elis; the Egyptian divinities begin to become known to the Greeks: whilst amongst Asiatics closely related to the culture and customs of the Egyptians there reigned active negotiation and a reciprocal influence, the Hellenes, of quite other disposition and more active in commerce, remained strangers to the Egyptians. They were met with suspicion, and restrictions were laid upon them. Aahmes was the first to assign them a place in Naucratis, south of Sais, where they gained influence and property and could organize themselves as an independent community, but the Greek merchants were forbidden to navigate in any other branch of the Nile.

Internally the 26th dynasty in every sense bears the stamp of restoration. The end of a formidable crisis had come, and the endeavour was made to re-establish conditions as they were conceived to have been of old – that is to say – to introduce the abstract ideal.

Therefore, the Egyptians held themselves more aloof from the strangers, most carefully observing all laws as to cleanliness; the god of the strangers and hostile powers, the till-now-honoured Set, was cast out of the Pantheon, his name and image effaced everywhere: also the divinities taken up from the Syrian neighbours, such as Astarte and Anata, completely disappeared. In religion they turned back to the oldest laws; the dead formulas of the tombs of the Pyramids were revived, the worship of the early kings of Memphis, Sneferu, Khufu, Sahu-Ra, was again taken up.

THE PERSIAN CONQUEST AND THE END OF EGYPTIAN AUTONOMY

596–572 BCE

With the 26th Dynasty the curtain was practically drawn for all time on Egyptian autonomy. The recurrent struggle between Asia and Africa was renewed with disastrous consequences to the people of the Nile. We have here to do with the Persian conquest, and in particular with the deeds of Cambyses.

Neku reigned six years according to Manetho, 16 according to Herodotus, and this latter figure is confirmed by two steles at Florence and Leyden. His son, Psamthek II, whom Herodotus calls Psammis (596), reigned six years and died on his return from an expedition into Ethiopia. It was probably during this expedition that some Greek and Phoenician soldiers carved their names on the leg of one of the colossi of Abu-Simbel.

In the reign of Uah-ab-Ra, the Apries of the Greeks (591), Syria and Palestine were the theatre of important events. The petty people of these countries, threatened by the Chaldean power, tried to save their independence by the help of Egypt.

Nebuchadnezzar, king of Babylon, first turned his forces against the kingdom of Judah, which succumbed in spite of Egypt's tardy and inefficient intervention. Jerusalem was taken, and the people led away to captivity. The Jewish prophets, in their anger against Egypt, announced for it the fate of Judah, and, if we are to believe Josephus, these predictions were accomplished; for Nebuchadnezzar is said to have defeated and killed Uah-ab-Ra and subdued Egypt. But Herodotus and Diodorus say nothing of this defeat, and speak, on the contrary, of a naval victory of Apries over the Phoenicians and Cypriotes. M. [Joseph Ernest] Renan's explorations have brought to light the ruins of a temple raised by the Egyptians at Gebel, a fact which seems to indicate that they remained masters of the country.

Uah-ab-Ra undertook to subdue the Greek colony of Cyrene, and, as it would not have been prudent to oppose his Greek auxiliaries to a people of the same race, he employed only native troops on this expedition, which was an unfortunate one. The Egyptian soldiers, believing he had undertaken it solely in order to get rid of them, revolted. To appease them, Uah-ab-Ra sent an officer named Aahmes, whose good nature pleased the soldiers. As he was speaking to them, one of them put a helmet on his head, and there was a cry that they ought to make him their king. He did not wait to be persuaded, and immediately put himself at the head of the rebels.

Uah-ab-Ra, learning this, gave orders to one of those who remained faithful to him to bring Aahmes to him, dead or alive. The envoy received only a very coarse answer, and when he returned, the king had his nose and ears cut off. The indignant Egyptians instantly went over to Aahmes. Uah-ab-Ra at the head of his Carian and Ionian mercenaries, to the number of 30,000, marched against the rebels, who were far more numerous. He was beaten and led back, a prisoner, into the palace which had been his. Aahmes at first treated him with consideration, but the Egyptians insisted that he should be delivered up to them, and strangled. He had reigned 20 years. Aahmes had him buried in the tomb of his ancestors, and espoused a daughter of Psamthek II in order to graft himself on the Saitic dynasty.

572–525 BCE

Aahmes II, though he had become king by a reaction of the national party against the foreigner, nevertheless showed himself still more favourable to the Greeks than his predecessors had been. He permitted them to establish themselves at Naucratis, on the Canopic branch of the Nile, and to raise temples to their gods. One of these temples, the Hellenion, was built at the public expense by the principal Greek towns in Asia. Particular temples were consecrated to Apollo by the Milesians, to Hera by the Samians and to Zeus by the Aeginians. Aahmes sent his statue to several towns in Greece, and when the temple of Delphi was destroyed by fire, he desired to contribute to the subscription opened for its reconstruction, and offered a talent of alum from Egypt. He entered into an alliance with the Cyrenaeans, and married one of the daughters of the country; he also allied himself with Polycrates, tyrant of Samos, and with Croesus, king of the Lydians.

He made no war except against the Cypriotes, whom he subjected to a tribute. He chiefly occupied himself, as Psamthek had done, in developing the trade of Egypt. Like him, he erected monuments at Sais and Memphis, which are no longer in existence, but of which Herodotus speaks with admiration. There is at the Louvre a monolithic chapel in pink granite, which dates from the reign of Aahmes, and the British Museum possesses the sarcophagus of one of his wives, Queen Ankhnes, who long resided at Thebes. It is believed that the hypogees of Assassif, near Gurnah, belong to the Saitic epoch. There is one of them which, in extent and richness, yields to none of the tombs of Biban-el-Moluk. This is the tomb of a high priest who was at the same time a royal functionary.

Aahmes was nothing more than a soldier of fortune, and it appears that the ceremonious etiquette of the ancient kings of Egypt wearied him. When he had employed his morning in administering justice, he passed the rest of the time at table with his friends. Certain courtiers represented to him that he was compromising his dignity. He answered that a bowstring could not always be stretched. At the beginning of his reign the obscurity of his birth made him despised. Perceiving this, he had melted a gold basin, in which he used to wash his feet, made from it the golden statue of a god and offered it to the public veneration.

'Thus it was with me,' he said; 'I was a plebeian, now I am your king; render me, then, the honour and respect which are due me.' The people understood the allegory, and ended by becoming attached to this sensible man, who took his trade of king seriously. It was from him, according to Herodotus, that the Athenians borrowed their famous law against idleness.

'He ordered each Egyptian to declare to the nomarch, every year, what were his means of subsistence. He who did not comply with the law, or could not prove that he lived by honest means, was punished with death. Solon, the Athenian, borrowed this law from Egypt, and established it in Athens, where it is still in force, because it is a wise one and no fault can be found with it.'

Herodotus says that Egypt was never happier or more flourishing than in the reign of Aahmes, and that there were then in that country 20,000 well-peopled towns or villages.

All this prosperity was to disappear in one day, for Egypt was about to founder like Nineveh and Jerusalem and Sardis and Babylon, without previous decay, in one of those sudden and overwhelming storms which sweep monarchies away.

A new empire had just arisen in Asia. Persia had absorbed Media and subdued Chaldea and Asia Minor. Lydia had succumbed so quickly that Aahmes had not been able to succour his ally, Croesus. Cyrus, the founder of the Persian Empire, left Egypt in peace, and she took good care not to stir; but his son Cambyses felt the need of aggrandizing his states, and as in default of reasons wars never lack pretexts, here is the one he gave, or which was perhaps invented as an afterthought.

It was said that Cyrus had asked Aahmes to send him the best physician for diseases of the eye to be found in his dominion. This physician wished to avenge himself on the king of Egypt, who had torn him from the arms of his wife and children to send him into Persia. He persuaded Cambyses to demand the daughter of Aahmes, counting on a refusal, which would not fail to be considered as an insult. Aahmes knew well that Cambyses would not make his daughter a queen, but a slave of the harem; he sent a daughter of Uah-ab-Ra. The latter disclosed the ruse to the king of Persia, and demanded of him to avenge her father, whose murderer Aahmes had been. Cambyses flew into a violent rage and resolved to carry war into Egypt.

A desert that an army could not cross in less than three days' march protected Egypt on the side of Asia. Following the advice of Phanes, a Greek officer and deserter from the Egyptian army, Cambyses secured for himself the alliance of the Arab king, who stationed camels laden with skins full of water, all along the route the Persians were to follow. The town of Pelusium, which was the key of Egypt, was besieged by Cambyses. Polyaenus relates that he caused dogs, cats and ibises to be collected, and placed them in front of his army; the Egyptians dared not fly their arrows for fear of hitting the sacred animals, and the town was taken without resistance. Aahmes had just died, after a reign of 44 years (528 BCE). His son, Psamthek III, the Psammenitus of Herodotus, came to meet the enemy. The Greek and Carian mercenaries in the pay of the king of Egypt, learning the treason of Phanes, their former chief, revenged themselves on his children.

'They led them into the camp,' says Herodotus, 'and, having placed a mixing bowl between the two armies, they cut their throats under the eyes of their father, mingled their blood with wine and water in the bowl, and, when all the auxiliaries had drunk, rushed into battle.'

It was fierce and bloody; many perished on either side; but at last the Egyptians had the worst of it and fled in disorder to Memphis. Cambyses summoned the town to surrender; the crowd destroyed the Mytilenean vessel which carried the ambassadors, massacred those who manned it and dragged their limbs through the citadel. The town was taken, and Psamthek brought before the conqueror. He had reigned only six months.

THE ATROCITIES OF CAMBYSES

525 BCE

Cambyses treated him with the utmost severity, and had him led before the town, together with some other Egyptians.

'The king's daughter,' says Herodotus, 'was clad as a slave and sent, pitcher in hand, in search of water, with several other young girls of rank. They passed, weeping, in front of their captive fathers, who groaned at their humiliation. Psammenitus [Psamthek III] saw them and lowered his eyes towards the earth. Then Cambyses caused his son and 2,000 young men of the same age to pass before him, with cords round their necks and bridles in their mouths. They were being led to death to avenge the Mytileneans slain at Memphis, for the royal judges had ordained that, for every man killed on that occasion, 10 Egyptians of the first families should be put to death. Psammenitus saw them pass and recognized his son; but while the other Egyptians round him wept and lamented themselves, he preserved the same countenance as at the sight of his daughter. When the young men had passed, he perceived an old man who generally ate at his table. This man, despoiled of his goods, and reduced to live on charity, was imploring pity from the soldiers and even from Psammenitus and the Egyptian captives brought into the outskirts of the town. Psammenitus could not restrain his tears; he beat himself on the head and called to his friend. Three guards, deputed to watch him, made this known to Cambyses. He was astonished and sent a messenger to Psammenitus, who questioned him thus:

'"Cambyses, thy master, demands wherefore, having neither wept or groaned when thou sawest thy daughter treated as a slave and thy son marching to execution, thou shouldst interest thyself in the lot of this beggar who, from what we learn, is neither thy relative nor ally."

'He answered, "Son of Cyrus, the misfortunes of my house are too great to be wept; but the fate of a friend, once happy, and reduced to begging in his old age, has seemed to me to deserve tears."

'This answer was reported, and appeared a just one. The Egyptians say that Croesus, who had come into Egypt in the train of Cambyses, wept, and the Persians who were present wept also. Even Cambyses felt some pity. He ordered Psammenitus brought before him and his son to be withdrawn from the number of those about to die.

'Those sent to seek the child did not find him alive; he had been the first struck. They made Psammenitus rise and conducted him into the presence of Cambyses. He remained in the retinue and suffered no violence. The government of Egypt would even have been restored to him if he had not been suspected of exciting disturbances; for the Persians are wont to honour the children of kings and to replace them on the thrones lost by their fathers. But Psammenitus, having conspired, received his reward. Convicted by Cambyses of having urged the Egyptians to revolt, he drank bull's blood and died of it on the spot.

'From Memphis, Cambyses went on to Sais, and as soon as he had reached the tomb of Amasis [Aahmes] he ordered the corpse to be exhumed, to be beaten with rods, to have the hair and beard torn out, to be pricked with goads – in short, to be subjected to all sorts of outrages. The executioners soon grew tired of maltreating a lifeless body, from which they could break off nothing, as it was embalmed. Then Cambyses had it burnt without any respect of holy things. Indeed, the Persians believe that fire is a god, and it is not permitted, either by their law or by that of the Egyptians, to burn the dead. Thus, Cambyses performed on this occasion an act equally condemned by the laws of both peoples.'

In violating the tomb of the man who had usurped the throne of Egypt, Cambyses perhaps counted on rallying the legitimists, for he thus presented himself as the avenger and heir of Uah-ab-Ra. From the inscriptions on a statuette in the Vatican, it appears that, in the early days of his conquest, he avoided giving offence to the religion of the vanquished. He caused the great temple of Nit, where some Persian troops had installed themselves, to be evacuated, and had it repaired at his own expense. He even carried his zeal so far as to be initiated into the mysteries of Osiris. But this apparent and wholly political deference could not last long.

The religious symbols of the Egyptians, the external forms of their worship, inspired profound aversion in the Persians, whose religion greatly resembled the strict monotheism of the Semitic peoples. This antipathy, which was only awaiting an opportunity to manifest itself, blazed out after an unfortunate expedition of Cambyses against Ethiopia. Instead of ascending the Nile as far as Napata, he had taken the shorter route of the desert.

The provisions gave out, and his soldiers were reduced to devouring each other. He returned, having lost many men, and then learnt the complete destruction of another army which he had sent against the Ammonians and which had been entombed under whirlwinds of sand. He was exasperated at this disaster, and, as the Egyptians naturally attributed it to the vengeance of the gods, his fury turned against the Egyptian religion.

'From Assuan to Thebes and from Thebes to Memphis,' says [French scholar, archaeologist and Egyptologist François Auguste Ferdinand] Mariette, 'he marked his route by ruin: the temples were devastated, the tombs of the kings were opened and pillaged.' The mummy of Queen Ankhnes, wife of Aahmes, was torn from its sarcophagus in the depths of a funeral vault behind the Ramesseum, and burned as that of Aahmes himself had been. When this sarcophagus, which is now in London, was discovered by a French officer, remains of charred bones were found in it, according to Champollion Figéac, some of them preserving traces of gilding.

'Cambyses having returned to Memphis,' says Herodotus, 'the god Apis, whom the Greeks call Epaphos, manifested himself to the Egyptians. As soon as he had shown himself, they donned their richest clothing and made great rejoicings. Cambyses, believing that they were rejoicing at the ill-success of his arms, called the magistrates of Memphis before him, and asked them why, having exhibited no joy the first time that they saw him in their town, they were exhibiting so much of it since his return and after he had lost part of his army. They told him that their god, who was generally very long in appearing, had just manifested himself, and that the Egyptians were accustomed to celebrate this epiphany by public festivities. Cambyses, hearing this, said that they lied, and punished them with death for liars. When they had been killed he sent for the priests to come into his presence, and, having received the same answer from them, he told them that if any god showed himself familiarly to the Egyptians, he would not hide himself from him, and he ordered them to bring Apis to him. The priests immediately went in search of him.

'This Apis, who is the same as Epaphos, is born of a cow which can bear no further offspring. The Egyptians say that this cow conceives Apis by lightning, which descends from heaven. These are the distinguishing signs of the calf they call Apis: it is black, and bears a white square on its forehead; it has the figure of an eagle on its back, on its tongue that of a beetle, and the hairs of its tail are double.

'As soon as the priest had brought Apis, Cambyses, like a maniac, drew his sword to pierce its belly, but only struck its thigh. Then, beginning to laugh, he said to the priests:

'"O blockheads, are there such gods, made of flesh and blood and susceptible to the stroke of steel? This god is well worthy of the Egyptians, but you shall have no cause to rejoice for having attempted to laugh at our expense."

'Thereupon he had them whipped by those deputed for that purpose, and ordered such Egyptians as were found celebrating a festival to be slain. Thus the festivities ceased and the priests were punished. Apis, wounded in the thigh, languished, lying in the temple, and when he was dead the priests buried him, unknown to Cambyses. As to him, who was already wanting in good sense, he was from that time smitten with madness, the Egyptians say, in punishment of his crime.'

Among the funeral steles of the Apis, found by Mariette in the excavations of the Serapeum at Memphis, and which are now in the Egyptian Museum at the Louvre, are two connected with the facts recounted by Herodotus: one, whose inscription is almost illegible, contained the epitaph of the Apis who died in the reign of Cambyses, and was born, as it seems, in the 25th year of Aahmes. We possess, the catalogue says, his sarcophagus, sculptured by order of Cambyses. The other is the epitaph of the bull who died in the fourth year of Darius.

'We think,' says M. de Rougé, 'that this is the same Apis whom Cambyses, in his fury, wounded when, on his return from the unfortunate Ethiopian expedition, he found the Egyptians abandoning themselves to the rejoicings which accompanied the festivities of the theophany of a new Apis (in 518 BCE).' If this be so, this Apis must have survived his wound nearly five years.

522–332 BCE

Darius wished to repair the mistakes of his predecessor, and tried to conciliate the Egyptians. He put to death the satrap Aryandes, whose tyranny was already provoking revolts, and, learning that the Apis had just died, he joined in the public mourning and promised 100 talents of gold to whoever should find a new Apis. He visited the great temple of Ptah and would have placed his statue there beside that of Sesostris [Ramses II]. The priests told him that he had not yet equalled the exploits of Sesostris, since he had not subdued the Scythians. Darius was not offended at this exhibition of national pride; he answered simply that if he lived as long as Sesostris he would endeavour to equal him. He had a great temple of Amen, whose ruins still exist, built in the oasis of Thebes. Finally, he finished the canal of communication which Seti I and Neku II had wished to establish between the Nile and the Red Sea. According to Diodorus, his memory was venerated by the Egyptians, who placed him in the number of their great legislators.

The kings of Persia who form the 27th dynasty did not, however, succeed in making themselves accepted by Egypt. They had not, like the Shepherd kings, adopted her religion, her language, her writing and her manners, and therefore they were always foreigners to her. Their dominion was rarely oppressive, and yet it was interrupted by insurrections which always found a support in the Greek republics.

After 120 years, Egypt recovered her independence under three native dynasties, the 28th, the 29th and the 30th. But she lost it 64 years after, through the cowardice of her king, who fled into Ethiopia without fighting, as Meneptah had fled before the Unclean. Egypt was a second time conquered by the Persians, and Ochus renewed the follies and pillaging of Cambyses (340 BCE).

The 28th dynasty is regarded as consisting of one king only, since at his death the rule passed to the princes of Mendes. This king was Amen-rut (Amyrtaeus), 405–399 BCE, son of Pausiris and grandson of that Amyrtaeus who was the ally of Inarus of Libya. Amen-rut revolted against Persia, and became independent on the death of Darius II.

Nia-faa-rut I, prince of Mendes (399–393), succeeded Amen-rut. He and his successors – Haker (393–380), Psamut (380) and Nia-faa-rut II (379) – form the 29th dynasty, and continued, by the alliances with Persia's enemies, to maintain the native rule of Egypt.

This state of affairs continued under the 30th dynasty, which ruled at Sebennytus. Under the first king, Nekht-Hor-heb (Nectanebo I), the Persians, 200,000 strong, made a desperate attempt, with the help of the Greek general Iphicrates and 20,000 of his countrymen, to invade the Delta, but Nectanebo defeated them near Mendes. This victory secured peace and independence to Egypt for a term of years, during which art and commerce revived.

Tachus' reign was short (364–361 BCE), and he had internal as well as external troubles to deal with. He died an exile at the court of Artaxerxes. Nekht-neb-ef (Nectanebo II), 361–340 BCE, brought his dynasty and the empire of the pharaohs, after a duration of over 4,000 years, to an end by succumbing to the Persians under Ochus (Artaxerxes III).

c. 322 BCE

It is not surprising that, after the eight years during which this second Persian dynasty lasted, Alexander should have been received as a liberator and proclaimed son of Amen, that is to say, legitimate successor of the ancient kings of Egypt. The most able of his generals, Ptolemy, son of Lagus, founded a dynasty which may, in spite of its foreign origin, be considered as national as that of the Ramessides or of the Saitic kings. Greek influence did not make itself felt outside Alexandria. The Lagides respected the religions and customs of Egypt, which became the most important of the Greek kingdoms, while still preserving her original civilization. She even preserved it under the Roman dominion; and if we did not read the inscriptions, we could never guess that the temples of Esneh, of Edfu, of Denderah and of Philae belong to the time of the Lagides, the Caesars and the Antonines.

CLEOPATRA

From Ptolemy I to Cleopatra VI the rulers identified themselves with the interests, and especially with the religion of the nation, with whom they were not allied by blood, built cities and temples and, the earlier members of the dynasty at least, wrought for the general good. In the case of most of the later kings, however, they were more cruel and oppressive, and revolts were more common than at first.

The architecture, especially the portrait sculpture of the Ptolemy period, was inferior to some of earlier date, but in the encouragement of literature, the building of libraries and other public edifices, and the extending of commerce the race distinguished itself.

As regents or independent rulers their queens held sway. The family intermarried to an extent shocking to Christian ideas, and Ptolemy after Ptolemy took his sister or other near relatives, usually called Arsinoe, Berenike or Cleopatra, to wife. These close relationships, however, did not seem to strengthen the family affections – it is a blood-stained history, and the murders were almost as numerous as the unions. Various towns were built and called after the queens, Arsinoe and Berenike, but though Cleopatra seems to have been a favourite name, and there were six or seven of them in succession, this name was not so often used as the cognomen of a town.

There are a few names in the world's history that stand alone. Many may share in the same, but to speak them is to call up one dominating image. In this sense there was but one Caesar, but one Washington, but one Eve, but one Semiramis, and to this class belongs Cleopatra. There are others, such as Helen of Troy and Mary Stuart, who have shared with these a high reputation, but in these cases further identification is needed than the single name. Cleopatra stands among the few daughters of Eve pre-eminent for wit, charm, power and perhaps beauty, and to this must be added ambition and vice.

But the woman who made men her slaves at a single interview surely lacked no charm that nature could bestow. Unbridled both in passions and ambitions, she knew no limit to either and grasped at universal empire.

The greatest men of her time bowed at her feet, and she changed the fate of battle with the turning of her vessel's prow. She was over 20 when she captivated Caesar, over 30 when Antony became her slave. Of her numerous lovers, Antony was the chosen of that wayward, passionate heart. She refused to survive his defeat and death and perished by her own hand. Though not, strictly speaking, Egyptian queens, the Ptolemy race were yet queens of Egypt – and thus ended the long line of female royalties, extending from the dim ages of mythology to the Roman period.

Cleopatra VI has been described by a late novelist, his picture drawn perhaps from some historical source, as having 'a broad head, wavy hair, deep-set eyes, full, eloquent mouth and a long, slender throat'. Charm and talent of the highest order are generally credited to her. She had a musical voice and was a linguist of ability, skilled in Greek and Latin and could converse with Ethiopians, Jews, Arabians, Syrians, Medes and Persians and was proficient in music. Tennyson says of her:

'Her warbling voice a lyre of wildest range,
Struck by all passions.'

And another writer [John P. Mahaffy], disputing the fact that she is sometimes depicted as swarthy, says she was 'a pure Macedonian of a race akin to and perhaps fairer than the Greeks'.

Ptolemy XIII, the so-called Auletes, came to the throne in a sense under the protection of the Romans, and again took possession of the kingdom. It was at this time that Antony first saw Cleopatra, a girl of 15, and was struck with her beauty, he being Master of Horse to the conquering general, Gabrinus. But the acquaintance, if such it was, and not merely a glimpse on Antony's part, went no further then, and neither probably anticipated their subsequent relations.

Auletes' will, demanding that his eldest son and daughter should succeed him, was accepted by the mixed populace of Alexandria, and in a degree by the whole country, and for the moment Rome did not interfere. It was a youthful pair to have laid upon them or undertake such a grave responsibility – a mere girl and a child. Cleopatra was but 16, Ptolemy only 10. But though young in years, Cleopatra soon showed that she had both the capacity and ambition of an older woman. The direct heritage perhaps from one or other parent included beauty and charm, but a worthless father had but little in the way of character or mental abilities with which to endow his children, and perhaps it was rather from her mother that she derived her superior characteristics. With such paternity and the traditions of the entire race we can hardly wonder at the instances of vice and cruelty which we find recorded of this last royal member of her family. That her story is so interwoven with Roman affairs gives us a clearer knowledge of it than of much of the previous history, which was included only in that of Egypt and Syria.

So Cleopatra, a mere girl of 16 or 17, and her brother of 10, succeeded to the throne and were accepted by the Alexandrians. But the boy was persuaded by his counsellors to oust his sister, who was forced to yield and fled to Syria. That she had both adherents and means, however, is proved by the fact that she did not tamely submit to this violation of the agreement, but promptly raised an army, and this alone seems to indicate that, young as she was, she already showed remarkable abilities and returned to recover her lawful heritage. To live at peace with each other seemed beyond the power of most of the Ptolemy race.

At this point Pompey, seeking for allies, turned toward Egypt, and the father of the young king having been under obligations to him he made overtures to the boy sovereign. But the party in power, who for the time being were 'the power behind the throne', decided to receive him with apparent friendliness, and then treacherously murdered him, hoping thereby to secure the more powerful friendship of his adversary, Caesar. Meanwhile the armies of the young king and his sister lay opposite to each other. Caesar at once came to Egypt and was revolted at the treacherous deed, but was not in a sufficiently strong position to punish the murderers. He was received somewhat coldly and had to proceed with caution, but summoning his legions he demanded that the youthful contestants for the crown should appear before him and discuss their claims peacefully, rather than by force of arms.

This was Cleopatra's opportunity; her strongest weapons were her personal charms rather than her military powers. At 20 years of age she must have been in the perfect bloom of her beauty, with exquisite eyes and colouring, the sweetest of voices, a fascinating manner, ample powers of wit and rare conversational abilities. To these she trusted, and not in vain. Her position, her very life was at stake; her adversaries, who could probably hope for no consideration at her hands should she again come into power, would no doubt have been glad to assassinate her had opportunity afforded. Fearing this, it is said, and time seems to give credit to the story, she hid herself in a bale of carpet and caused it to be carried to Caesar's palace by night. No device which her fertile brain and keen wit could invent, we may be sure, was lacking in the accessories of the toilette to produce the effect she desired, to move his pity and secure his assistance. She played a great stake, perhaps with confidence, perhaps with trembling of heart, but she won, for from that time forward till his death Caesar, elderly man though he was, between 50 and 60 years of age, became her fervent admirer. Rarely, if ever, had woman accomplished so much in a single interview. She must have been elated with triumph and renewed confidence in her powers. Yet Caesar did not attempt to make her sole monarch; he lost his heart, so to speak, but not his head, as Antony subsequently did. He decreed that the will of Auletes should be carried out, restored Cyprus to Egypt and proposed that the younger brother and sister, Ptolemy and Arsinoe, should be made its governors. He even insisted that the money Cleopatra's father had pledged to

Rome should be paid. For this purpose it is said the young king's plate was ostentatiously pawned.

The king's chief counsellor, Pothinos, not realizing the strength that Caesar could command, nor the personal ability of the man with whom he had to deal, recalled the army and virtually declared war. Cleopatra's troops had either been hired mercenaries, who deserted or whose time had expired, and who went over to what they considered the winning side, or they had been defeated, for in this emergency she seems to have been able to afford little support to Caesar. In defending himself he set fire to the ships in the harbour, and it is even reported that the great library was burnt, but as various authors make no mention of it this last disaster is questioned.

Caesar put to death the councillor, Pothinos, and kept with him in the fortress his new love, the beautiful Cleopatra, and the two boys, the young king and his brother. The Princess Arsinoe, probably also beautiful and attractive, and, young as she was, realizing perhaps the character and ambition of her elder sister, fled to the Egyptian camp, thus refusing to put herself under the protection of the conquering Roman, though it was to him she owed her position as ruler of Cyprus; but distrust was natural and perhaps not unfounded. The Egyptians then demanded the young king, and Caesar, though virtually master, was not yet in a sufficiently strong position to refuse, so, knowing that this mere boy could do him no harm, he released him. It was, however, but the poor youth's death warrant, for in the subsequent attack upon the Egyptians they were driven into the river, and the royal boy came to his end by drowning, saved by this possibly from even a worse fate.

The Egyptians, disheartened, now gave up the contest. Caesar treated them with comparative leniency, set Cleopatra with the youngest Ptolemy as her nominal husband over them and carried the poor Princess Arsinoe to Rome, where, led in chains, she was among the captives to grace the triumph. She did not prove to have the power of her sister's fascinations to melt his hard heart. Caesar may have considered that she was in debt to him and had proved ungrateful and treacherous, but this was an act unworthy of his character and is attributed to the evil influence of Cleopatra. There is no direct proof of this, though his subsequent treatment of her sister gives colour to the idea.

After Caesar's departure a child was born to Cleopatra, whom she stated to be his son, gave him the name of Caesarion, or some say the name was given by the Alexandrians, and always upheld his royal prerogative even as against later children of the more beloved Antony. These irregularities and evil doings seem to have been calmly accepted by the people, and in inscriptions the boy is entitled, 'Ptolemy, also Caesar, the god Philopator Philometor'. He is to be numbered among the young princes who came to an untimely end; a brief life and a sad one, yet it is possible, even probable, that it had its periods of the pleasure and joy natural to his age, if no prolonged happiness.

Sometime between 48 and 44 BCE Cleopatra left Egypt with her brother and joined Caesar in Rome. Possibly he summoned her to come to him, more probably it was of her own motion, fearing that out of sight was out of mind, or might prove so, and that her presence was necessary to retain over him the influence she had gained. It was a shameful connection, as Caesar already had a wife, Caepurnia, and caused much scandal, even in scandalous Rome. She is mentioned by Cicero and others, but it is not her beauty and her grace that he dwells upon, but her haughtiness. Knowing full well probably how she was regarded, she returned the latent contempt which she divined in her visitor, even if he did not make it apparent, with a proud and supercilious demeanour. She had nothing to gain from him and she did not seek to charm and conciliate as she had done with Caesar. She is, however, said to have promised him books from the Alexandrian library, which seems to suggest that there was some part of it yet remaining even if it had suffered damage by fire, but failed to perform her promise.

Many of Caesar's actions are credited to her influence, and it is even believed that she desired him to establish an empire with Alexandria rather than Rome for its capital. The ostensible cause of her visit to Rome was to negotiate a treaty between the former and the country over which she nominally ruled. She dwelt in Caesar's palace across the Tiber and held court, at which not only Caesar's adherents, but his opponents, appeared, and it is said that statues of her, beautiful probably as the Venus of Pauline Bonaparte, were erected in the temple of the goddess of Love and Beauty.

Yet this was no position of true dignity for the nominal queen of a foreign land, and when in 44 BCE Caesar's murder took from her his support and protection she sailed for Egypt, no broken-hearted mourner, but a woman still ambitious and grasping all the possibilities of life. The next year she disposed of her last incumbrance and is held responsible for the murder of her youngest and only surviving brother, the nominal king. Four years each is the period assigned to her joint rule with her two brothers. She had no love to spare for her own kin, and too evidently was glad to be rid of them, even if the suspicion of her having poisoned the last of her family, who appears to have died in the same year as Caesar, may chance to be unfounded.

Now for a time Cleopatra bided at home, waiting and watching for further opportunities of conquests in love or dominion. Life with her was devoted to self-seeking and pleasure, yet it must have had some serious moments, some space for display of maternal feeling, some days and hours devoted to actual study; though it is hard and unfamiliar to think of her in this aspect else could she not have been mistress of so many languages as are attributed to her. She, nominally at least, governed the kingdom, cautiously kept out of Roman entanglements and pleaded her inability to assist the contestants with subsidies, which, it is said, Cassius demanded from her on the score of poverty. And indeed Egypt was in no condition to be either a principal or an ally in warfare at this time. The people suffered, the queen probably still lived in luxury and abundance.

Now again came Cleopatra's opportunity. Antony, victorious in the battle of Philippi, turned his attention to the East, and summoned Cleopatra before him, she being accused, as it has been seen, perhaps untruly, of sending aid to his rival, Cassius. Antony was of the party of Caesar, had delivered his funeral oration and was in a sense his successor. Like Caesar, also he had a fair and devoted wife, the noble Fulvia, but no legal bonds could resist 'the Sorceress of the Nile'.

Dellius, Antony's messenger, at once foresaw the probable result of a meeting between his master and the fascinating Egyptian, advised her to go in her 'best style' and vaunted his chief as the 'gentlest and kindliest of soldiers'. But Cleopatra was no subservient slave to hasten at the first bidding, and, disregarding many summons, took her own time and way to comply.

Her interview with Antony was in singular contrast with her first meeting with Caesar. As a fugitive and suppliant she conquered the one, with regal pomp and magnificence the other. Perhaps each method appealed most directly to the man she had to deal with, and her keen perception indicated the different modes. Caesar might have shown himself less malleable to the dominant queen, Antony to the pleading and powerless maiden.

Josephus speaks of her corrupting Antony with her 'love trick', and says he was bewitched and utterly conquered by her charms – her 'tricks' were of large and magnificent description. She made great preparations and gathered together splendid ornaments and costly gifts. At last, with full and well-deserved confidence in her own powers of fascination she started. Plutarch's words will best describe the gorgeous pageant she devised. 'She came sailing up the River Cydnus' (Antony was in Cilicia) 'in a barge with gilded stem and outspread sails of purple, while oars of silver beat time to the music of flutes and pipes and harps. She herself lay all along under a canopy of cloth of gold, dressed as Venus in a picture, and beautiful young boys, like painted Cupids, stood on each side to fan her. Her maids were dressed like sea Nymphs and Graces, some steered at the rudder, some working at the ropes. The perfumes diffused themselves from the vessel to the shore, which was covered with multitudes.' The people vacated the whole place and hastened to gaze upon the wondrous and beautiful sight, while Antony remained alone, awaiting the humble petitioner whom perhaps he expected to appear before him. But finally as Cleopatra intended he went to her.

This beginning was the keynote of their future intercourse, amusements, banquets, entertainments of all sorts. Cleopatra sent Antony the whole gold service which he admired, and, according to the familiar story, dissolved her pearl earring in a cup of vinegar or sour wine, which she made him drink. Pleasure was the goddess whom they worshipped. Unworthy though it might be of her fine powers and abilities, this was perhaps the happiest time of Cleopatra's life. Antony tried to vie with her in the splendour of his entertainments, but laughingly confessed she far outdid him.

Something like true love for him seems to have inspired the fickle queen. Caesar was but three years dead, but he was unmourned and forgotten.

Meanwhile, Antony's wife was fighting his battles at Rome and beseeching him to return, which he finally promised to do, but the Circe who held him in thrall willed rather that he should go with her to Alexandria, and prevailed, for he basely yielded to her arguments and spent the winter there, giving himself with her wholly up to the pursuit of pleasure in every form and the wildest revelry.

The inferior officers must have fulfilled their duties more faithfully than their superiors or the whole land would have been plunged in anarchy and destruction. The laws were administered, industry and commerce flourished and Alexandria continued to be a large, populous and busy city, full of life and animation and adorned with many magnificent buildings. The Pharos steadily cast its beneficent light across the waters to be a guide to mariners; the Temple of Serapis, on its high platform, called attention to the worship of the gods; the Library was as yet the casket of valuable treasures; the Museum was thronged with students and scholars; palaces and public buildings adorned the beautiful streets, forts and castles, breakwaters and harbour were laid out and perfected and Alexandria was alone rivalled by Rome.

The gods, too, no matter what might be the moral aspect of the private life of royalty, were worshipped and revered, and with the temples of Denderah and Philae the name of Cleopatra VI is especially associated. Though less gigantic than some of the others, the Temple of Hathor, the Goddess of Love, at Denderah, with that at Philae were none the less beautiful. Here at Dendera or Denderah, the Tentyra of the Greeks, a yearly festival was conducted with great splendour. The original edifice dated back to the earliest period of Egyptian history; it was added to and altered by the monarchs of the 12th dynasty, by Tuthmosis III and by Rameses II and III. It is said to have contained no less than 12 crypts. On the site of this old building the later Ptolemies had re-erected a newer structure, and it is here, on the southern, rear wall was found the conventional portrait of Cleopatra VI, as Isis, and her son Caesarion.

But the blackest stain upon this period is the murder of the poor princess, Arsinoe, who had taken refuge at Miletus, in the temple of Artemis Leucophryne, and who was put to death there by Antony's orders, at the instigation of Cleopatra. Perhaps beautiful and attractive also, if to a less extent, how different were the experiences of the two sisters! It seems strange that Arsinoe was not already the wife of and under the protection of some powerful noble or king – but Fate decreed differently.

Their mad existence could not continue forever, and matters at Rome grew so serious for Antony that he finally tore himself away from his enchantress and returned. His wife came to meet him, but died on the journey, so that legally he was now a free man. One almost wonders that he did not marry Cleopatra and try to make himself king of Egypt, as the first Ptolemy had done. But probably his reason forbade the attempt, and old relations once more began to hold sway. He made peace with the new Caesar, Octavian, Julius' nephew, and accepted his offer of his half-sister, Octavia, the recent widow of Caius Marcellus, for his wife, the Senate dispensing with the law which obliged a widow to pay the respect of 10 months of single life to her late husband. Octavia was a fine and beautiful woman, and is spoken of as serious and gentle, worthy of a better fate than to be the mate of Antony. For a time, however, she won his regard and an influence for good over him, recalling him to his better self, and a return to public duties, till Antony undertook the campaign against Parthion, and came once more within reach of his former enslaver.

For four years he seems to have been separated from Cleopatra, who had borne him twins, and with strange patience bided her time. She is said to have maintained the claims of her eldest son Caesarion and during all this time to have made no demands on Antony. He had left her, spite of all she had done, or could do, to detain him, and wounded, mortified and indignant, perhaps, she held her peace.

Pride is sometimes as strong a motive as love itself. So for solace she turned, as so many before her had done, to the building and repairing of temples.

Once within reach of her, Antony's old passion revived, and he sent for her to Syria. Very differently she acted from the first time he had summoned her; she needed no second bidding, but came at his call, and all was as before between them. He made her numerous and valuable gifts, acknowledged the twins as his own, giving them the names of Alexander and Cleopatra, and as surnames the titles of 'Sun' and 'Moon', and utterly broke loose from all his obligations. Once more Cleopatra triumphed.

She then returned to Egypt, while Antony went further afield; she in the interval going in state to Jerusalem, to visit Herod the Great.

But in this instance Cleopatra did not make the usual conquest, though she doubtless exerted all her powers. Although (under unjust accusation) he was eventually persuaded to put her to death, Herod was at that time passionately attached to his wife, Mariamme, and withstood Cleopatra's fascinations. The reunion of Antony and Cleopatra was most alarming to him, and he even consulted his council as to whether she, being in his power, he might dare to make away with her, but the dread of Antony's vengeance prevented, and with much polite attention and many gifts, she was escorted back to Egypt.

Antony's campaign against Parthia was a failure, but as before two women stood ready to assist him. Cleopatra on the one hand, accused of having violated tombs and robbed temples, perhaps for this very purpose, hastened to Syria to meet him, with provisions and clothing for his distressed army, while on the other Octavia came to Athens with even larger supplies. But as against Fulvia, so now, Cleopatra was victor, and Antony accompanied her to Alexandria. Again he gave himself up to his mad infatuation, incensing the Romans (who regarded Cleopatra with horror and aversion) at every step.

But the folly of Antony's course was raising against him a powerful faction, and Caesar Octavian did everything to augment this feeling and prepared for war. Cleopatra now put all the resources of her kingdom at Antony's command and insisted on accompanying him to battle, herself in charge of the Egyptian fleet. They went to Samos and to Actium, where Antony gathered together his army and it is said would have fought on land, but Cleopatra insisted that the strength of the rivals should be tested at sea. One dominant thought possessed her, as strong, or stronger, than her love for Antony – it was an invincible dread of being taken captive by and made to grace the triumph of the brother of the outraged Octavia. At sea she might hope to escape as she could not on land. It was this doubtless, more than cowardice, for however wicked she certainly was a brave woman and not lacking in physical courage, that made her at the first evidence that the battle was going against Antony, turn her vessel's prow and seek safety in flight.

Losing heart and head at once Antony blindly followed. For years Cleopatra had been his inspiration, his passion, his lodestar; where else to fly he knew not, his old world was, all too deservedly, against him. Yet it was not now for romance that he sought, though he followed her; he steeled his heart against her sorceries, and shut himself up in morbid communings with his own spirit. He would not see her and for some time it was in vain that her maidens pleaded with and tried to comfort him.

It seemed for the moment as if Cleopatra's power, she who 'governed men by change', had failed.

But a reconciliation finally ensued. Not to be at peace with Cleopatra was to give up his last hope, and apparently his only chance for a renewal of life and power. His army, deserted by its officers, made submission to Caesar, who thus remained complete victor.

Arrived in Africa, Cleopatra proceeded to Alexandria, while Antony remained alone, wandering about in comparative solitude, with only one of two friends. Reaching home, the queen pretended to have conquered rather than been defeated, and proceeded to put to death people, official and otherwise, of whom she wished to be rid. Not for one moment does she seem to have sat down and given up to despair, as did Antony. One project after another was entered upon and put in execution, and when Antony, weary of wandering, at last joined her again, he found her busy endeavouring to have her fleet dragged across the Isthmus of Suez, from the Mediterranean to the Red Sea, that she might escape to the other side and find a place of refuge and safety. But the Arabians burnt her ships and she was forced to abandon her gigantic scheme. She also sent embassies to Caesar, praying that she might be allowed to retain Egypt for herself and her children and that Antony might dwell there or in Athens as a private individual. Caesar professed to be willing to grant her anything that was reasonable, but was inexorable as regards Antony. If she would murder Antony, get him out of the way by whatever means, then her own prospects would be better.

But wicked, ambitious and cruel as Cleopatra undoubtedly was, the most sincere sentiment of her wayward life seems her attachment to Antony. To this she clung, preferring to share his fate – even death itself, than abandon or kill him.

Nevertheless, Antony was jealous and suspicious of her, and once more shut himself up in moody solitude. That her star had set, the knell of her doom sounded, Cleopatra must have clearly foreseen, but to the very end she held her head proudly and showed unbroken spirit. Not for her in modern parlance was 'the white feather'. Once more and for the last time she tempted Antony to her side. It must have been impossible for him to withhold his meed of admiration from this undaunted soul. Once more it was for them both, 'Let us eat and drink for tomorrow we die!' and they plunged into the same revelry, almost on the brink, as it were, of the grave. For them life had held little that was better, but the fine flavour of earlier times must have departed and there could not but be bitterness in their souls as they partook of their 'dead sea fruit'.

Cleopatra now completed her tomb, which, like so many Egyptian monarchs, she had begun before; in which she gathered together all her treasures and made strange experiments, with various poisons, on her unfortunate slaves, seeking to know how death might be most easily attained. While inexorable fate in the person of the world conqueror, Octavius Caesar, moved steadily and surely towards the besotted pair, Cleopatra would not put herself in the power of the conqueror, she would not grace his triumph. Rather than that welcome death!

Caesar on his part was most anxious to possess himself of her valuables and to prevent her from killing herself, as he feared she might do, and continued to send her plausible messages, but she did not trust him. He had taken Pelusium and now advanced to invest Alexandria. The walls were tightening around the tiger queen, like the iron tower which enshrouded the prisoner and daily grew smaller, so misfortune closed in upon her. She deserved her fate, she had even done much to provoke it, but one cannot withhold some pity and admiration from the dauntless, if wicked, woman.

Antony plucked up his spirit and made one successful sally against the surrounding host, but it was but the dying flicker of the candle; defeat followed, and his fleet and troops deserted to the conqueror. He accused Cleopatra of treachery, rushing through the streets and decrying her aloud in his mad fury. She fled and shut herself up with her maidens and attendants in her well-guarded tomb, while Antony retired to his palace. She then caused word to be sent to him that she had committed suicide, and a wave of tenderness overwhelmed him, while he lauded her bravery and begged his attendant to kill him, but the faithful servant only thrust his sword into his own body, and fell dead at his master's feet. In despair Antony wounded himself, but not at once fatally, and word being brought him that Cleopatra still lived, he demanded and entreated to be carried to her.

Fearful of Caesar's emissaries, she refused to unbar the great stone door, but she and her maidens drew her dying lover up to the balcony, exerting all their strength, and laid his on a bed, where he expired in her arms.

Then she gave herself up to a passionate grief, of which we cannot doubt the sincerity, children – country – all was forgotten in her wild outburst of sorrow, and still the pitiful story drew to its close. Cleopatra attempted suicide, but Caesar's messengers having now reached the upper story, with scaling ladders, arrived in time to prevent, and drew her dagger away, even threatening her with the destruction of all her children if she did not desist. Now for a space she changed her policy, but probably never her mind, which was evidently bent on self-destruction. She arrayed herself in fine garments and received Caesar, delivering over to him, nominally, all her treasures, but flying into a furious passion with a servant who betrayed that she was withholding a part; alternate gusts of fury and grief swayed the now enfeebled and broken body, and the tormented soul. At one instant she drew herself up in queenly dignity, at another threw herself at Caesar's feet, bathed in tears. He raised and tried to reassure her, pretending that he intended her no harm, but never relinquishing the fixed purpose of having her grace his triumph. While she, on her part, allowing herself to seem comforted, was equally unchanged in her determination. 'Tis said that during this interview Octavius kept his eyes upon the ground that neither the sight of her beauty nor her grief might move him.

And now comes the last act of the theatrical and tragic story. A basket of figs was sent up to the queen, and hidden in that, or in the apartment, was the asp, the messenger of death. Crowned and arrayed as for a festival she laid herself upon the bed where Antony had expired, and received a bite from the irritated snake, which she had tormented to his fatal task, she breathed her last. The passionate devotion she had inspired was proven by the self-destruction of her two maidens, Iras and Charmian, both of whom followed her example. Many old stories have been, by modern criticism and research, proved to be mythical tales, but this seems to hold its own. She had written a pitiful entreaty to Caesar that she might be buried in the same tomb with Antony, the last proof that her love for him was indeed a true affection. No sooner had Octavius received this than he suspected her design, and again sent his messengers, if possible, to prevent it. But they were too late. So expired the last and most noted queen of Egypt and Rome, long virtually master, took full possession. Balked in his scheme of carrying Cleopatra captive, Caesar showed what his fixed determination had been by having a golden statue of her made, with the asp upon her arm, and carried in his triumphal procession.

Of the fate of Cleopatra's children, history makes brief mention. The young Caesarion, whose rights his mother had always so carefully guarded, had been sent away with his tutor to the town of far Berenike, but the faithless man betrayed him to Octavian, who had both him and Antony's son, Antyllus, who had been declared a hereditary prince, cruelly murdered. The younger children, though they soon pass from the records and are lost to sight, had perchance a happier fate. The young princess Cleopatra, Antony's daughter, who doubtless possessed at least a portion of her mother's beauty, was married to Juba, the so-called 'literary king' of Mauritania, and Octavian, having removed those members of the family that he considered in any way dangerous to his own autocratic authority, permitted the sister to carry with her the two younger brothers, Alexander and Ptolemy, and thus the once mighty kingdom of Egypt lay prostrate under the foot of the temporary master of the world and became a Roman province; and the history of the Ptolemy race virtually ends with that of the world renowned queen, as Tennyson says, 'a name forever'.

ANCIENT KINGS & LEADERS

Ancient cultures often traded with and influenced each other, while others grew independently. This section provides the key leaders from a number of regions, to offer comparative insights into developments across the ancient world.

SUMERIAN KING LIST

This list is based on the *Sumerian King List* or *Chronicle of the One Monarchy*. The lists were often originally carved into clay tablets and several versions have been found, mainly in southern Mesopotamia. Some of these are incomplete and others contradict one another. Dates are based on archaeological evidence as far as possible but are thus approximate. There may also be differences in name spellings between different sources. Nevertheless, the lists remain an invaluable source of information.

As with many civilizations, lists of leaders often begin with mythological and legendary figures before they merge into the more solidly historical, hence why you will see some reigns of seemingly impossible length.

After the kingship descended from heaven, the kingship was in Eridug.

Alulim	28,800 years (8 *sars**)
Alalngar	36,000 years (10 *sars*)

Then Eridug fell and the kingship was taken to Bad-tibira.

En-men-lu-ana	43,200 years (12 *sars*)
En-mel-gal-ana	28,800 years (8 *sars*)
Dumuzid the Shepherd (or Tammuz)	36,000 years (10 *sars*)

Then Bad-tibira fell and the kingship was taken to Larag.

En-sipad-zid-ana 28,800 years (8 *sars*)

Then Larag fell and the kingship was taken to Zimbir.

En-men-dur-ana 21,000 years (5 *sars* and 5 *ners*)

Then Zimbir fell and the kingship was taken to Shuruppag.

Ubara-Tutu 18,600 years (5 *sars* and 1 *ner**)

Then the flood swept over.

*A *sar* is a numerical unit of 3,600; a *ner* is a numerical unit of 600.

FIRST DYNASTY OF KISH

After the flood had swept over, and the kingship had descended from heaven, the kingship was in Kish.

Jushur	1,200 years	Zuqaqip	900 years
Kullassina-bel	960 years	Atab (or A-ba)	600 years
Nangishlisma	1,200 years	Mashda (son of Atab)	840 years
En-tarah-ana	420 years	Arwium (son of Mashda)	720 years
Babum	300 years		
Puannum	840 years	Etana the Shepherd	1,500 years
Kalibum	960 years	Balih (son of Etana)	400 years
Kalumum	840 years	En-me-nuna	660 years

Melem-Kish (son of Enme-nuna) 900 years
Barsal-nuna (son of Enme-nuna) 1,200 years
Zamug (son of Barsal-nuna) 140 years
Tizqar (son of Zamug) 305 years
Ilku 900 years
Iltasadum 1,200 years
Enmebaragesi 900 years (earliest proven ruler based on archaeological sources; Early Dynastic Period, 2900–2350 BCE)
Aga of Kish (son of Enmebaragesi) 625 years (Early Dynastic Period, 2900–2350 BCE)

Then Kish was defeated and the kingship was taken to E-anna.

FIRST RULERS OF URUK

Mesh-ki-ang-gasher (son of Utu) 324 years (Late Uruk Period, 4000–3100 BCE)
Enmerkar (son of Mesh-ki-ang-gasher) 420 years (Late Uruk Period, 4000–3100 BCE)
Lugal-banda the shepherd 1200 years (Late Uruk Period, 4000–3100 BCE)
Dumuzid the fisherman 100 years (Jemdet Nasr Period, 3100–2900 BCE)
Gilgamesh 126 years (Early Dynastic Period, 2900–2350 BCE)
Ur-Nungal (son of Gilgamesh) 30 years
Udul-kalama (son of Ur-Nungal) 15 years
La-ba'shum 9 years

En-nun-tarah-ana	8 years
Mesh-he	36 years
Melem-ana	6 years
Lugal-kitun	36 years

Then Unug was defeated and the kingship was taken to Urim (Ur).

FIRST DYNASTY OF UR

Mesh-Ane-pada	80 years
Mesh-ki-ang-Nuna (son of Mesh-Ane-pada)	36 years
Elulu	25 years
Balulu	36 years

Then Urim was defeated and the kingship was taken to Awan.

DYNASTY OF AWAN

Three kings of Awan	356 years

Then Awan was defeated and the kingship was taken to Kish.

SECOND DYNASTY OF KISH

Susuda the fuller	201 years
Dadasig	81 years
Mamagal the boatman	360 years

Kalbum (son of Mamagal)	195 years
Tuge	360 years
Men-nuna (son of Tuge)	180 years
Enbi-Ishtar	290 years
Lugalngu	360 years

Then Kish was defeated and the kingship was taken to Hamazi.

DYNASTY OF HAMAZI

Hadanish	360 years

Then Hamazi was defeated and the kingship was taken to Unug (Uruk).

SECOND DYNASTY OF URUK

En-shag-kush-ana	60 years (*c.* 25th century BCE)
Lugal-kinishe-dudu	120 years
Argandea	7 years

Then Unug was defeated and the kingship was taken to Urim (Ur).

SECOND DYNASTY OF UR

Nanni	120 years
Mesh-ki-ang-Nanna II (son of Nanni)	48 years

Then Urim was defeated and the kingship was taken to Adab.

DYNASTY OF ADAB

Lugal-Ane-mundu	90 years (*c.* 25th century BCE)

Then Adab was defeated and the kingship was taken to Mari.

DYNASTY OF MARI

Anbu	30 years	Zizi of Mari, the fuller	20 years
Anba (son of Anbu)	17 years	Limer the 'gudug' priest	30 years
Bazi the leatherworker	30 years	Sharrum-iter	9 years

Then Mari was defeated and the kingship was taken to Kish.

THIRD DYNASTY OF KISH

Kug-Bau (Kubaba)	100 years (*c.* 25th century BCE)

Then Kish was defeated and the kingship was taken to Akshak.

DYNASTY OF AKSHAK

Unzi	30 years	Undalulu	6 years

Urur	6 years
Puzur-Nirah	20 years
Ishu-Il	24 years
Shu-Suen (son of Ishu-Il)	7 years

Then Akshak was defeated and the kingship was taken to Kish.

FOURTH DYNASTY OF KISH

Puzur-Suen (son of Kug-bau)	25 years (*c.* 2350 BCE)
Ur-Zababa (son of Puzur-Suen)	400 years (*c.* 2300 BCE)
Zimudar	30 years
Usi-watar (son of Zimudar)	7 years
Eshtar-muti	11 years
Ishme-Shamash	11 years
Shu-ilishu	15 years
Nanniya the jeweller	7 years

Then Kish was defeated and the kingship was taken to Unug (Uruk).

THIRD DYNASTY OF URUK

Lugal-zage-si	25 years (*c.* 2296–2271 BCE)

Then Unug was defeated and the kingship was taken to Agade (Akkad).

DYNASTY OF AKKAD

Sargon of Akkad	56 years (*c.* 2270–2215 BCE)
Rimush of Akkad (son of Sargon)	9 years (*c.* 2214–2206 BCE)
Manishtushu (son of Sargon)	15 years (*c.* 2205–2191 BCE)
Naram-Sin of Akkad (son of Manishtushu)	56 years (*c.* 2190–2154 BCE)
Shar-kali-sharri (son of Naram-Sin)	24 years (*c.* 2153–2129 BCE)

Then who was king? Who was not the king?

Irgigi, Nanum, Imi and Ilulu	3 years (four rivals who fought to be king during a three-year period; *c.* 2128–2125 BCE)
Dudu of Akkad	21 years (*c.* 2125–2104 BCE)
Shu-Durul (son of Duu)	15 years (*c.* 2104–2083 BCE)

Then Agade was defeated and the kingship was taken to Unug (Uruk).

FOURTH DYNASTY OF URUK

Ur-ningin	7 years (*c.* 2091?–2061? BCE)
Ur-gigir (son of Ur-ningin)	6 years
Kuda	6 years
Puzur-ili	5 years
Ur-Utu (or Lugal-melem; son of Ur-gigir)	6 years

Unug was defeated and the kingship was taken to the army of Gutium.

GUTIAN RULE

Inkišuš	6 years (*c.* 2147–2050 BCE)
Sarlagab (or Zarlagab)	6 years
Shulme (or Yarlagash)	6 years
Elulmeš (or Silulumeš or Silulu)	6 years
Inimabakeš (or Duga)	5 years
Igešauš (or Ilu-An)	6 years
Yarlagab	3 years
Ibate of Gutium	3 years
Yarla (or Yarlangab)	3 years
Kurum	1 year
Apilkin	3 years
La-erabum	2 years
Irarum	2 years
Ibranum	1 year
Hablum	2 years
Puzur-Suen (son of Hablum)	7 years
Yarlaganda	7 years
Si'um (or Si-u)	7 years
Tirigan	40 days

Then the army of Gutium was defeated and the kingship taken to Unug (Uruk).

FIFTH DYNASTY OF URUK

Utu-hengal	427 years / 26 years / 7 years (conflicting dates; *c.* 2055–2048 BCE)

THIRD DYNASTY OF UR

Ur-Namma (or Ur-Nammu)	18 years (*c.* 2047–2030 BCE)
Shulgi (son of Ur-Namma)	48 years (*c.* 2029–1982 BCE)
Amar-Suena (son of Shulgi)	9 years (*c.* 1981–1973 BCE)
Shu-Suen (son of Amar-Suena)	9 years (*c.* 1972–1964 BCE)
Ibbi-Suen (son of Shu-Suen)	24 years (*c.* 1963–1940 BCE)

Then Urim was defeated. The very foundation of Sumer was torn out. The kingship was taken to Isin.

DYNASTY OF ISIN

Ishbi-Erra	33 years (*c.* 1953–1920 BCE)
Shu-Ilishu (son of Ishbi-Erra)	20 years
Iddin-Dagan (son of Shu-Ilishu)	20 years
Ishme-Dagan (son of Iddin-Dagan)	20 years
Lipit-Eshtar (son of Ishme-Dagan or Iddin Dagan)	11 years
Ur-Ninurta (son of Ishkur)	28 years
Bur-Suen (son of Ur-Ninurta)	21 years
Lipit-Enlil (son of Bur-Suen)	5 years
Erra-imitti	8 years
Enlil-bani	24 years
Zambiya	3 years
Iter-pisha	4 years
Ur-du-kuga	4 years
Suen-magir	11 years
Damiq-ilishu (son of Suen-magir)	23 years

ANCIENT EGYPTIAN PHARAOHS

There is dispute about the dates and position of pharaohs within dynasties due to several historical sources being incomplete or inconsistent. This list aims to provide an overview of the ancient Egyptian dynasties, but is not exhaustive and dates are approximate. There may also be differences in name spellings between different sources. Also please note that the throne name is given first, followed by the personal name – more commonly they are known by the latter.

ANCIENT EGYPTIAN DEITIES

Ancient Egyptian gods and goddesses were worshipped as deities. They were responsible for maat (divine order or stability), and different deities represented different natural forces, such as Ra the Sun God. After the Egyptian state was first founded in around 3100 BCE, pharaohs claimed to be divine representatives of these gods and were thought to be successors of the gods.

While there are many conflicting Egyptian myths, some of the significant gods and goddesses and their significant responsibilities are listed here.

Amun/Amen/Amen-Ra — Creation
Atem/Tem — Creation, the sun

Ra	The sun
Isis	The afterlife, fertility, magic
Osiris	Death and resurrection, agriculture
Hathor	The sky, the sun, motherhood
Horus	Kingship, the sky
Set	Storms, violence, deserts
Maat	Truth and justice, she personifies *maat*
Anubis	The dead, the underworld

PREDYNASTIC AND EARLY DYNASTIC PERIODS (*c.* 3000–2686 BCE)

First Dynasty (*c.* 3150–2890 BCE)

The first dynasty begins at the unification of Upper and Lower Egypt.

Narmer (Menes/M'na?)	*c.* 3150 BCE
Aha (Teti)	*c.* 3125 BCE
Djer (Itej)	54 years
Djet (Ita)	10 years
Merneith (possibly the first female Egyptian pharaoh)	*c.* 2950 BCE
Khasti (Den)	42 years
Merybiap (Adjib)	10 years
Semerkhet (Iry)	8.5 years
Qa'a (Qebeh)	34 years
Sneferka	*c.* 2900 BCE
Horus-Ba (Horus Bird)	*c.* 2900 BCE

Second Dynasty (*c.* 2890–2686 BCE)

Little is known about the second dynasty of Egypt.

Hetepsekhemwy (Nebtyhotep)	15 years
Nebra	14 years
Nynetjer (Banetjer)	43–45 years
Ba	unknown
Weneg-Nebty	*c.* 2740 BCE
Wadjenes (Wadj-sen)	*c.* 2740 BCE
Nubnefer	unknown
Senedj	*c.* 47 years
Peribsen (Seth-Peribsen)	unknown
Sekhemib (Sekhemib-Perenmaat)	*c.* 2720 BCE
Neferkara I	25 years
Neferkasokkar	8 years
Horus Sa	unknown
Hudejefa (real name missing)	11 years
Khasekhemwy (Bebty)	18 years

OLD KINGDOM (*c.* 2686–2181 BCE)

Third Dynasty (*c.* 2686–2613 BCE)

The third dynasty was the first dynasty of the Old Kingdom. Its capital was at Memphis.

Djoser (Netjerikhet)	*c.* 2650 BCE
Sekhemkhet (Djoser-Teti)	2649–2643 BCE
Nebka? (Sanakht)	*c.* 2650 BCE
Qahedjet (Huni?)	unknown
Khaba (Huni?)	2643–2637 BCE
Huni	2637–2613 BCE

Fourth Dynasty (*c.* 2613–2498 BCE)

The fourth dynasty is sometimes known as the 'golden age' of Egypt's Old Kingdom.

Snefru (Nebmaat)	2613–2589 BCE
Khufu, or Cheops (Medjedu)	2589–2566 BCE
Djedefre (Kheper)	2566–2558 BCE
Khafre (Userib)	2558–2532 BCE
Menkaure (Kakhet)	2532–2503 BCE
Shepseskaf (Shepeskhet)	2503–2498 BCE

Fifth Dynasty (*c.* 2498–2345 BCE)

There is some doubt over the succession of pharaohs in the fifth dynasty, especially Shepseskare.

Userkaf	2496/8–2491 BCE
Sahure	2490–2477 BCE
Neferirkare-Kakai	2477–2467 BCE
Neferefre (Izi)	2460–2458 BCE
Shepseskare (Netjeruser)	few months between 2458 and 2445 BCE
Niuserre (Ini)	2445–2422 BCE
Menkauhor (Kaiu)	2422–2414 BCE
Djedkare (Isesi)	2414–2375 BCE
Unis (Wenis)	2375–2345 BCE

Sixth Dynasty (*c.* 2345–2181 BCE)

Teti	2345–2333 BCE
Userkare	2333–2332 BCE
Meryre (Pepi I)	2332–2283 BCE

Merenre I (Nemtyemsaf I)	2283–2278 BCE
Neferkare (Pepi II)	2278–2183 BCE
Merenre II (Nemtyemsaf II)	2183 or 2184 BCE
Netjerkare (Siptah I) or Nitocris	2182–2179 BCE

FIRST INTERMEDIATE PERIOD (*c.* 2181–2040 BCE)

Seventh and Eighth Dynasties (*c.* 2181–2160 BCE)

There is little evidence on this period in ancient Egyptian history, which is why many of the periods of rule are unknown.

Menkare	*c.* 2181 BCE
Neferkare II	unknown
Neferkare III (Neby)	unknown
Djedkare (Shemai)	unknown
Neferkare IV (Khendu)	unknown
Merenhor	unknown
Sneferka (Neferkamin I)	unknown
Nikare	unknown
Neferkare V (Tereru)	unknown
Neferkahor	unknown
Neferkare VI (Peiseneb)	unknown to 2171 BCE
Neferkamin (Anu)	*c.* 2170 BCE
Qakare (Ibi)	2175–2171 BCE
Neferkaure	2167–2163 BCE
Neferkauhor (Khuwihapi)	2163–2161 BCE
Neferiirkkare (Pepi)	2161–2160 BCE

Ninth Dynasty (*c.* 2160–2130 BCE)

There is little evidence on this period in ancient Egyptian history which is why many of the periods of rule are unknown.

Maryibre (Khety I)	2160 BCE to unknown
Name unknown	unknown
Naferkare VII	unknown
Seneh (Setut)	unknown

The following pharaohs and their dates of rule are unknown or widely unconfirmed.

Tenth Dynasty (*c.* 2130–2040 BCE)

Rulers in the Tenth dynasty were based in Lower Egypt.

Meryhathor	2130 BCE to unknown
Neferkare VIII	2130–2040 BCE
Wahkare (Khety III)	unknown
Merykare	unknown to 2040 BCE
Name unknown	unknown

Eleventh Dynasty (*c.* 2134–1991 BCE)

Rulers in the eleventh dynasty were based in Upper Egypt.

Intef the Elder	unknown
Tepia (Mentuhotep I)	unknown to 2133 BCE
Sehertawy (Intef I)	2133–2117 BCE
Wahankh (Intef II)	2117–2068 BCE
Nakhtnebtepefer (Intef III)	2068–2060/40 BCE

MIDDLE KINGDOM (*c.* 2040–1802 BCE)

Eleventh Dynasty Continued (*c.* 2134–1991 BCE)

This period is usually known as the beginning of the Middle Kingdom.

Nebhepetre (Mentuhotep II) 2060–2040 BCE as king of Upper Egypt, 2040–2009 BCE as King of Upper and Lower Egypt
Sankhkare (Mentuhotep III) 2009–1997 BCE
Nebtawyre (Mentuhotep IV) 1997–1991 BCE

Twelfth Dynasty (*c.* 1991–1802 BCE)

The twelfth dynasty was one of the most stable prior to the New Kingdom, and is often thought to be the peak of the Middle Kingdom.

Sehetepibre (Amenemhat I) 1991–1962 BCE
Kheperkare (Senusret I / Sesostris I) 1971–1926 BCE
Nubkaure (Amenemhat II) 1929–1895 BCE
Khakheperre (Senusret II / Sesostris II) 1898–1878 BCE
Khakaure (Senusret III / Sesostris III) 1878–1839 BCE
Nimaatre (Amenemhat III) 1860–1815 BCE
Maakherure (Amenemhat IV) 1815–1807 BCE
Sobekkare (Sobekneferu/Nefrusobek) 1807–1802 BCE

SECOND INTERMEDIATE PERIOD (*c.* 1802–1550 BCE)

Thirteenth Dynasty (*c.* 1802–*c.* 1649 BCE)

There is some ambiguity on the periods of rule of the thirteenth dynasty, but it is marked by a period of several short rules. This dynasty is often combined with the eleventh, twelfth and fourteenth dynasties under the Middle Kingdom.

Sekhemre Khutawy (Sobekhotep I)	1802–1800 BCE
Mehibtawy Sekhemkare (Amenemhat Sonbef)	1800–1796 BCE
Nerikare (Sobek)	1796 BCE
Sekhemkare (Amenemhat V)	1796–1793 BCE
Ameny Qemau	1795–1792 BCE
Hotepibre (Qemau Siharnedjheritef)	1792–1790 BCE
Lufni	1790–1788 BCE
Seankhibre (Amenemhat VI)	1788–1785 BCE
Semenkare (Nebnuni)	1785–1783 BCE
Sehetepibre (Sewesekhtawy)	1783–1781 BCE
Sewadijkare I	1781 BCE
Nedjemibre (Amenemhat V)	1780 BCE
Khaankhre (Sobekhotep)	1780–1777 BCE
Renseneb	1777 BCE
Awybre (Hor)	1777–1775 BCE
Sekhemrekhutawy Khabaw	1775–1772 BCE
Djedkheperew	1772–1770 BCE
Sebkay	unknown
Sedjefakare (Kay Amenemhat)	1769–1766 BCE
Khutawyre (Wegaf)	c. 1767 BCE
Userkare (Khendjer)	c. 1765 BCE
Smenkhkare (Imyremeshaw)	started in 1759 BCE
Sehetepkare (Intef IV)	c. 10 years
Meribre (Seth)	ended in 1749 BCE
Sekhemresewadjtawy (Sobekhotep III)	1755–1751 BCE
Khasekhemre (Neferhotep I)	1751–1740 BCE
Menwadjre (Sihathor)	1739 BCE

Khaneferre (Sobekhotep IV)	1740–1730 BCE
Merhotepre (Sobekhotep V)	1730 BCE
Knahotepre (Sobekhotep VI)	c. 1725 BCE
Wahibre (Ibiau)	1725–1714 BCE
Merneferre (Ay I)	1714–1691 BCE
Merhotepre (Ini)	1691–1689 BCE
Sankhenre (Sewadjtu)	1675–1672 BCE
Mersekhemre (Ined)	1672–1669 BCE
Sewadjkare II (Hori)	c. 5 years
Merkawre (Sobekhotep VII)	1664–1663 BCE
Seven kings (names unknown)	1663–? BCE

Note: the remaining pharaohs of the thirteenth dynasty are not listed here as they are either unknown or there is a lot of ambiguity about when they ruled.

Fourteenth Dynasty (*c.* 1805/1710–1650 BCE)

Rulers in the fourteenth dynasty were based at Avaris, the capital of this dynasty.

Sekhaenre (Yakbim)	1805–1780 BCE
Nubwoserre (Ya'ammu)	1780–1770 BCE
Khawoserre (Qareh)	1770–1745 BCE
Aahotepre ('Ammu)	1760–1745 BCE
Maaibre (Sheshi)	1745–1705 BCE
Aasehre (Nehesy)	c. 1705 BCE
Khakherewre	unknown
Nebefawre	c. 1704 BCE
Sehebre	1704–1699 BCE
Merdjefare	c. 1699 BCE

Note: the remaining pharaohs of the fourteenth dynasty are not listed here as they are either unknown or there is a lot of ambiguity about when they ruled.

Fifteenth Dynasty (*c.* 1650–1544 BCE)

The fifteenth dynasty was founded by Salitas and covered a large part of the Nile region.

Salitas	c. 1650 BCE
Semqen	1649 BCE to unknown
'Aper-'Anat	unknown
Sakir-Har	unknown
Seuserenre (Khyan)	*c.* 30 to 35 years
Nebkhepeshre (Apepi)	1590 BCE?
Nakhtyre (Khamudi)	1555–1544 BCE

Sixteenth Dynasty (*c.* 1650–1580 BCE)

Rulers in the sixteenth dynasty were based at Thebes, the capital of this dynasty. The name and date of rule of the first pharaoh is unknown.

Sekhemresementawy (Djehuti)	3 years
Sekhemresemeusertawy (Sobekhotep VIII)	16 years
Sekhemresankhtawy (Neferhotep III)	1 year
Seankhenre (Mentuhotepi)	less than a year
Sewadjenre (Nebiryraw)	26 years
Neferkare (?) (Nebiryraw II)	c. 1600 BCE
Semenre	c. 1600 BCE
Seuserenre (Bebiankh)	12 years
Djedhotepre (Dedumose I)	*c.* 1588–1582 BCE

Djedneferre (Dedumose II)	c. 1588–1582 BCE
Djedankhre (Montensaf)	c. 1590 BCE
Merankhre (Mentuhotep VI)	c. 1585 BCE
Seneferibre (Senusret IV)	unknown
Sekhemre (Shedwast)	unknown

Seventeenth Dynasty (*c.* 1650–1550 BCE)

Rulers in the seventeenth dynasty ruled Upper Egypt.

Sekhemrewahkhaw (Rahotep)	c. 1620 BCE
Sekhemre Wadjkhaw (Sobekemsaf I)	c. 7 years
Sekhemre Shedtawy (Sobekemsaf II)	unknown to c. 1573 BCE
Sekhemre-Wepmaat (Intef V)	c. 1573–1571 BCE
Nubkheperre (Intef VI)	c. 1571–1565 BCE
Sekhemre-Heruhirmaat (Intef VII)	late 1560s BCE
Senakhtenre (Ahmose)	c. 1558 BCE
Seqenenre (Tao I)	1558–1554 BCE
Wadkheperre (Kamose)	1554–1549 BCE

NEW KINGDOM (*c.* 1550–1077 BCE)

Eighteenth Dynasty (*c.* 1550–1292 BCE)

The first dynasty of Egypt's New Kingdom marked the beginning of ancient Egypt's highest power and expansion.

Nebpehtire (Ahmose I)	c. 1550–1525 BCE
Djeserkare (Amenhotep I)	1541–1520 BCE
Aakheperkare (Thutmose I)	1520–1492 BCE

Aakheperenre (Thutmose II)	1492–1479 BCE
Maatkare (Hatshepsut)	1479–1458 BCE
Menkheperre (Thutmose III)	1458–1425 BCE
Aakheperrure (Amenhotep II)	1425–1400 BCE
Menkheperure (Thutmose IV)	1400–1390 BCE
Nebmaatre 'the Magnificent' (Amehotep III)	1390–1352 BCE
Neferkheperure Waenre (Amenhotep IV)	1352–1336 BCE
Ankhkheperure (Smenkhkare)	1335–1334 BCE
Ankhkheperure mery Neferkheperure (Neferneferuaten III)	1334–1332 BCE
Nebkheperure (Tutankhamun)	1332–1324 BCE
Kheperkheperure (Aya II)	1324–1320 BCE
Djeserkheperure Setpenre (Haremheb)	1320–1292 BCE

Nineteenth Dynasty (*c.* 1550–1292 BCE)

The nineteenth dynasty is also known as the Ramessid dynasty as it includes Ramesses II, one of the most famous and influential Egyptian pharaohs.

Menpehtire (Ramesses I)	1292–1290 BCE
Menmaatre (Seti I)	1290–1279 BCE
Usermaatre Setpenre 'the Great', 'Ozymandias' (Ramesses II)	1279–1213 BCE
Banenre (Merneptah)	1213–1203 BCE
Menmire Setpenre (Amenmesse)	1203–1200 BCE
Userkheperure (Seti II)	1203–1197 BCE
Sekhaenre (Merenptah Siptah)	1197–1191 BCE
Satre Merenamun (Tawosret)	1191–1190 BCE

Twentieth Dynasty (*c.* 1190–1077 BCE)

This, the third dynasty of the New Kingdom, is generally thought to mark the start of the decline of ancient Egypt.

Userkhaure (Setnakht)	1190–1186 BCE
Usermaatre Meryamun (Ramesses III)	1186–1155 BCE
Heqamaatre Setpenamun (Ramesses IV)	1155–1149 BCE
Heqamaatre Setpenamun (Ramesses IV)	1155–1149 BCE
Usermaatre Sekheperenre (Ramesses V)	1149–1145 BCE
Nebmaatre Meryamun (Ramesses VI)	1145–1137 BCE
Usermaatre Setpenre Meryamun (Ramesses VII)	1137–1130 BCE
Usermaatre Akhenamun (Ramesses VIII)	1130–1129 BCE
Neferkare Setpenre (Ramesses IX)	1128–1111 BCE
Khepermaatre Setpenptah (Ramesses X)	1111–1107 BCE
Menmaatre Setpenptah (Ramesses XI)	1107–1077 BCE

Twenty-first Dynasty (*c.* 1077–943 BCE)

Rulers in the twenty-first dynasty were based at Tanis and mainly governed Lower Egypt.

Hedjkheperre-Setpenre (Nesbanadjed I)	1077–1051 BCE
Neferkare (Amenemnisu)	1051–1047 BCE
Aakkheperre (Pasebakhenniut I)	1047–1001 BCE
Usermaatre (Amenemope)	1001–992 BCE
Aakheperre Setepenre (Osorkon the Elder)	992–986 BCE
Netjerikheperre-Setpenamun (Siamun)	986–967 BCE
Titkheperure (Pasebakhenniut II)	967–943 BCE

Twenty-second Dynasty (*c.* 943–728 BCE)

Sometimes called the Bubastite dynasty. Its pharaohs came from Libya.

Hedjkheneperre Setpenre (Sheshonq I)	943–922 BCE
Sekhemkheperre Setepenre (Osorkon I)	922–887 BCE
Heqakheperre Setepenre (Sheshonq II)	887–885 BCE
Tutkheperre (Sheshonq Llb)	*c.* the 880s BCE
Hedjkheperre Setepenre (Takelot I Meriamun)	885–872 BCE
Usermaatre Setpenre (Sheshonq III)	837–798 BCE
Hedjkheperre Setepenre (Sheshonq IV)	798–785 BCE
Usermaatre Setpenre (Pami Meriamun)	785–778 BCE
Aakheperre (Sheshonq V)	778–740 BCE
Usermaatre (Osorkon IV)	740–720 BCE

Twenty-third and Twenty-fourth Dynasties (*c.* 837–720 BCE)

These dynasties were led mainly by Libyans and mainly ruled Upper Egypt.

Hedjkheperre Setpenre (Takelot II)	837–813 BCE
Usermaatre Setpenamun (Meriamun Pedubaste I)	826–801 BCE
Usermaatre Meryamun (Sheshonq VI)	801–795 BCE
Usermaatre Setpenamun (Osorkon III)	795–767 BCE
Usermaatre-Setpenamun (Takelot III)	773–765 BCE
Usermaatre-Setpenamun (Meriamun Rudamun)	765–762 BCE
Shepsesre (Tefnakhte)	732–725 BCE
Wahkare (Bakenrenef)	725–720 BCE

Twenty-fifth Dynasty (*c.* 744–656 BCE)

Also known as the Kushite period, the twenty-fifth dynasty follows the Nubian invasions.

Piankhy (Piye)	744–714 BCE
Djedkaure (Shebitkku)	714–705 BCE
Neferkare (Shabaka)	705–690 BCE
Khuinefertemre (Taharqa)	690–664 BCE

LATE PERIOD (*c.* 664–332 BCE)

Twenty-sixth Dynasty (*c.* 664 – 525 BCE)

Also known as the Saite period, the twenty-sixth dynasty was the last native period before the Persian invasion in 525 BCE.

Wahibre (Psamtik I)	664–610 BCE
Wehemibre (Necho II)	610–595 BCE
Neferibre (Psamtik II)	595–589 BCE
Haaibre (Apreis)	589–570 BCE
Khemibre (Amasis II)	570–526 BCE
Ankhkaenre (Psamtik III)	526–525 BCE

Twenty-seventh Dynasty (*c.* 525–404 BCE)

The twenty-seventh dynasty is also known as the First Egyptian Satrapy and was ruled by the Persian Achaemenids.

Mesutre (Cambyses II)	525–1 July 522 BCE
Seteture (Darius I)	522–November 486 BCE
Kheshayarusha (Xerxes I)	November 486–December 465 BCE
Artabanus of Persia	465–464 BCE
Arutakhshashas (Artaxerxes I)	464–424 BCE
Ochus (Darius II)	July 423–March 404 BCE

Twenty-eighth Dynasty (*c.* 404–398 BCE)

The twenty-eighth dynasty consisted of a single pharaoh.

Amunirdisu (Amyrtaeus)	404–398 BCE

Twenty-ninth Dynasty (*c.* 398–380 BCE)

The twenty-ninth dynasty was founded following the overthrow of Amyrtaeus.

Baenre Merynatjeru (Nepherites I)	398–393 BCE
Khnemmaatre Setepenkhnemu (Hakor)	*c.* 392–391 BCE
Userre Setepenptah (Psammuthis)	*c.* 391 BCE
Khnemmaatre Setepenkhnemu (Hakor)	*c.* 390–379 BCE
Nepherites II	*c.* 379 BCE

Thirtieth Dynasty (*c.*379–340 BCE)

The thirtieth dynasty is thought to be the final native dynasty of ancient Egypt.

Kheperkare (Nectanebo I)	*c.* 379–361 BCE
Irimaatenre (Teos)	*c.* 361–359 BCE
Snedjemibre Setepenanhur (Nectanebo II)	*c.* 359–340 BCE

Thirty-first Dynasty (*c.* 340–332 BCE)

The thirty-first dynasty is also known as the Second Egyptian Satrapy and was ruled by the Persian Achaemenids.

Ochus (Artaxerxes III)	*c.* 340–338 BCE
Arses (Artaxerxes IV)	338–336 BCE
Darius III	336–332 BCE

MACEDONIAN/ARGEAD DYNASTY (*c.* 332–309 BCE)

Alexander the Great conquered Persia and Egypt in 332 BCE.

Setpenre Meryamun (Alexander III of Macedon 'the Great')	332–323 BCE
Setpenre Meryamun (Philip Arrhidaeus)	323–317 BCE
Khaibre Setepenamun (Alexander IV)	317–309 BCE

PTOLEMAIC DYNASTY (*c.* 305–30 BCE)

The Ptolemaic dynasty in Egypt was the last dynasty of ancient Egypt before it became a province of Rome.

Ptolemy I Soter	305–282 BCE
Ptolemy II Philadelphos	284–246 BCE
Arsinoe II	c. 277–270 BCE
Ptolemy III Euergetes	246–222 BCE
Berenice II	244/243–222 BCE
Ptolemy IV Philopater	222–204 BCE
Arsinoe III	220–204 BCE
Ptolemy V Epiphanes	204–180 BCE
Cleopatra I	193–176 BCE
Ptolemy VI Philometor	180–164, 163–145 BCE
Cleopatra II	175–164 BCE, 163–127 BCE and 124–116 BCE
Ptolemy VIII Physcon	171–163 BCE, 144–131 BCE and 127–116 BCE
Ptolemy VII Neos Philopator	145–144 BCE

Cleopatra III	142–131 BCE, 127–107 BCE
Ptolemy Memphites	113 BCE
Ptolemy IX Soter	116–110 BCE
Cleopatra IV	116–115 BCE
Ptolemy X Alexander	110–109 BCE
Berenice III	81–80 BCE
Ptolemy XI Alexander	80 BCE
Ptolemy XII Auletes	80–58 BCE, 55–51 BCE
Cleopatra V Tryphaena	79–68 BCE
Cleopatra VI	58–57 BCE
Berenice IV	58–55 BCE
Cleopatra VII	52–30 BCE
Ptolemy XIII Theos Philopator	51–47 BCE
Arsinoe IV	48–47 BCE
Ptolemy XIV Philopator	47–44 BCE
Ptolemy XV Caesar	44–30 BCE

In 30 BCE, Egypt became a province of the Roman Empire.

ANCIENT GREEK MONARCHS

This list is not exhaustive and dates are approximate. Where dates of rule overlap, emperors either ruled jointly or ruled in opposition to one another. There may also be differences in name spellings between different sources.

Because of the fragmented nature of Greece prior to its unification by Philip II of Macedon, this list includes mythological and existing rulers of Thebes, Athens and Sparta as some of the leading ancient Greek city-states. These different city-states had some common belief in the mythological gods and goddesses of ancient Greece, although their accounts may differ.

KINGS OF THEBES (*c.* 753–509 BCE)

These rulers are mythological. There is much diversity over who the kings actually were, and the dates they ruled.

Calydnus (son of Uranus)
Ogyges (son of Poseidon, thought to be king of Boeotia or Attica)
Cadmus (Greek mythological hero known as the founder of Thebes, known as Cadmeia until the reign of Amphion and Zethus)
Pentheus (son of Echion, one of the mythological Spartoi, and Agave, daughter of Cadmus)

Polydorus (son of Cadmus and Harmonia, goddess of harmony)
Nycteus (like his brother Lycus, thought to be the son of a Spartoi and a nymph, or a son of Poseidon)
Lycus (brother of Nyceteus)
Labdacus (grandson of Cadmus)
Lycus (second reign as regent for Laius)
Amphion and Zethus (joint rulers and twin sons of Zeus, constructed the city walls of Thebes)
Laius (son of Labdacus, married to Jocasta)
Oedipus (son of Laius, killed his father and married his mother, Jocasta)
Creon (regent after the death of Laius)
Eteocles and Polynices (brothers/sons of Oedipus; killed each other in battle)
Creon (regent for Laodamas)
Laodamas (son of Eteocles)
Thersander (son of Polynices)
Peneleos (regent for Tisamenus)
Tisamenus (son of Thersander)
Autesion (son of Tisamenes)
Damasichthon (son of Peneleos)
Ptolemy (son of Damasichton, 12 century BCE)
Xanthos (son of Ptolemy)

KINGS OF ATHENS

Early legendary kings who ruled before the mythological flood caused by Zeus, which only Deucalion (son of Prometheus) and a few others survived (date unknown).

Periphas (king of Attica, turned into an eagle by Zeus)
Ogyges (son of Poseidon, thought to be king of either Boeotia or Attica)
Actaeus (king of Attica, father-in-law to Cecrops I)

Erechtheid Dynasty (1556–1127 BCE)

Cecrops I (founder and first king of Athens; half-man, half-serpent who married Actaeus' daughter)	1556–1506 BCE
Cranaus	1506–1497 BCE
Amphictyon (son of Deucalion)	1497–1487 BCE
Erichthonius (adopted by Athena)	1487–1437 BCE
Pandion I (son of Erichthonius)	1437–1397 BCE
Erechtheus (son of Pandion I)	1397–1347 BCE
Cecrops II (son of Erechtheus)	1347–1307 BCE
Pandion II (son of Cecrops II)	1307–1282 BCE
Aegeus (adopted by Pandion II, gave his name to the Aegean Sea)	1282–1234 BCE
Theseus (son of Aegeus, killed the minotaur)	1234–1205 BCE
Menestheus (made king by Castor and Pollux when Theseus was in the underworld)	1205–1183 BCE
Demophon (son of Theseus)	1183–1150 BCE
Oxyntes (son of Demophon)	1150–1136 BCE
Apheidas (son of Oxyntes)	1136–1135 BCE
Thymoetes (son of Oxyntes)	1135–1127 BCE

Melanthid Dynasty (1126–1068 BCE)

Melanthus (king of Messenia, fled to Athens when expelled)	1126–1089 BCE
Codrus (last of the semi-mythological Athenian kings)	1089–1068 BCE

LIFE ARCHONS OF ATHENS (1068–753 BCE)

These rulers held public office up until their deaths.

Medon	1068–1048 BCE	Pherecles	864–845 BCE
Acastus	1048–1012 BCE	Ariphon	845–825 BCE
Archippus	1012–993 BCE	Thespieus	824–797 BCE
Thersippus	993–952 BCE	Agamestor	796–778 BCE
Phorbas	952–922 BCE	Aeschylus	778–755 BCE
Megacles	922–892 BCE	Alcmaeon	755–753 BCE
Diognetus	892–864 BCE		

From this point, archons led for a period of ten years up to 683 BCE, then a period of one year up to 485 CE. Selected important leaders – including archons and tyrants – in this later period are as follows:

SELECTED LATER LEADERS OF ATHENS

Peisistratos 'the Tyrant of Athens'	561, 559–556, 546–527 BCE
Cleisthenes (archon)	525–524 BCE
Themistocles (archon)	493–492 BCE
Pericles	c. 461–429 BCE

KINGS OF SPARTA

These rulers are mythological and are thought to be descendants of the ancient tribe of Leleges. There is much diversity over who the kings actually were, and the dates they ruled.

Lelex (son of Poseidon or Helios, ruled Laconia) c. 1600 BCE
Myles (son of Lelex, ruled Laconia) c. 1575 BCE
Eurotas (son of Myles, father of Sparta) c. 1550 BCE

From the Lelegids, rule passed to the Lacedaemonids when Lacedaemon married Sparta.

Lacedaemon (son of Zeus, husband of Sparta)
Amyklas (son of Lacedaemon)
Argalus (son of Amyklas)
Kynortas (son of Amyklas)
Perieres (son of Kynortas)
Oibalos (son of Kynortas)
Tyndareos (first reign; son of Oibalos, father of Helen of Troy)
Hippocoon (son of Oibalos)
Tyndareos (second reign; son of Oibaos, father of Helen of Troy)

From the Lacedaemons, rule passed to the Atreids when Menelaus married Helen of Troy.

Menelaus (son of Atreus, king of Mycenae, and husband of Helen) c. 1250 BCE
Orestes (son of Agamemnon, Menelaus' brother) c. 1150 BCE
Tisamenos (son of Orestes)
Dion c. 1100 BCE

From the Atreids, rule passed to the Heraclids following war.

Aristodemos (son of Aristomachus, great-great-grandson of Heracles)

Theras (served as regent for Aristodemes' sons, Eurysthenes and Procles)
Eurysthenes c. 930 BCE

From the Heraclids, rule passed to the Agiads, founded by Agis I. Only major kings during this period are listed here.

Agis I (conceivably the first historical Spartan king) c. 930–900 BCE
Alcamenes c. 740–700 BCE, during First Messenian War
Cleomenes I (important leader in the Greek resistance against the Persians) 524 – 490 BCE
Leonidas I (died while leading the Greeks – the 300 Spartans – against the Persians in the Battle of Thermopylae, 480 BCE) 490–480 BCE
Cleomenes III (exiled following the Battle of Sellasia) c. 235–222 BCE

KINGS OF MACEDON

Argead Dynasty (808–309 BCE)

Karanos	c. 808–778 BCE	Alcetas I	c. 576–547 BCE
Koinos	c. 778–750 BCE	Amyntas I	c. 547–498 BCE
Tyrimmas	c. 750–700 BCE	Alexander I	c. 498–454 BCE
Perdiccas I	c. 700–678 BCE	Alcetas II	c. 454–448 BCE
Argaeus I	c. 678–640 BCE	Perdiccas II	c. 448–413 BCE
Philip I	c. 640–602 BCE	Archelaus I	c. 413–339 BCE
Aeropus I	c. 602–576 BCE	Craterus	c. 399 BCE

Orestes	*c.* 399–396 BCE	Perdiccas III	*c.* 368–359 BCE
Aeropus II	*c.* 399–394/93 BCE	Amyntas IV	*c.* 359 BCE
Archelaus II	*c.* 394–393 BCE	Philip II	*c.* 359–336 BCE
Amyntas II	*c.* 393 BCE	Alexander III 'the Great' (also King of Persia and Pharaoh of Egypt by end of reign)	*c.* 336–323 BCE
Pausanias	*c.* 393 BCE		
Amyntas III	*c.* 393 BCE; first reign		
Argeus II	*c.* 393–392 BCE	Philip III	*c.* 323–317 BCE
Amyntas III	*c.* 392–370 BCE	Alexander IV	*c.* 323/317–309 BCE
Alexander II	*c.* 370–368 BCE		

Note: the Corinthian League or Hellenic League was created by Philip II and was the first time that the divided Greek city-states were unified under a single government.

Post-Argead Dynasty (309–168 BCE, 149–148 BCE)

Cassander	*c.* 305–297 BCE
Philip IV	*c.* 297 BCE
Antipater II	*c.* 297–294 BCE
Alexpander V	*c.* 297–294 BCE

Antigonid, Alkimachid and Aeacid Dynasties (294–281 BCE)

Demetrius	*c.* 294–288 BCE
Lysimachus	*c.* 288–281 BCE
Pyrrhus	*c.* 288–285 BCE; first reign

Ptolemaic Dynasty (281–279 BCE)

Ptolemy Ceraunus (son of Ptolemy I of Egypt)	*c.* 281–279 BCE
Meleager	279 BCE

Antipatrid, Antigonid, Aeacid Dynasties, Restored (279–167 BCE)

Antipater	*c*. 279 BCE
Sosthenes	*c*. 279–277 BCE
Antigonus II	*c*. 277–274 BCE; first reign
Pyrrhus	*c*. 274–272 BCE; second reign
Antigonus II	*c*. 272–239 BCE; second reign
Demetrius II	*c*. 239–229 BCE
Antigonus III	*c*. 229–221 BCE
Philip V	*c*. 221–179 BCE
Perseus (deposed by Romans)	*c*. 179–168 BCE
Revolt by Philip VI (Andriskos)	*c*. 149–148 BCE

SELEUCID DYNASTY (*c*. 320 BCE–63 CE)

Seleucus I Nicator	*c*. 320–315, 312–305, 305–281 BCE
Antiochus I Soter	*c*. 291, 281–261 BCE
Antiochus II Theos	*c*. 261–246 BCE
Seleucus II Callinicus	*c*. 246–225 BCE
Seleucus III Ceraunus	*c*. 225–223 BCE
Antiochus III 'the Great'	*c*. 223–187 BCE
Seleucus IV Philopator	*c*. 187–175 BCE
Antiochus (son of Seleucus IV)	*c*. 175–170 BCE
Antiochus IV Epiphanes	*c*. 175–163 BCE
Antiochus V Eupater	*c*. 163–161 BCE
Demetrius I Soter	*c*. 161–150 BCE
Alexander I Balas	*c*. 150–145 BCE
Demetrius II Nicator	*c*. 145–138 BCE; first reign
Antiochus VI Dionysus	*c*. 145–140 BCE

Diodotus Tryphon	c. 140–138 BCE
Antiochus VII Sidetes	c. 138–129 BCE
Demetrius II Nicator	c. 129–126 BCE; second reign
Alexander II Zabinas	c. 129–123 BCE
Cleopatra Thea	c. 126–121 BCE
Seleucus V Philometor	c. 126/125 BCE
Antiochus VIII Grypus	c. 125–96 BCE
Antiochus IX Cyzicenus	c. 114–96 BCE
Seleucus VI Epiphanes	c. 96–95 BCE
Antiochus X Eusebes	c. 95–92/83 BCE
Demetrius III Eucaerus	c. 95–87 BCE
Antiochus XI Epiphanes	c. 95–92 BCE
Philip I Philadelphus	c. 95–84/83 BCE
Antiochus XII Dionysus	c. 87–84 BCE
Seleucus VII	c. 83–69 BCE
Antiochus XIII Asiaticus	c. 69–64 BCE
Philip II Philoromaeus	c. 65–63 BCE

Ptolemaic Dynasty (305–30 BCE)

The Ptolemaic dynasty in Greece was the last dynasty of ancient Egypt before it became a province of Rome.

Ptolemy I Soter	305–282 BCE
Ptolemy II Philadelphos	284–246 BCE
Arsinoe II	c. 277–270 BCE
Ptolemy III Euergetes	246–222 BCE
Berenice II	244/243–222 BCE
Ptolemy IV Philopater	222–204 BCE
Arsinoe III	220–204 BCE
Ptolemy V Epiphanes	204–180 BCE

Cleopatra I	193–176 BCE
Ptolemy VI Philometor	180–164, 163–145 BCE
Cleopatra II	175–164 BCE, 163–127 BCE and 124–116 BCE
Ptolemy VIII Physcon	171–163 BCE, 144–131 BCE and 127–116 BCE
Ptolemy VII Neos Philopator	145–144 BCE
Cleopatra III	142–131 BCE, 127–107 BCE
Ptolemy Memphites	113 BCE
Ptolemy IX Soter	116–110 BCE
Cleopatra IV	116–115 BCE
Ptolemy X Alexander	110–109 BCE
Berenice III	81–80 BCE
Ptolemy XI Alexander	80 BCE
Ptolemy XII Auletes	80–58 BCE, 55–51 BCE
Cleopatra V Tryphaena	79–68 BCE
Cleopatra VI	58–57 BCE
Berenice IV	58–55 BCE

In 27 BCE, Caesar Augustus annexed Greece and it became integrated into the Roman Empire.

ANCIENT ROMAN LEADERS

This list is not exhaustive and some dates are approximate. The legitimacy of some rulers is also open to interpretation. Where dates of rule overlap, emperors either ruled jointly or ruled in opposition to one another. There may also be differences in name spellings between different sources.

KINGS OF ROME (753–509 BCE)

Romulus (mythological founder and first ruler of Rome)	753–716 BCE
Numa Pompilius (mythological)	715–672 BCE
Tullus Hostilius (mythological)	672–640 BCE
Ancus Marcius (mythological)	640–616 BCE
Lucius Tarquinius Priscus (mythological)	616–578 BCE
Servius Tullius (mythological)	578–534 BCE
Lucius Tarquinius Superbus (Tarquin the Proud; mythological)	534–509 BCE

ROMAN REPUBLIC (509–27 BCE)

During this period, two consuls were elected to serve a joint one-year term. Therefore, only a selection of significant consuls are included here.

Lucius Junius Brutus (semi-mythological)	509 BCE
Marcus Porcius Cato (Cato the Elder)	195 BCE
Scipio Africanus	194 BCE
Cnaeus Pompeius Magnus (Pompey the Great)	70, 55 and 52 BCE
Marcus Linius Crassus	70 and 55 BCE
Marcus Tullius Cicero	63 BCE
Caius Julius Caesar	59 BCE
Marcus Aemilius Lepidus	46 and 42 BCE
Marcus Antonius (Mark Anthony)	44 and 34 BCE
Marcus Agrippa	37 and 28 BCE

PRINCIPATE (27 BCE–284 CE)

Julio-Claudian Dynasty (27 BCE–68 CE)

Augustus (Caius Octavius Thurinus, Caius Julius Caesar, Imperator Caesar Divi filius)	27 BCE–14 CE
Tiberius (Tiberius Julius Caesar Augustus)	14–37 CE
Caligula (Caius Caesar Augustus Germanicus)	37–41 CE
Claudius (Tiberius Claudius Caesar Augustus Germanicus)	41–54 CE
Nero (Nero Claudius Caesar Augustus Germanicus)	54–68 CE

Year of the Four Emperors (68–69 CE)

Galba (Servius Sulpicius Galba Caesar Augustus)	68–69 CE
Otho (Marcus Salvio Otho Caesar Augustus)	Jan–Apr 69 CE
Vitellius (Aulus Vitellius Germanicus Augustus)	Apr–Dec 69 CE

Note: the fourth emperor, Vespasian, is listed below.

Flavian Dynasty (66–96 CE)

Vespasian (Caesar Vespasianus Augustus)	69–79 CE
Titus (Titus Caesar Vespasianus Augustus)	79–81 CE
Domitian (Caesar Domitianus Augustus)	81–96 CE

Nerva-Antonine Dynasty (69–192 CE)

Nerva (Nerva Caesar Augustus)	96–98 CE
Trajan (Caesar Nerva Traianus Augustus)	98–117 CE
Hadrian (Caesar Traianus Hadrianus Augustus)	138–161 CE
Antonius Pius (Caesar Titus Aelius Hadrianus Antoninus Augustus Pius)	138–161 CE
Marcus Aurelius (Caesar Marcus Aurelius Antoninus Augustus)	161–180 CE
Lucius Verus (Lucius Aurelius Verus Augustus)	161–169 CE
Commodus (Caesar Marcus Aurelius Commodus Antoninus Augustus)	180–192 CE

Year of the Five Emperors (193 CE)

Pertinax (Publius Helvius Pertinax)	Jan–Mar 193 CE
Didius Julianus (Marcus Didius Severus Julianus)	Mar–Jun 193 CE

Note: Pescennius Niger and Clodius Albinus are generally regarded as usurpers, while the fifth, Septimius Severus, is listed below

Severan Dynasty (193–235 CE)

Septimius Severus (Lucius Septimus Severus Pertinax)	193–211 CE
Caracalla (Marcus Aurelius Antonius)	211–217 CE
Geta (Publius Septimius Geta)	Feb–Dec 211 CE
Macrinus (Caesar Marcus Opellius Severus Macrinus Augustus)	217–218 CE
Diadumenian (Marcus Opellius Antonius Diadumenianus)	May–Jun 218 CE
Elagabalus (Caesar Marcus Aurelius Antoninus Augustus)	218–222 CE
Severus Alexander (Marcus Aurelius Severus Alexander)	222–235 CE

Crisis of the Third Century (235–285 CE)

Maximinus 'Thrax' (Caius Julius Verus Maximus)	235–238 CE
Gordian I (Marcus Antonius Gordianus Sempronianus Romanus)	Apr–May 238 CE
Gordian II (Marcus Antonius Gordianus Sempronianus Romanus)	Apr–May 238 CE
Pupienus Maximus (Marcus Clodius Pupienus Maximus)	May–Aug 238 CE
Balbinus (Decimus Caelius Calvinus Balbinus)	May–Aug 238 CE
Gordian III (Marcus Antonius Gordianus)	Aug 238–Feb 244 CE
Philip I 'the Arab' (Marcus Julius Philippus)	244–249 CE
Philip II 'the Younger' (Marcus Julius Severus Philippus)	247–249 CE
Decius (Caius Messius Quintus Traianus Decius)	249–251 CE
Herennius Etruscus (Quintus Herennius Etruscus Messius Decius)	May/Jun 251 CE

Trebonianus Gallus (Caius Vibius Trebonianus Gallus)	251–253 CE
Hostilian (Caius Valens Hostilianus Messius Quintus)	Jun–Jul 251 CE
Volusianus (Caius Vibius Afinius Gallus Veldumnianus Volusianus)	251–253 CE
Aemilian (Marcus Aemilius Aemilianus)	Jul–Sep 253 CE
Silbannacus (Marcus Silbannacus)	Sep/Oct 253 CE
Valerian (Publius Licinius Valerianus)	253–260 CE
Gallienus (Publius Licinius Egnatius Gallienus)	253–268 CE
Saloninus (Publius Licinius Cornelius Saloninus Valerianus)	Autumn 260 CE
Claudius II Gothicus (Marcus Aurelius Claudius)	268–270 CE
Quintilus (Marcus Aurelius Claudias Quintillus)	Apr–May/Jun 270 CE
Aurelian (Luciua Domitius Aurelianus)	270–275 CE
Tacitus (Marcus Claudius Tacitus)	275–276 CE
Florianus (Marcus Annius Florianus)	276–282 CE
Probus (Marcus Aurelius Probus Romanus; in opposition to Florianus)	276–282 CE
Carus (Marcus Aurelias Carus)	282–283 CE
Carinus (Marcus Aurelius Carinus)	283–285 CE
Numerian (Marcus Aurelius Numerianus)	283–284 CE

DOMINATE (284–610)

Tetrarchy (284–324)

Diocletian 'Lovius' (Caius Aurelius Valerius Diocletianus)	284–305
Maximian 'Herculius' (Marcus Aurelius Valerius Maximianus; ruled the western provinces)	286–305/late 306–308

Galerius (Caius Galerius Valerius Maximianus; ruled the eastern provinces)	305–311
Constantius I 'Chlorus' (Marcus Flavius Valerius Constantius; ruled the western provinces)	305–306
Severus II (Flavius Valerius Severus; ruled the western provinces)	306–307
Maxentius (Marcus Aurelius Valerius Maxentius)	306–312
Licinius (Valerius Licinanus Licinius; ruled the western, then the eastern provinces)	308–324
Maximinus II 'Daza' (Aurelius Valerius Valens; ruled the western provinces)	316–317
Martinian (Marcus Martinianus; ruled the western provinces)	Jul–Sep 324

Constantinian Dynasty (306–363)

Constantine I 'the Great' (Flavius Valerius Constantinus; ruled the western provinces then whole)	306–337
Constantine II (Flavius Claudius Constantinus)	337–340
Constans I (Flavius Julius Constans)	337–350
Constantius II (Flavius Julius Constantius)	337–361
Magnentius (Magnus Magnentius)	360–353
Nepotianus (Julius Nepotianus)	Jun 350
Vetranio	Mar–Dec 350
Julian 'the Apostate' (Flavius Claudius Julianus)	361–363
Jovian (Jovianus)	363–364

Valentinianic Dynasty (364–392)

Valentinian I 'the Great' (Valentinianus)	364–375
Valens (ruled the eastern provinces)	364–378

Procopius (revolted against Valens)	365–366
Gratian (Flavius Gratianus Augustus; ruled the western provinces then whole)	375–383
Magnus Maximus	383–388
Valentinian II (Flavius Valentinianus)	388–392
Eugenius	392–394

Theodosian Dynasty (379–457)

Theodosius I 'the Great' (Flavius Theodosius)	Jan 395
Arcadius	383–408
Honorius (Flavius Honorius)	395–432
Constantine III	407–411
Theodosius II	408–450
Priscus Attalus; usurper	409–410
Constantius III	Feb–Sep 421
Johannes	423–425
Valentinian III	425–455
Marcian	450–457

Last Emperors in the West (455–476)

Petronius Maximus	Mar–May 455
Avitus	455–456
Majorian	457–461
Libius Severus (Severus III)	461–465
Anthemius	467–472
Olybrius	Apr–Nov 472
Glycerius	473–474
Julius Nepos	474–475
Romulus Augustulus (Flavius Momyllus Romulus Augustulus)	475–476

Leonid Dynasty (East, 457–518)

Leo I (Leo Thrax Magnus)	457–474
Leo II	Jan–Nov 474
Zeno	474–475
Basiliscus	475–476
Zeno (second reign)	476–491
Anastasius I 'Dicorus'	491–518

Justinian Dynasty (East, 518–602)

Justin I	518–527
Justinian I 'the Great' (Flavius Justinianus, Petrus Sabbatius)	527–565
Justin II	565–578
Tiberius II Constantine	578–582
Maurice (Mauricius Flavius Tiberius)	582–602
Phocas	602–610

LATER EASTERN EMPERORS (610–1059)

Heraclian Dynasty (610–695)

Heraclius	610–641
Heraclius Constantine (Constantine III)	Feb–May 641
Heraclonas	Feb–Nov 641
Constans II Pogonatus ('the Bearded')	641–668
Constantine IV	668–685
Justinian II	685–695

Twenty Years' Anarchy (695–717)

Leontius	695–698
Tiberius III	698–705

Justinian II 'Rhinometus' (second reign)	705–711
Philippicus	711–713
Anastasius II	713–715
Theodosius III	715–717

Isaurian Dynasty (717–803)

Leo III 'the Isaurian'	717–741
Constantine V	741–775
Artabasdos	741/2–743
Leo V 'the Khazar'	775–780
Constantine VI	780–797
Irene	797–802

Nikephorian Dynasty (802–813)

Nikephoros I 'the Logothete'	802–811
Staurakios	July–Oct 811
Michael I Rangabé	813–820

Amorian Dynasty (820–867)

Michael II 'the Amorian'	820–829
Theophilos	829–842
Theodora	842–856
Michael III 'the Drunkard'	842–867

Macedonian Dynasty (867–1056)

Basil I 'the Macedonian'	867–886
Leo VI 'the Wise'	886–912
Alexander	912–913
Constantine VII Porphyrogenitus	913–959
Romanos I Lecapenus	920–944

Romanos II	959–963
Nikephoros II Phocas	963–969
John I Tzimiskes	969–976
Basil II 'the Bulgar-Slayer'	976–1025
Constantine VIII	1025–1028
Romanus III Argyros	1028–1034
Michael IV 'the Paphlagonian'	1034–1041
Michael V Kalaphates	1041–1042
Zoë Porphyrogenita	Apr–Jun 1042
Theodora Porphyrogenita	Apr–Jun 1042
Constantine IX Monomachos	1042–1055
Theodora Porphyrogenita (second reign)	1055–1056
Michael VI Bringas 'Stratioticus'	1056–1057
Isaab I Komnenos	1057–1059

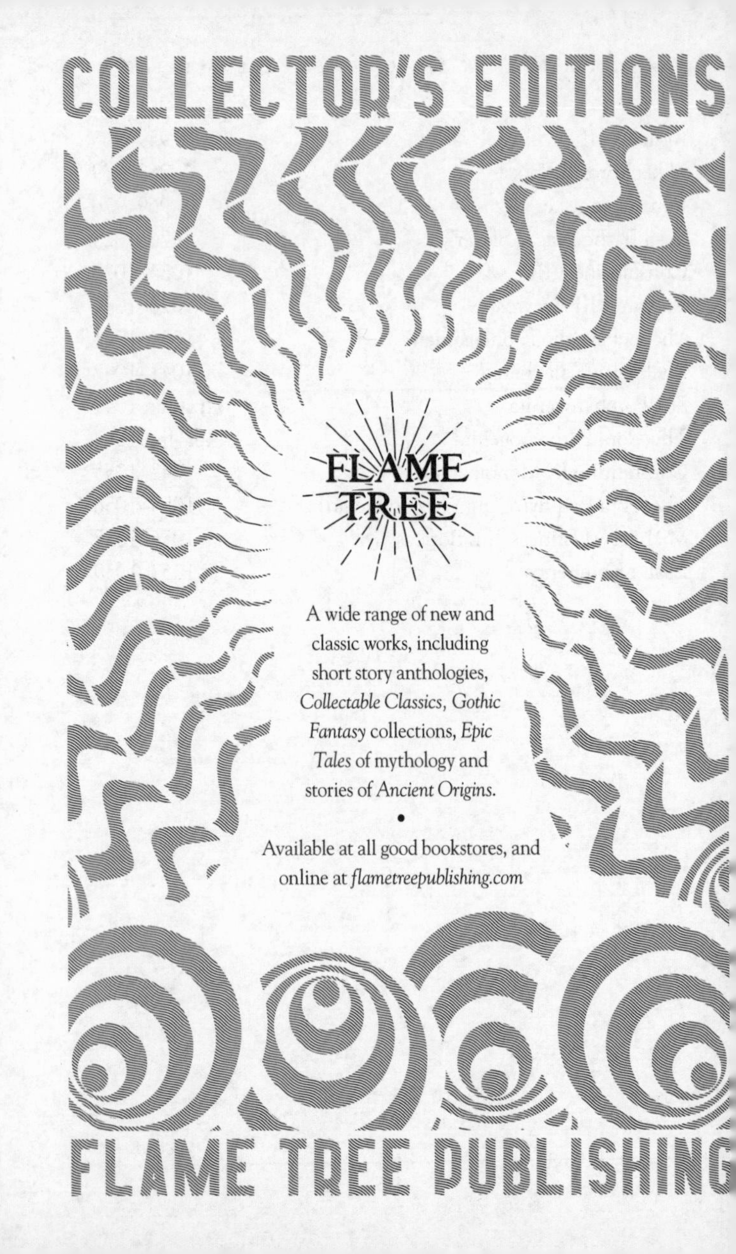
COLLECTOR'S EDITIONS
FLAME TREE
A wide range of new and classic works, including short story anthologies, Collectable Classics, Gothic Fantasy collections, Epic Tales of mythology and stories of Ancient Origins.
•
Available at all good bookstores, and online at flametreepublishing.com
FLAME TREE PUBLISHING